D0699978

Joyce's Moraculous Sindbook

JOYCE'S MORACULOUS SINDBOOK

A Study of *Ulysses*

SUZETTE A. HENKE

Ohio State University Press: Columbus

Library of Congress Cataloguing in Publication Data

Henke, Suzette A.
    Joyce's moraculous sindbook.

    Bibliography: p.
    Includes index.
    1. Joyce, James, 1882–1941. Ulysses. I. Title
PR6019.09U6547   823'.9'12   77-18049
ISBN 0-8142-0275-6

 To my mother, Elizabeth Kish Henke,
and to all the cherished friends who
have offered support and encouragement
over the past decade

Contents

Acknowledgments

The roots of *Joyce's Moraculous Sindbook* go back at least seven years, to the time when this study began to take shape in the recesses of the intellectual imagination. An entire human age has passed, and those who have contributed inspiration or encouragement are far too numerous to be catalogued.

I owe a long-standing debt of gratitude to Professor Paul Ricoeur of the University of Paris for originally introducing me to the principles of phenomenology and existentialism. Professors David Halliburton and Albert Guerard of Stanford University generously read this text in its original form, and I am extremely grateful for their editorial comments and for their unfailing professional assistance. David Riggs and Robert Polhemus of Stanford welcomed me as an auditor in several of their Joyce seminars, where a number of my critical perspectives on *Ulysses* were clarified.

I wish to thank Richard Ellmann, Goldsmiths' Professor of

English at Oxford, for greeting me as a ''fellow-worker in the Irish bog'' at a time when a few words of interest made a difference. I am indebted to Robert Kellogg and Robert Langbaum, colleagues at the University of Virginia, for reading and commenting on this manuscript at several stages of composition. Finally, I would like to express my gratitude to Morris Beja, of the Ohio State University, for reading *Joyce's Moraculous Sindbook* with meticulous care and for making editorial suggestions that have proved invaluable. I doubt that even he fully understands the effect that his sharp critical eye, combined with earnest enthusiasm, has had on the final development of this study.

In *A Room of One's Own,* Virginia Woolf declared that ''surely it is time that the effect of discouragement upon the mind of the artist should be measured.'' And we might say the same thing about encouragement, as well. Certainly, the impact of supportive friendships, both professional and personal, can never fully be counted. I hope that the friends to whom this book is dedicated will recognize my tribute and understand my deep appreciation.

For enduring companionship throughout my years in California, I am grateful to Samuel Tabor, who has contributed more than any other nuclear physicist I know to the study of matters Joycean. For inspiration, criticism, and humor, I thank the students who have participated in my Joyce seminars at the University of Virginia, especially John Sack and James MacQueen, fellow-spirits in the existential quest. For long hours of proofreading and much else, I would like to thank Michael Hubbard, whose Joycean wit and abundant good cheer have lightened life in the academical village.

For much that is non-Joycean, I am grateful to Bobbie Sanger and Judy Ward, who have always been willing to share their advice and experience. Finally, I can only begin to express my sincere appreciation to my mother, Elizabeth Kish Henke, whose faith, courage, and *amor matris* have offered me the gift of lifelong love and support.

For help with the tasks of typing and bibliographical research, I wish to thank Janet Mullaney; Karen Tidmarsh and Kathleen Fogarty, my research assistants; and the secretarial staff at the University of Virginia, including Darnell McGhee and Peggy Dorrier.

For a financial grant in seedtime, I would like to acknowledge the Mabelle McCleod Lewis Memorial Fund of Stanford, California, whose award in 1971–72 made it possible for me to begin work on this study.

University of Virginia
Charlottesville, 1977

Joyce's Moraculous Sindbook

Introduction

In the beginning was the Word.—John 1:1
*In the virgin womb of the imagination the word was
made flesh.*—*"A Portrait of the Artist as a Young Man"*

The theme of Saint John's gospel is also the motif of James
Joyce's *Ulysses,* a work that preaches the "good news" of the
Logos and offers the promise of a "new Bloomusalem in the
Nova Hibernia of the future."[1] Like Stephen Dedalus, Joyce
was determined to use his artistic talents for the transformation
of mankind. Throughout the canon of his work, he utters the
"word known to all men" (p. 581)—the Logos that defines
being, engenders sympathy, and identifies the symbol-system
of the race. From the material of words, the artist creates
worlds: with godlike omniscience, he fashions an aesthetic
microcosm, a fictional "postcreation" that expands the collective horizons of human awareness.

Joyce's earlier novel, *A Portrait of the Artist as a Young
Man,* traces its hero's gradual discovery of the awesome power
of the word. Pain is the goad that inspires Stephen Dedalus to

3

construct an imaginary world of poetry and song. While Baby Stephen cowers beneath the kitchen table, a rhyme about eagles and authority consigns the figures of parental justice to a play frame. A later scene of torment with Heron, Boland, and Nash unfolds as a drama of static perception: Stephen is "divested of his suddenwoven anger as easily as a fruit is divested of its soft ripe peel."[2] The torturous experiences of youth and adolescence are stripped of their anguish and dramatically controlled by the use of elaborate metaphor. Poetry offers aesthetic compensation for the dawning pangs of frustrated erotic desire: in Stephen's Byronic verses "To E—C—," "the kiss, which had been withheld by one, was given by both" (*P* 71). Art "transubstantiates" the bread of everyday life into the sanctified wafer of beauty. It transmutes the disappointments of mundane reality into cathartic experiences of pity, terror, and joy.

The structure of Stephen's aesthetic theory in *Portrait* is based on Aristotle's *Poetics,* filtered through the writings of Thomas Aquinas. The function of the artist is to perceive the "thing in itself" as it really is, shown forth in wholeness, harmony, and radiance. *Claritas* gives birth to the notion of epiphany, the revelation of the "whatness" of an object or event. An epiphany connotes "a sudden spiritual manifestation, whether in the vulgarity of speech or of gesture or in a memorable phase of the mind itself."[3] In this "most delicate and evanescent of moments" (*SH* 211), the "soul of the commonest object . . . seems to us radiant" (*SH* 213). Stephen leads us through an Aristotelian maze, but he ultimately discards the categorical nets that bind his artistic vision. His description of epiphany initiates an aesthetic celebration of phenomenal reality, perceived and sanctified in the present moment.

In the "Telemachus" episode of *Ulysses,* Stephen again finds himself enveloped by widening circles of asphyxiation. Threatened by the claustrophobic forces of Irish society, he struggles for the physical and psychological space necessary to function as a priest of art, forging in the smithy of his soul the uncreated conscience of his race. Most of the Dubliners who surround him have been trapped in a stultified world of spiritual

4

paralysis. The citizens have been psychologically reduced to particles of matter and energy that function mechanically, according to predetermined modes of behavior. The past, whether racial, social, or personal, constitutes a dead weight of determinism that destroys individual freedom.

The nets of family, church, and state all are supported by a philosophical vision grounded in Aristotelian categories. "History . . . is a nightmare from which I am trying to awake" (p. 34), Stephen proclaims—whether it be his own personal history of irrational guilt, a religious history of subservience to Irish Catholicism, or a national history of British political oppression. The historical model is linear and archetypal: it depends on a serial repetition of instants progressing toward "one great goal" (p. 34). A character like Garrett Deasy claims to be in total possession of the light and looks forward to the manifestation of an "allbright" deity. In contrast, Stephen peers into the darkness of private consciousness and turns to the shadowy regions of his own creative will. As a modern, "vivisective" artist, he rejects the nightmare of tradition and clings to the present moment: "Hold to the now, the here, through which all future plunges to the past" (p. 186).

As early as *Stephen Hero,* Joyce's protagonist rejects Aristotle as a guide to the "inexact sciences" of human behavior. When Lynch wonders what Aristotle would have thought of Stephen as a poet, his companion angrily replies: "I'm damned if I would apologise to him at all. Let him examine me if he is able" (*SH* 186). "I do not think that he is the special patron of those who proclaim the usefulness of a stationary march" (*SH* 187). Stephen disdains both the "toy life" of the "docile young men" in the college and the "marionette life" of his Jesuit masters: "And yet both these classes of puppets think that Aristotle has apologised for them before the eyes of the world. Kindly remember the monstrous legend upon which all their life is regulated—how Aristotelian it is!" (*SH* 187). Although Stephen chooses to reiterate a number of premises from the *Poetics,* he feels nothing but scorn for the "hemiplegia of the will" supposedly sanctioned by Aristotle.

5

In the course of *Ulysses,* Stephen moves from an enclosed world of determinism to the existential liberation of artistic consciousness. With a Luciferian gesture of independence in "Circe," he professes moral and creative freedom in a realm of infinite possibilities. He becomes the *Übermensch* who embodies "the new, the unique, the incomparable, making laws for ourselves and creating ourselves."[4] Joyce's artist-hero is a Nietzschean overman, the messiah and priest of a new religion, who affirms the "spirit of man in literature" (p. 666) and "creates a meaning for the earth."[5] Declaring aesthetic autocracy, the artist becomes godlike in his power to fashion a new reality from the "flesh made word": "In woman's womb word is made flesh but in the spirit of the maker all flesh that passes becomes the word that shall not pass away. This is the postcreation" (p. 391).

The movement toward phenomenal reality makes possible both art and human relationship, activities that require the suspension of categorical assumptions and the exercise of "negative capability." The literary artist creates imaginary worlds from the revelation of things in themselves, made radiant in a moment of epiphany. Similarly, what Joyce calls "interindividual relations" (p. 667) take root in an act of mind contingent on creative sympathy. Suspending the limits of his own ego, the individual stands open to the *claritas* of another personality. The process involves a spontaneous psychodrama initiated by the perceiver, who reconstructs and identifies with a life-world beyond the scope of his immediate experience.

If Stephen Dedalus is a self-declared artist of the beautiful, Leopold Bloom functions as an unselfconscious artist of sympathy. By contemplating the unknown lives of others, Bloom moves toward an imaginative identification with familiar qualities that make alien sensibilities keenly intelligible. Long acquainted with exile and suffering, he is constantly in the process of creating miniature works of art—empathic stories that reconcile him to an apparently hostile environment.

Using the word of life to structure his own experience, Bloom applies a parallactic perspective to every situation he encoun-

6

ters. Like Homer's mythic hero, he is "Everyman" and "Noman." In the persona of *Outis* or Noman, Bloom reduces his ego to a "parenthesis of infinitesimal brevity" (p. 698) in the cosmos. He refuses to think as "One does," or to obey the social precepts established by *das Man,* Heidegger's term for "the crowd." As "Noman," Bloom is able to question perceptual models that reinforce prejudice or feed on social bigotry.[6]

Like Stephen Dedalus, Bloom discovers that he can fashion his own reality from the shards of historical chaos. Bloom's equanimity allows him to defy traditional categories of behavior. He rejects conditioned responses of sexual jealousy and successfully exorcises the specters of compulsion. Bloom is able to conquer past phantoms and to take effective action in the present—to proffer his hand to Stephen in paternal solicitude and to slay Molly's suitors on the battleground of his psyche. By the end of the novel, he transforms a potentially tragic situation into a comedy of personal triumph.

There is little resemblance between Leopold Bloom and the brawny titans of ancient Greece and Rome. In the modern world, traditional bravado is outmoded. The true hero is the individual endowed with sufficient courage to challenge tribal patterns of violence, wrath, and aggression. Bloom embodies the injunction to salvation uttered by the thunder in Eliot's *Waste Land.* In full recognition of the limitations that bind his life, he manifests charity, sympathy, and the wisdom of self-control. He creates hope out of despair and presents the twentieth century with a model of contemporary heroism.

By suspending moral judgments, Bloom abstracts from contingent circumstances the victimized consciousness of "the other." He becomes the "new womanly man" (p. 493) who unites scientific curiosity with feminine compassion. In the role of androgynous artist, Bloom makes of his own life a miniature work of art through negative capability. He dramatically acts out the aesthetic ideal, not only of Keats, but of Stephen Dedalus. One might say of Bloom, as Stephen declares of Shakespeare, that he finds "in the world without as actual what was in his world within as possible" (p. 213).

"Love loves to love love" (p. 333). If all flesh comes to nothing, then the only hope of conquering the beastliness of a "dogsbody" existence is to liberate the mind in a sympathetic gesture of understanding: "I mean the opposite of hatred" (p. 333). Leopold Bloom offers a new gospel that celebrates the power of the word in human consciousness. The Logos entails more than verbal felicity. It releases symbols that put us in touch with the inchoate experience of the human race. Static art is itself a kinetic reagent: it stimulates the ecstatic response of consciousness to communal perception. The Logos takes on a sacramental, semi-religious function. It evokes spontaneous associations that fuse private perceptions with those of the entire human community. Verbal expression makes possible the articulation of shared experience, and thus, of "at-one-ment" with others through a wellspring of common feeling.

The three protagonists of *Ulysses*—Stephen, Bloom, and Molly—all exult in the playground of the mind. Stephen's intellect is well stocked with erudition, but he must learn through a long, somewhat torturous apprenticeship, to connect word with flesh. Bloom is more adept at associating verbal symbols with visceral experience. Endowed with a cosmic, "parallactic" perspective, he recognizes the triviality of words that evoke an archaic emotional resonance and no longer describe the human condition.

Bloom warrants our pity, but not our tears. Like Shakespeare, he has forfeited spousal possession and paternal ownership for a life of creative sympathy. Despite the sadness and disappointments of middle age, he lives, grows, and refuses to be paralyzed. He exhibits a mind rich in curiosity, rife with fantasy, and burgeoning with an artistic comprehension of universal pain. From his own experience of domestic isolation, Bloom can re-create his wife's loneliness, fear, and sexual hunger. He is able to imagine the frustrations of motherhood, the terror of physical inadequacy, and the sheer pathos of erotic desertion. Given the cold of interstellar space, charity is the only appropriate gesture. Eros is transient, agape transcendent.

Leopold Bloom brings "light to the Gentiles" by introducing

Stephen to the arts of love and personal relationship. He leads the younger man to the altar of the flesh made word—not to worship, but to behold. Bloom acquaints Stephen, at least verbally, with the "warm, fullblooded life" of Gea-Tellus.

And in some sense, Molly Bloom may be the most prolific artist in *Ulysses*. Working in the most universal of all media, she builds a fictional microcosm from the materials of passionate reverie. Through Molly, Joyce celebrates the powers of the Logos residual in every human being. As art improves on life, so dream and fantasy embellish quotidian reality. Molly recollects her daily experiences in the magical mode of amorous transcendence. She re-creates life out of life, weaving a tapestry of events into a mythic story that defies the limits of factual history. The past becomes grist for the mill of art. From moment to moment, Molly exists in a continuous present, turning "like the huge earth ball . . . round and round spinning."[7] Her thoughts explode spontaneously from a central, controlling consciousness that spins in cyclical repetition around the axis of imaginative fantasy.

Molly escapes from linear time and mentally enclosed space by celebrating the "ecstatic moment." She creates her own reality from the experiences of the day-self filtered through the uncensored imagination. All those possibilities never actualized by history come alive in a psychodrama of prolific enjoyment. The artistic faculty of Molly's dream-self gives birth to fictive worlds that associate and recombine in fascinating permutation. Molly represents the anima, the side of the mind that refurbishes the past and illumines the future. Joyce's Penelope is "posthuman," and as such, she captures the ideal of postcreation.

In *Ulysses*, the gods have come down to earth. Art is redemptive in its power to transform the mythic heritage of humankind. It reveals to us the imaginative potential of ourselves: "In the intense instant of imagination, when the mind, Shelley says, is a fading coal, that which I was is that which I am and that which in possibility I may come to be" (p. 194). Art illumines the reality of what we are and divulges the secret of what we might become.

9

Bloom is an artist of compassion; Molly, an artist of passion. Both function as "artists of life." And Stephen, as poetic observer, will eventually give verbal form and aesthetic stasis to the movement of love that unites the Bloom ménage. Together, the three characters affirm the spirit of humanity through literature, sympathy, and desire.

In *Finnegans Wake,* Joyce describes *Ulysses* as his "moraculous . . . sindbook," an epithet that came to seem increasingly appropriate as the world of *Ulysses* began to reveal itself.[8] In German, *sind* is a form of the verb "to be"; and the noun *Sinn* denotes "meaning" or "sense." The title conflates a number of Joycean themes: the concepts of morality and of sin; the authorial preoccupation with *Sein* or "being"; and Joyce's artistic celebration of the miraculous powers of human consciousness.

Throughout the canon of his work, Joyce retained a sense of the priestly vocation he attributes to Stephen Dedalus in *Portrait*—a vocation to forge the uncreated conscience of his race. The author himself never forgot this priesthood of the imagination or its call to arouse the dormant conscience of Ireland. In *Ulysses,* Joyce sets forth a new gospel and a new morality: he substitutes the principles of existential humanism for an outworn ethic of defilement. "Sin" and "guilt" belong to a dead past solidified into paralytic stasis; they are part of the historical nightmare that Stephen, Bloom, and Molly all attempt to destroy. In the course of the novel, the three protagonists escape from "sin" into a realization of existential *Dasein*.[9] By virtue of the intellectual imagination made possible by language, they transcend inherited modes of perception and begin to fashion a new reality from the present, "epiphanic" moment.

Although most critics acknowledge the innovative nature of Joyce's stylistic experiments, few have called attention to the radical content of *Ulysses* or to the revolutionary view of consciousness implicit in the novel. The mind imprisoned in traditional thinking is trapped in a sequence of historical events that demand categorical response. To be truly free, the psyche must uproot itself from conditioned experience and move backward and forward in time, with the liberty of four-dimensional vision. Consciousness not only perceives history but completes it through imaginative postcreation. The "world without as actual" is re-created, once again, as "possible" within the landscape of the mind.

In the later, more experimental episodes of *Ulysses*, Joyce provides us with subtle keys to the interpretation of his novel. He insists that the reader, like the characters, explore the ramifications of both temporal and ethical relativity. We are expected to be "time-travelers," defying Gotthold Lessing's serial definition of literature. We are forced to apprehend the entire novel as a contemporaneous object of consciousness, an autotelic and self-referential phenomenon. The ultimate subject of *Ulysses* becomes the mind beholding itself in an act of transcendental, creative perception.

Joyce's Moraculous Sindbook is an attempt to re-create *Ulysses* as an existential act of mind and a phenomenological life-world. The methods I employ are closely allied with those of the Geneva school, represented by Georges Poulet in Europe and by J. Hillis Miller in America. "Criticism of consciousness" studies the repetition of words, phrases, and themes within a particular text in order to reconstruct a fictional world. It traces a work of literature back to its point of conception and tries to analyze the consciousness of an "implied" or "incarnate" author—a non-biographical persona, born in a literary work at the moment of genesis, and coexistent with the final artistic product.[10]

Both criticism of consciousness and phenomenology take their origins from Edmund Husserl, and both have been influenced by Heidegger and Sartre. Phenomenological criticism examines the existential problems of time, space, and being within a literary context. It acknowledges the work of art as an "object of intentionality" for the author and for his reader, both of whom regard the text as an intersubjective drama of mutual creation.[11]

11

Joyce's Moraculous Sindbook takes much of its impetus from the principles of phenomenology, a philosophy that stands open to the eclectic use of diverse critical methods. In the following discussion, I rely on the techniques of the Geneva school, and of "new criticism" when close textual analysis proves illuminating. I refer to the ideas of Sigmund Freud and of Carl Jung when traditional psychoanalytic theory substantiates phenomenological observation. And in all cases, I try to allow Joyce's fictional microcosm to dictate both principles of interpretation and critical conclusions.

Ulysses is not a tour de force but a work of literature that takes its meaning "from and in life," and is significant to us as moral beings. In the course of the novel, Joyce's characters move from a world of psychological enclosure to an existential liberation of consciousness. Joyce was far ahead of his contemporaries in his understanding of social interaction and psychological development. In *Ulysses*, he questions traditional notions of identity and reality, of conjugal appropriation and egocentric privilege. He delights in the capaciousness of the human imagination and implies that every individual can become an "artist of life" through myth, sympathy, and creative fantasy.

1. James Joyce, *Ulysses,* p. 484, published by The Bodley Head. All quotations from *Ulysses* will be cited from the 1961 Random House reprint edition and will be indicated by page number only, unless corrections are made from earlier editions of the text.

2. James Joyce, *A Portrait of the Artist as a Young Man*, p. 82. Hereafter cited in the text as *PA*.

3. James Joyce, *Stephen Hero*, p. 211. Hereafter cited in the text as *SH*. Grateful acknowledgment is made to The Society of Authors as the literary representative of the Estate of James Joyce and to the Executors of the James Joyce Estate for permission to reprint.

4. Friedrich Nietzsche, *Joyful Wisdom*, p. 168. According to Richard Ellmann, Joyce became familiar with the writings of Nietzsche at the age of twenty-two, "and it was probably upon Nietzsche that Joyce drew when he expounded to his friends a neo-paganism" (*James Joyce*, p. 147). Joyce, in fact, signed a 1904 letter as "James Overman." In *The Consciousness of Joyce,* Ellmann cites the existence of three volumes by Nietzsche in Joyce's

Trieste library: *The Birth of Tragedy*, trans. W. A. Hausmann; *The Case of Wagner, Nietzsche Contra Wagner, Selected Aphorisms*, trans. A. M. Ludovici; and *The Joyful Wisdom*, trans. Thomas Common (Appendix, p. 121).

5. Friedrich Nietzsche, "Thus Spoke Zarathustra: First Part" (1883) in *The Portable Nietzsche*, p. 144. Nietzsche writes: "A new pride my ego taught me, and this I teach men: no longer to bury one's head in the sand of heavenly things, but to bear it freely, an earthly head, which creates a meaning for the earth" (p. 144). Compare *Stephen Hero:* "To walk nobly on the surface of the earth, to express oneself without pretence, to acknowledge one's own humanity! You mustn't think I rhapsodise: I am quite serious. I speak from my soul" (p. 142).

6. According to Richard Ellmann, "Joyce used to insist upon a 'thirteenth-century' etymology for the Greek form of Ulysses' name, Odysseus; he said it was a combination of *Outis*—nobody, and *Zeus*—god. The etymology is merely fanciful, but it is a controlled fancy which helps to reinforce Joyce's picture of the modern Ulysses. For Bloom is a nobody . . . yet there is a god in him. . . . The divine part of Bloom is simply his humanity—his assumption of a bond between himself and other created beings" (*James Joyce*, p. 372).

7. James Joyce, *Letters of James Joyce*, 1:170.

8. James Joyce, *Finnegans Wake*, p. 627. Hereafter cited in the text as *FW*.

9. According to Richard Ellmann, "the whole conception of sin became repugnant to him. He allowed instead for 'error.' To quarrel with the Church . . . led him to quarrel with his mother and by extension with his motherland, in which he saw a secret collusion of Catholic and British authorities threatening hell or jail" (*The Consciousness of Joyce*, p. 2).

10. As Sarah Lawall explains, "These writers share the existential view of literature as a mental act. . . . They have been called the new 'Geneva School' or, more recently, the 'Genetic' critics. . . . Their accents are moral and humanistic, and their method a kind of spiritual historicism based upon the existential evidence provided by literature. . . . As 'genetic' critics, all these men . . . analyze the human consciousness in literature at its very focal point or genesis. As practical critics, they try to coexist with a creative consciousness at the moment when experience ceases to be mute and takes on the appearance of words and the structure of words" (Sarah N. Lawall, *Critics of Consciousness*, p. 3). According to Lawall, "The idea of literary consciousness leads to an analysis of the work as a mental universe, a self-contained world where human experience takes shape as literature. . . . This creation in mental space attempts to fuse human perceptions of subject and object, and is thus an 'experience' of life and an 'act' of consciousness. The criticism aimed at this consciousness sees literature as an act or genesis and analyzes it as a drama taking place in the mind. . . . This empathetic reading is evidently not aimed at a formal analysis of the text. It views literature as an existential experience and act of cognition, and consequently attributes to the

reader only the task of extracting the work's original creative experience. The reader cannot view the text 'from outside,' in an aesthetic, formal, or evaluative judgment, for he must attempt to coincide with its very being and identity'' (*ibid.*, p. 8).

11. Literature marks the intersection between the subjective expression of the author and the subjective apprehension of the reader. As Roger Poole declares, literature should be a "significant human study." "The kind of enquiry begun by Dilthey might here be taken for our guide. The 'understanding' which he opposes to mere 'explanation' . . . considers a work of literature as existing in the medium of life and therefore as demanding a reading from and in life. . . . Literature finally matters to us as moral beings. And since literature emanates from moral beings, . . . we cannot accept as sufficient an analytical method which offers us no means of access whatsoever to this inner meaning which literature has'' (Roger C. Poole, "Structuralism and Phenomenology: A Literary Approach," p. 8).

"Telemachus": Ghosts and Cannibals

A tale told of Shaun or Shem?—*"Finnegans Wake"*
A tale told of Stephen Dedalus

At the outset of *Ulysses,* Stephen Dedalus no longer seems to be
the cold, esoteric aesthete who had recourse to Dante's
"spiritual-heroic refrigerating apparatus" at the end of *Portrait*
(*PA* 252). Chastened by an abortive flight to Paris, lapwing
Stephen has begun to mature. His theories have been tempered,
at least intellectually, by the developing conviction that art must
take root in personal experience. As a nascent poet, Stephen
demands the rights of self-expression so long denied the Celtic
bard. He refuses to chronicle sagas of Irish history or to heed the
church's strictures concerning art. He wants to create from the
fabric of his soul, and his heated pursuit of aesthetic freedom is
tantamount to a personal quest for the liberty of self-determination.[1]

   Beneath the mask of paradox, Stephen harbors a secret terror
of betrayal and martyrdom. In "Telemachus," he inhabits a
closed, almost paranoid world of physical and mental asphyxia-

tion. He nervously hovers in the dark Martello tower and mounts the stairs like a caged, suspicious animal. The fortress is the "omphalos" of the earth; yet despite its uterine interior, Stephen never feels secure in its belly. He fears being overwhelmed by the claustrophobic objects of a hostile, foreign environment.

The sea terrifies Stephen because it portends engulfment—a sinking down into matter and the annihilation of personal identity. It calls up womb images and metaphorically functions as a giant placenta, encompassing Ireland in viscous amniotic fluid. The unborn souls of men float paralyzed in the "deep jelly of the water" (p. 21).[2]

Stephen is further alienated from his surroundings by the private experience of "Agenbite of Inwit"—a medieval "prick of conscience" that suggests the free-floating anxiety of existential dread. Ethical horror emanates from the ghost of Mary Dedalus, who indicts her son for his refusal to kneel and pray at her deathbed:[3]

> —The aunt thinks you killed your mother. . . . That's why she won't let me have anything to do with you.
> —Someone killed her, Stephen said gloomily.
> —You could have knelt down, damn it, Kinch, when your dying mother asked you, Buck Mulligan said. I'm hyperborean as much as you. But to think of your mother begging you with her last breath to kneel down and pray for her. And you refused. There is something sinister in you . . . (P. 5)

Already Mulligan has proved himself worthy of Stephen's telegram quoting *Richard Feverel*: "*The sentimentalist is he who would enjoy without incurring the immense debtorship for a thing done*" (p. 199). Mulligan cares little about his friend's departed mother and less about the sin of apostasy. He uses all the sentimental rhetoric at his command to arouse Stephen's unconscious guilt, and he enjoys watching his victim squirm.[4] Buck is not emotionally involved in the demise and has incurred none of the "immense debtorship" associated with the nominal murder. By using such maudlin clichés as "dying mother" and

16

"begging you with her last breath," he appeals to the subliminal guilt that every individual retains from the vague, primordial "memory, more and more galling, of his having consented to live in his mother, then to leave her."[5] Mulligan conflates the guilt of existence with the "debtorship" of a murderer toward his victim. His melodramatic language vies with the sticky romanticism of Gerty MacDowell. Like Iago, he plants the seeds of psychological agony in Stephen's mind and grimaces at his victim's self-torture:

> Stephen, an elbow rested on the jagged granite, leaned his palm against his brow and gazed at the fraying edge of his shiny black coat-sleeve. Pain, that was not yet the pain of love, fretted his heart. Silently, in a dream she had come to him after her death, her wasted body within its loose brown graveclothes giving off an odour of wax and rosewood, her breath, that had bent upon him, mute, reproachful, a faint odour of wetted ashes. Across the threadbare cuffedge he saw the sea hailed as a great sweet mother by the wellfed voice beside him. The ring of bay and skyline held a dull green mass of liquid. A bowl of white china had stood beside her deathbed holding the green sluggish bile which she had torn up from her rotting liver by fits of loud groaning vomiting. (P. 5)

All of Stephen's senses are sharply attuned to perceive his mother's specter. He feels tactile pain "fretting" his heart and experiences the gustatory horror of imagining the phlegm spit up from her cancerous liver. Tortured vicariously, he re-creates the sensation of an internal organ slowly being ripped apart by Promethean vultures.

Mary Dedalus appears to her son with the detailed visual clarity of a pre-Raphaelite painting. She reeks of "wax and rosewood" and "a faint odour of wetted ashes." The "once beautiful May Goulding" resembles Rossetti's Blessed Damozel peering down from her golden perch in heaven. She approaches her son like a departed mistress courting erotic favor, evoking an amorous distraction "not yet the pain of love." She recriminates him as both son and lover, roles that the Freudian censor makes psychologically exclusive.

By publicly refusing his mother's deathbed request, Stephen

hoped to free himself from a double bondage to home and church; and perhaps, simultaneously, to renounce preconscious incestuous desires. Now, if he fails to yield to the phantom temptress, he offends the *sanctum sanctorum,* "mother love." If, in turn, he violates the ideal virginity of his maiden-mother, he offends the most primitive strictures of social behavior.

Looking out from his tower prison, Stephen is surrounded by a "ring of bay and skyline." The circle that binds his vision becomes cramped until the sea-ring shrinks in his anxious imagination. He recalls a much smaller circle, the rim of a white china bowl that stood by his mother's deathbed. Inside the dish, the "snotgreen sea" changes to "green sluggish bile," a minute quantity of liquid that drowns his mind in a flood of excruciating memories.

Stephen muses on the secrets that had defined his mother's life: "old feather fans, tasselled dancecards, powdered with musk, a gaud of amber beads in her locked drawer" (p. 9). The once beautiful May Goulding is now "folded away in the memory of nature with her toys" (p. 10). Stephen senses the acute pathos of these nostalgic mementoes. Death is terrible because human life can be reduced to so little: a collection of shadows and reflections too trivial to bear the weight of personal sorrow. One need not believe in Irish fairies or in Catholic spirits to perceive the ghost of Mary Dedalus. She is painfully present in the "mode of absence," a shade negatively constituted by the remnants of a life-world once imbued with conscious meaning.

Stephen is enslaved to the memory of his mother, who in turn was bound to physical reminiscences. He is being suffocated by a morass of paralyzed matter: "Memories beset his brooding brain. Her glass of water from the kitchen tap when she had approached the sacrament. A cored apple, filled with brown sugar, roasting for her at the hob on a dark autumn evening. Her shapely fingernails reddened by the blood of squashed lice from the children's shirts" (p. 10). Stephen mentally associates food and drink with cannibalism, since Mary Dedalus partook of

18

"the body and blood of Christ" in the Eucharist, just as she ingested "a cored apple" and squashed the lice feeding on her children's bodies. The mother returns after death in ghoulish fashion, "her glazing eyes, staring out of death, to shake and bend my soul" (p. 10). Her son becomes the eucharistic victim to be consumed in holy Viaticum, the Catholic communion for the dying. He will be masticated like a cored apple, assimilated back into the maternal body shunned at birth. Enraged by the ghost's psychic cannibalism, Stephen wakes from his reverie in violent protest: "Ghoul! Chewer of corpses! / No mother. Let me be and let me live" (p. 10). Mary Dedalus wants to devour her son's life fluid as the lice had fed on his blood. Stephen fears she would annihilate his personality in a sacramental attempt to save his immortal soul.[6]

The phantasm defends a religion of decay and of mouldering devotion:

> In a dream, silently, she had come to him, her wasted body within its loose graveclothes giving off an odour of wax and rosewood, her breath bent over him with mute secret words, a faint odour of wetted ashes.
> . . . On me alone. . . . Her eyes on me to strike me down.
> *Liliata rutilantium.* . . . (P. 10)

Resembling a priest of the grave, Mary Dedalus wears sacramental vestments. Her garb reeks of strange incense, and she utters "mute secret words" of religious ritual. Her ashen breath recalls the rites of Ash Wednesday, the *memento mori* preached by a rotting corpse. Stephen remembers his mother on her deathbed—a hard, frenzied creature trying to subjugate his rebellious spirit. Her ghost calls him to a eucharistic feast in which he himself will be the sacrificial victim.

In the womb of mother Ireland, in the lap of the ocean, Stephen is haunted by Mary Dedalus. Physically confined in a round, granite bastion, he is being mentally asphyxiated by a ghost who fills every *space* available. No crevice is safe from the phantom's ashen breath. Like the sea, that "great sweet mother," Mary Dedalus is a castrating female who evokes

19

"scrotumtightening" anxiety. Part of the dead past, she threatens to engulf the present in paralytic stasis.

Because drowning serves as a synecdoche for death, the shade of Stephen's mother is a sea-ghost. At the mere mention of water, Stephen recalls Agenbite of Inwit, the guilt evinced by her imputed murder. Mulligan, Haines, and Mary Dedalus all are symbolically connected with the ocean's claustrophobia. They inhabit a dead world of determined essences where nothing is new, nothing created. All is categorized, mechanical, and automatic.

In opposition to the forces of engulfment, Stephen is fighting to become a bardic "priest of the imagination," capable of transmuting the materials of common experience into the sanctified wafer of art.[7] His aesthetic vocation is undermined by Mulligan, the usurper who tries to drown his companion in a sea of undifferentiated matter. Preaching the joys of pagan decadence, Mulligan dons a mask of public gaiety to cloak cruelty, envy, and jealousy. Superficially a "stage Irishman" who will do anything for a laugh, Buck is in fact a *poseur* with the malevolence of a Faustian Mephistopheles.[8]

Mulligan is masculine and aggressive, a "naturalistic man." He wields the razor blade, an instrument of butchery, for the purpose of cutting through aesthetic images reflected in the mirror of art. He wants to reduce the literary world to palpably sensuous terms: "The bard's noserag. A new colour for our Irish poets: snotgreen. You can almost taste it, can't you?" (p. 5). The jest has a tinge of malice intended to denigrate poets who, despite esoteric cries of "art for art's sake," live by the same bodily functions as common men. Algernon Charles Swinburne becomes "Algy"—but more appropriately, the vegetative parasite, "algae," attached to the womb of the "great sweet mother, / Mother and lover of men, the sea" ("The Triumph of Time"). Buck deliberately misquotes Swinburne's verses and conflates the ocean with Whistler's "grey sweet mother" (p. 5).

Mulligan perpetually chides Stephen for aesthetic "mumming" and for his failure to use art as a vehicle of Zolaesque

20

naturalism. He wants Kinch to recognize the bloody knife and razor perched on the mirror of art, to think in excretory images, and to regard death in terms of "beastly" medical cadavers.

Throughout "Telemachus," Mulligan is described in non-human imagery: his face is "equine"; his "untonsured" hair resembles "pale oak." "He swept the mirror a half circle in the air to flash the tidings abroad in sunlight now radiant on the sea. His curling shaven lips laughed and the edges of his white glittering teeth. Laughter seized all his strong wellknit trunk" (p. 6).

Behind a veneer of elegance, Mulligan harbors predatory instincts. He suddenly becomes an animal with "curling lips," a wolf anxious to sink "his white glittering teeth" into the soft flesh of "poor dogsbody." Buck is metamorphosed into a sentient automaton, a machine no longer in control of its actions. His bodily parts seem to function independently. Mulligan *himself* does not laugh: "His curling shaven lips laughed and the edges of his white glittering teeth." His body responds automatically to external stimuli until even the muscles are denied initiative. His frame is controlled entirely from without: "Laughter seized all his strong wellknit trunk."

Joyce's language changes Mulligan from a rational animal to a sentient predator, and finally to an inanimate vegetable. In a single paragraph, Buck has descended the Thomistic scale of being. He starts out as angelic messenger to the heavens, a wizard-priest flashing circles in the air. In the next sentence, he becomes a snarling beast, flashing nothing more than glittering white fangs. Ultimately, he is reduced to arboreal immobility: like the oak, he can boast of a "strong wellknit trunk."

Mulligan judges himself and his companions by the mask of "being-for-others." He tries to annihilate Stephen's self-image by forcing the poet to turn his attention from inward brooding to external identity:

—Look at yourself, he said, you dreadful bard.
Stephen bent forward and peered at the mirror held out to him, cleft by a crooked crack, hair on end. As he and others see me. Who

21

chose this face for me? This dogsbody to rid of vermin. It asks me too. (P. 6)

Stephen is rightfully befuddled by Mulligan's crude mimesis. He looks at the physical image of himself "as he and others see me." As the language slips from external description to interior monologue, Joyce reflects Stephen's mental confusion through syntactical ambiguity. Stephen "peered at the mirror held out to him, cleft by a crooked crack, hair on end." Of the three phrases that succeed "mirror," the first two are introduced by participles that modify the noun. The glass is "held out" by a hand and "cleft" by a crack. The third phrase, "hair on end," fails to balance the triplet. It refers back to Stephen, the subject, who notices a coiffure so disheveled that even he is startled.

One might further extend the verbal ambiguity by associating the word "cleft" with the preceding pronoun, "him"—reflexively, "Stephen." The sudden shock of seeing his image has proved psychically "cleaving" to the bard. He feels disoriented, torn between introspective self-consciousness and an external mirror image. Stephen experiences a split in existence, a psychological extension of the Cartesian mind-body dichotomy. On the one hand, he identifies with the "transcendental ego," the self as it perceives itself in the process of conscious activity. Simultaneously, he apprehends his body as "other," alienated from the mind by its failure to respond to mental and volitional control. A man cannot *will* his heart to beat, his body to stay young, or his hair to lie flat. The body as a material organism constitutes a separate, foreign identity.[9]

Confused by this sudden sensation of duality, Stephen asks, "Who chose this face for me?" He speaks of his *ego* as "first person" and of his body as objective "third person." He distinguishes the conscious "I" from the "me" confined to matter. His physical identity seems to be composed of arbitrary parts put together by an unknown artisan from prefabricated faces, hands, feet, and bodily organs. Stephen has yielded to Buck's degrading epithets. He regards his image

22

as a louse-ridden "dogsbody," a hunk of meat breeding maggots. The physical self has become "it," a thing "not-I" that joins the mass of oppressive matter sealing the poet into a confined space and crushing his potential expansion.

Stephen feels "the rage of Caliban at not seeing his face in the mirror."[10] He has not been shown a reflection of the *self* he identifies as "I." He has viewed, instead, an image of "poor dogsbody," a Caliban whose animal body houses the consciousness of a man. Stephen is unable to bridge the gap between physical and spiritual existence. Hence his vertiginous sense of personal disintegration.

Unlike Cranly in *Portrait,* Mulligan cannot get close to Stephen, even though he boasts that "I'm the only one that knows what you are" (p. 7). He employs the relative pronoun "what" rather than "who"; and by his choice of language, he answers his own question, "Why don't you trust me more?" (p. 7). Mulligan takes pains to define *what* Stephen is—a physically alienated *object* and a man guilty of matricide. While Stephen meditates, Buck proposes that the two join forces to establish a new religion of pagan materialism. "To ourselves . . . new paganism . . . omphalos" (p. 7). For Buck, contemplation will involve navel-gazing at a body that is "beastly" alive. His cult is more hedonistic than meditative, a religion of egotistical self-involvement. No matter how long Mulligan looks at his *omphalos,* he will never see more than a symbol of physical birth.

Mulligan is so self-centered that he uses egotism as an excuse for his jibes against Stephen. "I can't remember anything," he argues. "I remember only ideas and sensations" (p. 8). His mode of perception is both Lockean and solipsistic. He recalls only those things that impinge directly on his ego, and he takes refuge in a private world from which he is loath to escape. He lives on a sentient, instinctual level, affected only by random stimuli and by "ideas" that touch his mind as passive sensations. Because Buck dwells so close to the bestial, he interprets life in animal terms. He strips "poor dogsbody" of his integrity and casually remarks that

Stephen's mother is "beastly dead." If, in fact, Mary Dedalus can be described as "beastly dead," then Stephen might rightfully be addressed by his jeering companion as a "dogsbody," little more than a walking carcass. The dam of "dogsbody" could be labeled a "bitch"; and Buck's derogatory nickname would brand Stephen as an S.O.B., one of the lowest figures of Dublin vulgarity.

"And what is death, he asked, your mother's or yours or my own? . . . I see them pop off every day in the Mater and Richmond and cut up into tripes in the dissecting room. It's a beastly thing and nothing else. It simply doesn't matter" (p. 8). Death "does not matter" if life is only a beastly exaltation of animal enjoyment. A dead man becomes food for the dissecting room, since the human machine is no more than the sum of its parts, "cut up into tripes" the moment it stops functioning. Mulligan's language suggests cannibalism and invites us to taste human entrails, "tripes" cut out of a cadaver.

Such flippant remarks offer a direct challenge to Stephen's spiritual definition of his own aesthetic vocation. When Mulligan protests, "I didn't mean to offend the memory of your mother," Stephen retorts:

—I am not thinking of the offence to my mother.
—Of what, then? Buck Mulligan asked.
—Of the offence to me, Stephen answered (Pp. 8–9)

Buck's pagan mockery constitutes a genuine threat to the notion of sacramental creation. The reduction of human life to "beastliness" invalidates the role of the artist-god. If the poet is to function as priest of the eternal imagination, his identity is contingent on the spiritual dimensions of human existence. More than denying the reality of the soul, Mulligan is negating the primacy of consciousness as the source of personal integrity. He defends a mechanistic view of life and refuses to recognize the unity of physical, intellectual, and emotional experience.

Surprised that Stephen should take offense at his profanity, Mulligan complains that his friend is too exacting, too discrim-

24

inating and jesuitical: "Look at the sea. What does it care about offences? Chuck Loyola, Kinch, and come on down" (p. 9). Buck invites Stephen to abandon judgment and to sink into the bliss of hedonistic materialism. But yielding to pagan irresponsibility would entail forfeiting personal will and drowning in a whirlpool of spiritual annihilation.

Psychologically, the "gloomy domed livingroom of the tower" reinforces Stephen's terror of asphyxiation. The belly of the tower is a smoky pit worthy of Beelzebub. Dark gloom, the yellow glow of the hearth, and "a cloud of coalsmoke and fumes of fried grease" create a hellish atmosphere.[11] "We'll be choked," Mulligan screams; and he soon translates his frenzy into the present tense. "Janey Mack, I'm choked. He howled without looking up from the fire:—Kinch!" (p. 11). Mulligan is looking *at* the fire, but the prepositional phrase is sufficiently ambiguous to place him in the midst of the flames. Like a howling devil, he seems to address his companion from a Luciferian abyss. We know rationally that Buck is staring *at* the flames; but we are encouraged linguistically to visualize him yelling "from the fire," screaming to Kinch-Christ for the key to salvation.

Within the tower, the infernal environment destroys individual identity. Human beings no longer function as volitional agents, but as "forms," material objects externally animated: "Buck Mulligan's gowned *form* moved briskly about the hearth to and fro. . . . A tall *figure* rose from the hammock where *it* had been sitting, went to the doorway and pulled open the inner doors" (p. 11; italics mine). Even after the door has been opened to "welcome light and bright air," the draught does nothing to alleviate the tower's enclosedness. Mulligan continues to describe himself in similes that refer to inanimate objects: "I'm melting, he said, as the candle remarked" (p. 12).

Themes of violence and cannibalism dominate the morning repast. When Old Mother Grogan figuratively appears in the person of an aged Irish milkwoman, Buck responds to her exclamation of "Glory be to God" with the wry remark: "The

islanders . . . speak frequently of the collector of prepuces"
(p. 13). His medical reference to the Hebrew-Christian God as
barbaric foreskin-hunter is as meaningless to the old lady as
Haines's Gaelic-French. "Are you a medical student, sir?" (p.
14), the woman inquires.

The crone panders to her medicine man, and Stephen
cynically envisions her "unclean loins" as prey to the phallic
serpent. But like the old woman, the poet is himself an
"unclean bard" who refuses to perform ritual ablutions: "They
wash and tub and scrub. Agenbite of inwit. Conscience. Yet
here's a spot" (p. 16). He recognizes the darkness endemic to
the human soul and refuses the ineffectual waters of
sacramental cleansing. He will listen only to the chaste moon,
Diana, who bids him purify his body once a month.

When Stephen scorns Buck's "puppet" pose of gaiety and
demands money from Haines, he is rhetorically metamorphosed
into a hoofed quadruped, then into a parasitic louse: "You put
your hoof in it now . . . your lousy leer and your gloomy jesuit
jibes" (p. 16). In Mulligan's sphere, human beings are stripped
of personal volition, and physical objects take on independent
existence. Buck speaks to his "rebellious tie," "stiff collar,"
and "dangling watchchain," chiding them for insubordination.
Despite his Whitmanian egotism, the mocker is not in control:
"Do I contradict myself? Very well then, I contradict myself.
Mercurial Malachi. A limp black missile flew out of his talking
hands" (p. 17). Hands talk and hats fly in a realm of automata
presided over by a human machine.

Once outside the tower, Mulligan continues to fight quixotic
dragons, clubbing "with his heavy bathtowel the leader shoots
of ferns or grasses," and crying, "Down, sir. How dare you,
sir?" (p. 17). Buck is a prime example of mechanical perverseness. Believing himself a Nietzschean superman, he is in fact a
slave to the world of physical matter. His actions are perverse
and impulsive, predetermined by automatic responses. Bellicose Buck is appropriately housed in a Martello tower of war,
built by "Billy Pit . . . when the French were on the sea" (p.

26

17). But he has an enemy closer than France—the pseudo-French bard sporting a Latin-quarter hat.

Because Stephen is fervidly concerned with personal freedom, he resists the dehumanizing powers of "mechanical man." In the "bright silent instant" of "Telemachus," he experiences a sudden epiphany: he recognizes himself as a melancholic Hamlet figure cramped between Mulligan and Haines. He walks alone, isolated in garb and identity, and hemmed in by two malevolent stage jesters, Rosencrantz and Guildenstern. Brightness falls from the air, but the luminescence is a Luciferian glow from Mulligan's twinkling eyes. In Buck's stare, Stephen confronts a psychological rather than a physical reflection of himself; he becomes painfully aware of his body as the object of a penetrating "Medusa gaze." In a grotesque way, Mulligan is an inverted double who turns on his victim a diabolical "evil eye."[12]

Like Mulligan, Haines allies himself with the light and has eyes "pale as the sea" (p. 18). The invader gazes over the bright skyline, dazzled by his empire. Stephen identifies the Saxon conqueror with oceanic dominion and sees the Englishman as a representative of the threatening, all-encompassing sea. The Irish poet refuses to play "jester at the court of his master" (p. 25). He will not prostitute his wit to the arrogant Oxonian, and he deliberately withholds his theory proving "by algebra that Hamlet's grandson is Shakespeare's grandfather and that he himself is the ghost of his own father" (p. 18).

In anticipation of Stephen's aesthetic discussion, Haines introduces a "theological interpretation" of *Hamlet:* "The Father and the Son idea. The Son striving to be atoned with the Father" (p. 18). He flippantly offers a paradigm of all religious myth—from the classical Zeus-Jove hurling thunderbolts to a Christian God demanding the death of his only Son in expiation of Adam's sin. All religion might be defined as a "striving to be atoned with the Father," if we interpret the word "atone" both in its primary sense of "suffering to make up for a debt due"

27

and in the synthetic sense of being "at one" with a supernatural power. Shakespeare's Hamlet is striving to be atoned with the displeased shade of a murdered king, but he cannot be united with Hamlet senior until he himself has embraced death. Stephen is similarly frustrated in his quest for atonement: he can never be spiritually reconciled with Simon Dedalus, a sentimental Irishman who lives on wine, song, and nostalgia. The young poet is searching for the "shade of Kinch the elder," a man in some way worthy of consanguinity.

Clownish Buck Mulligan feels he can make himself "one" with the Father by reducing the Godhead to the level of vulgar materialism. At the mention of Christian atonement, Mulligan puts on "a blithe broadly smiling face." He becomes a Renaissance fool with eyes "blinking with mad gaiety" and moves "a doll's head to and fro" like a puppet or a machine. Even his words are automated, as he chants "in a quiet happy foolish voice" the "ballad of Joking Jesus":

> *–I'm the queerest young fellow that ever you heard.*
> *My mother's a jew, my father's a bird.*
> *With Joseph the joiner I cannot agree,*
> *So here's to disciples and Calvary.*

(P. 19)

Mulligan's song begins with a mock-definition of Christ's identity in terms of biblical parentage. Christ is alien, an *isolé*. His "mother's a jew," a member of the outcast race of Leopold Bloom and Lunita Laredo. His father is the Holy Spirit, usually represented in Christian iconography as a dove; or, as Joyce suggests in *Stephen Hero,* a "spermatozoon with wings" (*SH* 141). "The ballad of Joking Jesus" is a *reductio ad absurdum* of the doctrine of virginal conception. Like Yeats in "The Second Coming," Mulligan draws on the bestial element of pre-Christian mythology. He makes Christ's father subhuman, rather than supernatural. And he parodies earlier myths of apparent bestiality: Leda coupled with swan-Zeus; Deirdre raped by a "grey hawk." For the Messiah described in Mulli-

28

gan's ballad, atonement is impossible: the Savior could never be "at one" with an incompatible "bird-father."[13]

According to Mulligan, Christ "could not agree" with either his heavenly progenitor or his earthly father. Joseph the joiner remained skeptical of Mary's explanation of pregnancy, *"C'est le pigeon"* (p. 41). Alienated from both male parents, Christ became a wandering Messiah. Like Stephen, he could not identify his consubstantial father, the Holy Spirit, with his adopted protector, Joseph. Unable to achieve atonement, he embraced a "pseudo-paternity" over his disciples. Buck's poem is a theological parody of Stephen's *Hamlet* theory: both Christ and Shakespeare "atoned" to the Father by making themselves spiritual fathers of all mankind.

Chanting his song in the first person, Mulligan the mock-priest assumes the persona of Christ. He flutters "his hands at his sides like fins or wings of one about to rise in the air," recalling both the fish-symbol of Christ and the Messiah's parodic bird ancestry. *"What's bred in the bone cannot fail me to fly / And Olivet's breezy . . . Goodbye, now, goodbye"* (p. 19). Mulligan carries his thesis to absurdity by interpreting Christ's ascension into heaven as a literal manifestation of avian powers.

In contrast to the religious mockery in the "ballad of Joking Jesus," Stephen insists on a dogmatic definition of Catholicism. He rigidly pronounces himself an apostate:

> —You're not a believer, are you? Haines asked. I mean, a believer in the narrow sense of the word. Creation from nothing and miracles and a personal God.
> —There's only one sense of the word, it seems to me, Stephen said. . . .
> —Yes, of course, he said, as they went on again. Either you believe or you don't, isn't it? Personally I couldn't stomach that idea of a personal God. You don't stand for that, I suppose?
> —You behold in me, Stephen said with grim displeasure, a horrible example of free thought. (Pp. 19–20)

If Haines is a satanic figure, he is tempting Stephen not to deny God the Father but to relinquish a libertarian rebellion against Catholic doctrine. He tries to exact a profession of apathetic rationalism that would acknowledge an impersonal, deistic God. Stephen, emulating his patron saint, jealously guards the role of martyr. If the rebel is to fly above the labyrinth of dogma, religion must maintain its rigidity. Stephen willfully condemns himself to a Catholic hell. He wants to distinguish himself as "horrible" in freedom, just as Daedalus the Greek must have appeared terrible to the Cretans who witnessed his escape.[14]

Haines has unconsciously defined Christianity in terms of eucharistic consummation. He "personally" could not "stomach that idea of a personal God." The verbal repetition reiterates the theme of latent cannibalism associated with the Mass. According to Catholic doctrine, the individual "stomachs" the body and blood of a personal God, Jesus Christ, in the reception of Holy Communion. Haines unwittingly rejects the Eucharist and possibly reminds Stephen of his own refusal to "stand for" Easter communion in *Portrait*.

Ironically, the Englishman comments: "After all, I should think you are able to free yourself. You are your own master, it seems to me" (p. 20). Haines is referring to the "free thought" that would liberate Stephen from Irish Catholicism. His companion responds by implicating Haines and his countrymen in a bondage from which the Irishman can *not* free himself. "I am the servant of two masters, Stephen said, an English and an Italian. . . . And a third . . . there is who wants me for odd jobs" (p. 20). Contradicting the biblical injunction that "no man can serve two masters," Stephen is in servitude to three: Britain, the Roman church, and Malachi Mulligan.

The sudden appearance of two men searching for a drowned body focuses the theme of "Telemachus," once again, on the psychological terrors of enclosedness:

> Two men stood at the verge of the cliff, watching: businessman, boatman.
> —She's making for Bullock harbour.
> The boatman nodded towards the north of the bay with some disdain.

30

—There's five fathoms out there, he said. It'll be swept up that way when the tide comes in about one. It's nine days today.

The man that was drowned. A sail veering about the blank bay waiting for a swollen bundle to bob up, roll over to the sun a puffy face, salt white. Here I am. (P. 21)

The spectators await a corpse returning from its unholy novena in the womb of the sea. Like Lycidas, the drowned man has "sunk beneath the watery floor" and will rise again. But he will be resurrected as nothing more than a "swollen bundle" bobbing to the surface, a mutilated image with "puffy face, salt white." The corpse is a paradigm of the alien, the man who has become an object engulfed by inanimate matter. As part of a mechanistic universe, the dead body is reduced to the space it occupies. It can be identified numerically in temporal and spatial terms: "five fathoms out there"; "nine days today." The drowned man has become food for fishes, and his "salt white face" is reminiscent of the Dantesque "salt bread" of exile that Stephen himself consumes (p. 21).[15]

Stephen ironically concludes with the phrase "Here I am" placed in the mouth of the dead man. The corpse no longer enjoys a personal ego and cannot participate in *Being-there,* the *Dasein* described by Heidegger. The drowned man has been asphyxiated by total immersion in an alien environment. His remains are distinguished as "not-I," matter whose spatial location *here* is devoid of the existential *Being-there* that defines human experience. Stephen's satirical animation of the body is characteristic of an episode of metamorphoses. In the bizarre world of "Telemachus," dead men speak and living men are transformed into weird amphibians. "A young man clinging to a spur of rock near him moved slowly frogwise his green legs in the deep jelly of the water" (p. 21). In a reverse evolutionary process, individuals sink into matter and return to the primal fluid of the sea.

When nature does not objectify, other human beings do. "I got a card from Bannon," declares the frogman. "Says he found a sweet young thing down there. Photo girl he calls her" (p. 21). The man never identifies Milly Bloom; he describes her

31

as "a sweet young thing," the object of Bannon's male amusement. Similarly, Seymour, the medical student turned soldier, has been "stewing" around with female flesh, food for his sexual appetite.

The sudden appearance of an aged crab-man adds to the cast of metamorphosed characters: "An elderly man shot up near the spur of rock a blowing red face. He scrambled up by the stones, water glistening on his pate and on its garland of grey hair, water rilling over his chest and paunch and spilling jets out of his black sagging loincloth" (p. 22). Mulligan crosses himself piously at what seems to be the ghost of a resurrected corpse. The old man is an impotent Poseidon stripped of his powers over the sea. Despite immersion in the waters of fertility, his loincloth is sagging and black, spilling forth seedless rills of salt water. His decrepit body is one step removed from that of the dead man. In contrast to the spectral figure, Buck Mulligan declares himself a Nietzschean superman: "My twelfth rib is gone, he cried. I'm the *Uebermensch.* . . . Thus spake Zarathustra" (pp. 22–23).

Psychologically weakened, Stephen is easy prey to Mulligan, the "bird-man" who feeds on his victim's conscience. Stephen finds himself helpless to protest when Mulligan demands the key to the tower and "twopence . . . for a pint." But the final imperial command will not be obeyed: "The Ship . . . Half twelve" (p. 23). Like Homer's Telemachus, Stephen recognizes the ambush set by his friends and exiles himself to the life of a wanderer: "I will not sleep here tonight. Home also I cannot go" (p. 23). The poet romantically strikes out as an isolated and rebellious spirit. He casts off mental paralysis and determines to exercise the liberty of self-creation. "Horn of a bull, hoof of a horse, smile of a Saxon" (p. 23): none is to be trusted. Stephen will himself become the *Übermensch.*

The conclusion of "Telemachus" resembles a climactic moment in Joyce's earlier work *Stephen Hero.* Beset by "hemiplegia of the will," Stephen resolves to free himself from spiritual and psychological bondage: "The spectacle of the world in thrall filled him with the fire of courage. He, at least, though living at the farthest remove from the centre of European culture, marooned on an island in the ocean, though inheriting a will broken by doubt . . . would live his own life according to what he recognised as the voice of a new humanity, active, unafraid and unashamed'' (*SH* 194).

As Stephen turns to leave at the end of ''Telemachus,'' he witnesses Buck's final metamorphosis: ''A voice, sweettoned and sustained, called to him from the sea. Turning the curve he waved his hand. It called again. A sleek brown head, a seal's, far out on the water, round'' (p. 23). Mulligan has been attempting to reduce his companion to a fawning ''dogsbody''—an object of derision and a helpless being-for-others. Now Stephen can recognize the animality Buck has disguised as sophisticated paganism. He sees his opponent for what he is: a barking seal immersed in a sea of matter, a ''usurper'' drowning in the womb-tomb of a deterministic universe.[16]

Mulligan, Haines, and Mary Dedalus all have been overwhelmed by a claustrophobic world of mechanical action. The ghost of Mary Dedalus is a puppet of religion; Mulligan is enslaved to an Irish stage persona; and Haines is shackled to British imperialism. They are automata, particles of matter and energy being reabsorbed into the paralyzed Irish environment. It is precisely this ''hemiplegia'' that Stephen eschews in his search for the aesthetic vocation so dimly and so idealistically conceived in *A Portrait of the Artist as a Young Man.*

1. For a further discussion of Stephen as hero, see Thomas F. Staley's article ''Stephen Dedalus and the Temper of the Modern Hero,'' in *Approaches to ''Ulysses,''* ed. Thomas F. Staley and Bernard Benstock. As Staley remarks, ''Stephen's struggle in *Ulysses* . . . is Joyce's portrait of the creative individual's struggle in the modern world. Paradox and suffering emerge from the beginning of *Ulysses* as the inevitable conditions of the creative modern temper as it seeks to define itself in its own terms'' (p. 15).

2. ''Inauthenticity'' constitutes a metaphorical drowning—the total immersion of consciousness in a world of traditional values. As artist and rebel, Stephen refuses to sink down into the comfortable anonymity of what Heidegger terms *das Man*: ''the neuter, the 'they', which is nothing definite,

and which all are. . . . . Distantiality, averageness, and levelling down, as ways of Being for the 'they', constitute what we know as 'publicness'. . . . In these modes one's way of Being is that of inauthenticity and failure to stand by one's Self." As Heidegger declares, the third-person "they" "deprives the particular Dasein of its answerability. . . . Everyone is the other, and no one is himself" (Martin Heidegger, *Being and Time*, pp. 164–67).

3. As Thomas Staley reminds us, Stephen's "refusal to kneel and pray has been the one overt break with his past that has forced him to face directly the human consequences of his intellectual integrity" ("Stephen Dedalus," p. 18).

4. Mulligan's rhetoric is etymologically derisive. He calls Stephen "Kinch, the knife-blade," perhaps alluding to his sharp, caustic wit; but possibly insulting him, according to William York Tindall's derivation of "Kinch" from "kinchin" or "child" (*A Reader's Guide to James Joyce*, p. 139).

5. Samuel Beckett, *Three Novels: Molly, Malone Dies, The Unnamable*, p. 240.

6. Stephen is terrified of his mother's ghost because it embodies the threat of "immanence." As Simone de Beauvior explains in *The Second Sex*, "if the little boy remains in early childhood sensually attached to the maternal flesh, when he grows older, becomes socialized, and takes note of his individual existence, this same flesh frightens him." The feminine "presence calls him back to those realms of immanence whence he would fly, exposes roots from which he would tear himself loose. . . . To have been conceived and then born an infant is the curse that hangs over his destiny, the impurity that contaminates his being. And, too, it is the announcement of his death" (p. 136).

7. Stanislaus Joyce reports his brother Jim saying: "Don't you think . . . there is a certain resemblance between the mystery of the Mass and what I am trying to do? I mean that I am trying in my poems to give people some kind of intellectual pleasure or spiritual enjoyment by converting the bread of every-day life into something that has a permanent artistic life of its own . . . for their mental, moral, and spiritual uplift" (*My Brother's Keeper*, pp. 103–4). James Joyce ascribes the same artistic vocation to Stephen Dedalus in *Portrait* (p. 221).

8. In *Ulysses on the Liffey*, Richard Ellmann arrives at a similar conclusion about Mulligan: "Since Molly occupies the end of the book, it would follow that someone at the start must say, with Goethe's Mephistopheles, *Ich bin der Geist der stets verneint.*' This role was clearly apposite for Mulligan. . . . To the extent that Mulligan is the denying spirit, Joyce was faithful to the project he mentioned to his brother, of making *Ulysses* an Irish *Faust*'' (pp. 8, 11).

9. In Sartre's *Nausea*, Roquentin has a similar experience of alienation in front of his mirror image: "There is a white hole in the wall, a mirror. It is a trap. I know I am going to let myself be caught in it. I have. The grey thing appears in the mirror. I go over and look at it, I can no longer get away.

It is the reflection of my face. Often in these lost days I study it. I can understand nothing of this face. The faces of others have some sense, some

34

direction. Not mine. I cannot even decide whether it is handsome or ugly. . . . At heart, I am even shocked that anyone can attribute qualities of this kind to it, as if you called a clod of earth or a block of stone beautiful or ugly'' (Jean-Paul Sartre, *Nausea*, p. 27).

10. Buck's quotation is from Wilde's preface to *The Picture of Dorian Gray*.

11. Robert Boyle makes a similar observation in his essay ''The Priesthoods of Stephen and Buck.'' He remarks that the Martello Tower as ''not totally unlike, in smaller scale, the confines of the smoking and fuming prison of hell described in the retreat'' (*Approaches to ''Ulysses,''* ed. Staley and Benstock, p. 37).

12. For further discussion of ''impulses of perverseness'' and the role of the ''evil eye'' in Joyce's writing, see Maria Elisabeth Kronegger, *James Joyce and Associated Image Makers*, pp. 97–100. In *The Mechanics of Meaning*, David Hayman also remarks on the Shakespearean resonances of this scene.

13. It is quite possible that Joyce intended the theories proposed by Haines and by Mulligan as parodies of Ernest Jones's study, *The Problem of Hamlet and the Oedipus Complex*. See Ellmann, *The Consciousness of Joyce*, pp. 54, 114.

14. A. M. Klein interprets the dialogue between Haines and Stephen as a representation of the biblical temptation of Christ in the desert: '''And he was in the wilderness forty days, tempted of Satan: and was with the wild beasts' Mark 1:12). . . . Out of the very text the colloquy between Satan and his intended victim may thus be rendered. . . . The answer, as tradition required, was ambiguous. Free thought was confessed but was declared horrible. Despite his insinuating understatements, his 'rathers' and his 'somehows,' his feigned concession, . . . Satan is no further advanced than when he began his seduction.'' (''The Black Panther,'' pp. 142–43).

15. ''Now I eat his salt bread'' (p. 20). Don Gifford and Robert J. Seidman note that the phrase echoes Dante's *Paradiso*, XVII:55–65, in which ''Dante's great-great-grandfather, Cacciaguida, predicts the future course of Dante's life and the bitterness of his exile'' with the prophecy, ''Thou shalt make trial of how salt doth taste another's bread'' (*Notes for Joyce*, p. 14).

16. In *Epic Geography*, Michael Seidel reminds us that ''mockers are Protean parasites'' and that ''Proteus in the *Odyssey* was a keeper of seals. . . . Menelaus captured Proteus by disguising himself and his men in seals' hides and taking control of his domain'' (p. 140).

35

2

"Nestor": The Nightmare of History

In the "Nestor" and the "Proteus" episodes, Joyce extends the psychological boundaries of Irish paralysis: time and space become the limits of Stephen's claustrophobia, and enclosedness characterizes all of human history. The ghost of Mary Dedalus gives way to the haunting shadow of past time, the tower-prison to historical confinement. Stephen feels shackled to the temporal categories that define Western thought, the "nightmare" from which he must try to break free.

> You, Cochrane, what city sent for him?
> —Tarentum, sir.
> —Very good. Well?
> —There was a battle, sir.
> —Very good. Where?
> The boy's blank face asked the blank window.
> Fabled by the daughters of memory. And yet it was in some way if not as memory fabled it. A phrase, then, of impatience, thud of

Blake's wings of excess. I hear the ruin of all space, shattered glass and toppling masonry, and time one livid final flame. What's left us then? (P. 24)

Aristotle's definition of time as "the motion of matter" sets the precedent for Stephen's history lesson: "It must be a movement then, an actuality of the possible as possible. Aristotle's phrase" (p. 25).[1] Stephen forces himself, as well as his pupil, to spatialize temporal phenomena: "What city sent for him?" (p. 24). Cochrane gropes for a geographical location, then recreates the scene descriptively. "There was a battle," he murmurs, using "there" as an expletive. The teacher insists that "there" be employed adverbially: he demands an exact location, which he himself must verify by "glancing at the name and date in the gorescarred book" (p. 24). The whole phenomenon of history suggests temporal-spatial disjunction. Cochrane can remember the date of the battle, but not its location. The two facts exist separately as independent categories. History is defined in terms of time and place, as the intersection of two linear axes, with no further dimension for human imagination.

Stephen counterpoints the lesson with private reflections on William Blake's description of history as allegory, "a totally distinct and inferior kind of Poetry . . . Form'd by the daughters of Memory" from the "Vanities of Time and Space." In his notes for the "Vision of the Last Judgment," Blake insists that "Vision or Imagination is a Representation of what Eternally Exists, Really and Unchangeably."[2] The romantic poet would destroy the edifice of past history because it contradicts pure imaginative thought. But if time collapses into "one livid final flame," "What's left us then?" (p. 24). The Platonic form of eternal being ignores both perceptual reality and individual experience: it shuns the phenomenal world of empirical revelation. Stephen is determined to fly beyond the labyrinth of history without Blake's "wings of excess."

He thinks of Pyrrhus as "any general to any officers," murmuring words applicable to all historical triumphs: "*Another victory like that and we are done for*" (p. 24). Every individual, whether he wins or loses particular battles, is "done for" in the end. And every era of civilization gives way to the new, collapsing in Viconian spirals of repetition. All history is a "pier," a "disappointed bridge" that ostensibly leads to some teleological goal, but ends abruptly in the waves.

Stephen completes his dialectic by contemplating history in Aristotelian terms of act and potency: "Had Pyrrhus not fallen by a beldam's hand in Argos or Julius Caesar not been knifed to death? They are not to be thought away. Time has branded them and fettered they are lodged in the room of the infinite possibilities they have ousted. But can those have been possible seeing that they never were? Or was that only possible which came to pass?" (p. 25). The events of history are metaphorically lodged in a closed chamber where they occupy all available space, leaving no room for further contingencies. As a poet, Stephen is a "weaver of the wind" who fashions stories from the historical possibilities that were never actualized. In so doing, he asserts the superiority of creative consciousness over the solidified structure of a nightmare past.

For Stephen, the nightmare of history is a composite of deterministic forces that threaten individual creativity. Its landscape embraces the formidable night world of the unconscious, where specters of biographical trauma abide. Stephen wonders how much of his own life has been determined by consubstantial parents, Catholic training, Irish nationality, and a Celtic cultural heritage.[3]

One of the principal themes of the "Nestor" episode is the "burial of the dead." How can the individual dispose of his past and free himself from the viscosity of its presence? The shaggy dog riddle of a "fox burying his grandmother under a hollybush" (p. 27) is a pedestrian version of the resurrection myth in *Lycidas*. Stephen is frantically trying to bury the specter of his mother in the ground of past history. But like the fox, he feels compelled by "remorse of conscience" perpetually to resurrect her threatening apparition. He cannot dismiss her as a "poor soul gone to heaven" (p. 28), but must dig in the earth to

39

uncover the corpse of his guilt: "and on a heath beneath winking stars a fox, red reek of rapine on his fur, with merciless bright eyes scraped in the earth, listened, . . . scraped and scraped" (p. 28).

Stephen sees in the figure of Cyril Sergent the helplessness of childhood bending beside him. He painfully recalls his own vulnerability and youthful isolation: "Secrets, silent, stony sit in the dark palaces of both our hearts: secrets weary of their tyranny: tyrants willing to be dethroned" (p. 28). Only a "mother's love" protects the melancholic child. *"Amor matris:* subjective and objective genitive" seems to be the "only true thing in life" (pp. 27–28).

Stephen is desperately searching for a philosophy that will transcend the spectral past and confirm the uniqueness of a creative vision rooted in the present moment. At the heart of his colloquy with Garrett Deasy lies the antinomy between historical determinism and imaginative freedom. The schoolmaster's notion of history is linear and eschatological. It is, in a restricted sense, "Aristotelian." In his "Natural Science," Aristotle depicted the temporal moment spatially, as an individual point on a line; he visualized time as a serial progression of instants inexorably bound together. His model provided a basis for the Western conceptualization of temporality. Applied to human experience, the Aristotelian trope suggests that each individual is rolled along a track from birth to death, with little rational or volitional control over his destiny. He is bound to a "domino" set of causes and effects: the external categories of time and space govern an ineluctable progression toward the stasis of death.[4]

Christianity made use of Aristotle's metaphor to explain its own eschatology: human history moves forward to an apocalypse, a last judgment, and the second coming of Christ. Deasy's language is biblical, as well as Hegelian, when he declares that "all history moves towards one great goal, the manifestation of God" (p. 34). Evangelism provides a rationale for predestination, Protestant election, and anti-Semitism.

Deasy's office is a miniature replica of the decaying "room" of history from which imaginative possibilities have been ousted. The mouldering atmosphere of the enclosed chamber recalls Stephen's claustrophobia in the Martello tower: "Stale smoky air hung in the study with the smell of drab abraded leather of its chairs. As on the first day he bargained with me here. As it was in the beginning, is now. On the sideboard the tray of Stuart coins, base treasure of a bog: and ever shall be . . . world without end" (p. 29). Stephen muses: "And now his strongroom for the gold. . . . An old pilgrim's hoard, dead treasure, hollow shells" (p. 29). Like the tower room, Deasy's study is lifeless and suffocating, unchanged since the first day Stephen entered. The cloister provides sanctuary for the gold coins and hollow shells greedily amassed by the schoolmaster. The old man's "treasure hoard" is built on the skeleton of paralyzed time. Deasy believes that he has somehow captured the past in his collection of Apostle spoons and Stuart coins. He has tried to shut out the flux of life and to deny the changing phenomena of the present. His endeavor is as futile as it is naive. "A sovereign fell, bright and new, on the soft pile of the tablecloth" (p. 29). The Edwardian coin is an unheeded reminder that kings are continually falling in history and that even the "sovereign power" of a monarch is evanescent.

The schoolmaster is fettered to lifeless objects of the past, as well as to the archetypal categories of an outmoded tradition. He inhabits a mechanical, automatic world and is entranced by "enclosedness." His aim is to stockpile as much gold as possible, with little concern for output in a vital, operative economy. "Money is power," Deasy insists (p. 30), as he proudly displays proof of sovereignty. Deasy is evidently unfamiliar with either Keynesian economics or Freudian psychoanalytic theory. He sees virtue in greed, delights in controlling static objects, and manifests all the traits of a typically anal-retentive personality.

As in the tower, Stephen experiences the paralysis of a world where nothing lives of its own accord, nothing wills its own existence. In the stagnant cloister, he is hemmed in by inanimate objects that never change. "As it was in the beginning, is now . . . and ever shall be'' (p. 29). ''The same room and hour, the same wisdom: and I the same. Three times now. Three nooses round me here. Well. I can break them in this instant if I will'' (p. 30). Stephen is aware of the hangman's rope around his neck, for he perceives a direct correlation between the money he earns and the shells of history: both are dead relics of a living past. His third salary constitutes still another link with a claustrophobic death-world. Stephen realizes that there *is* a way to avoid the foredoomed noose. He need not subscribe to Deasy's Edwardian ethic or embrace a utilitarian definition of success. In a moment of self-determination, he can choose his own existence and break free of the paralyzed environment that threatens to destroy him.

Stephen recognizes Deasy's ''history'' as nothing more than a series of ''disappointed bridges'' by which greed for power drives men to automated, irrational behavior. The nightmare becomes another manifestation of the horrifying ''Ghoul, Chewer of corpses'': ''Time shocked rebounds, shock by shock. Jousts, slush and uproar of battles, the frozen deathspew of the slain, a shout of spear spikes baited with men's bloodied guts'' (p. 32). The children's field hockey is emblematic of the ''joust'' of life undertaken in a warlike, competitive society. Stephen realizes the grotesque nature of the game of ''getting ahead'' that Deasy plays with so little awareness.

History is indeed a nightmare. But Stephen questions the necessity of perpetuating the conflict—of contributing to the ''frozen deathspew of the slain'' until we ourselves taste the blood of battle. It must be possible to get beyond a Hobbesian state of nature to the freedom of artistic vision—to exist ''as gods,'' fashioning a ''postcreation'' from the fertile realm of human imagination. Stephen refuses to play the game of life as Deasy defines it. He will not capitulate to a society that measures success in terms of aggression and gives the prize to those who have ''paid their way'' with the shells of other men's bones.

The rhetoric of imperialism seals the bonds of historical imprisonment. When Deasy insists that ''we are a generous

42

people but we must also be just," Stephen complains that he fears "those big words . . . which make us so unhappy" (p. 31). He sees neither justice nor generosity in the subservience of his countrymen to a foreign power. The British have reduced Irish political history to a tale of poverty and subjugation. The vocabulary of rationalization sanctions atrocities in the name of manifest destiny.

Garrett Deasy can see the morbid conditions surrounding him, but he projects them onto the scapegoat Jews, "signs of a nation's decay." His conversation reflects a political terror of the Jewish financiers attached to the court of King Edward: "Wherever they gather they eat up the nation's vital strength" (p. 33). Deasy vilifies the Hebrew merchants for a work of destruction that he himself perpetuates. He fails to see the resemblance between his own greed for money, power, and relics of the past and the caricature by which he depicts the Jewish moneylender. In fact, he refuses to consider the possibility that guilt may be universal to mankind:

> —A merchant, Stephen said, is one who buys cheap and sells dear, jew or gentile, is he not?
> —They sinned against the light, Mr. Deasy said gravely. And you can see the darkness in their eyes. And that is why they are wanderers on the earth to this day. . . .
> —Who has not? Stephen said.
> —What do you mean? Mr. Deasy asked.
> He came forward a pace and stood by the table. His underjaw fell sideways open uncertainly. Is this old wisdom? He waits to hear from me.
> —History, Stephen said, is a nightmare from which I am trying to awake.
> From the playfield the boys raised a shout. A whirring whistle: goal. What if that nightmare gave you a back kick?
> —The ways of the Creator are not our ways, Mr. Deasy said. All history moves towards one great goal, the manifestation of God.
> Stephen jerked his thumb towards the window, saying:
> —That is God.
> Hooray! Ay! Whrrwhee!
> —What? Mr. Deasy asked.
> —A shout in the street, Stephen answered, shrugging his shoulders. (P. 34)

Deasy quotes the biblical statement "They sinned against the light" to reassure himself of Protestant election. He considers the Jews children of darkness and identifies subtlety as a characteristic of the enemy. He believes that Christian light shines on those who are prosperous and that wealth signifies divine approval. Despising the Hebrew merchants, Deasy paradoxically worships mercantile grandeur.

Earlier in the chapter, Stephen thought of Christ as a man with "dark eyes" whose mythic shadow lay over the earth. Jesus turned away from Caesar's coins of tribute and renounced political authority. He looked into the obscure depths of men's souls to proclaim the truth obliquely, through parable and metaphor: "To Caesar what is Caesar's, to God what is God's. A long look from dark eyes, a riddling sentence to be woven on the church's looms. Ay" (p. 26).

Deasy seems to have missed the purport of Christ's teachings: that he who is without charity is like a clanging cymbal. In his condemnation of the Jews, the schoolmaster has regressed to a mode of thinking far less sophisticated than the Judeo-Christian ethic. For Deasy, "darkness" signifies a stain of defilement, the "something" that infects the condemned scapegoat. Darkness is necessarily ambiguous: it constitutes a sign of moral turpitude, as well as a concrete blemish visible in the eyes of those contaminated. The Jews have been marked by communal guilt, a racial uncleanness imposed by a vengeful God. They have been condemned to wander over the earth as representatives of man's servile will. To a Deasy-mind, "evil is not nothing . . . it is posited; in this sense it is something to be 'taken away.'"[5] By persecuting the guilt-ridden scapegoat, the elect can reify its fear of impurity and purge itself of infection.

Insisting that the Jews must be wanderers, Deasy invokes the classical concept of atoning exile. He accuses the Hebrew race of "blood guilt" for the crucifixion of Christ. Every member of the Jewish family is an involuntary criminal who must atone for the tragic murder of God. The heirs of defilement have to be removed from contact with their fellow citizens. Persecution of the Jews becomes a virtue, a manifestation of justice, and an expression of exemption from the darkness of sin.

44

Deasy's morality of contamination comes full circle when he interprets the historical suffering of the Jews as evidence of transgression. He believes that the Hebrews have been dispossessed of Israel, their homeland, in just punishment for their sins. "That is why they are wanderers on the earth," Deasy argues. The schoolmaster appeals to history as proof of guilt. He has reverted to a pre-ethical stage of thinking, "in which evil and misfortune have not been dissociated, in which the ethical order of doing ill has not been distinguished from the cosmo-biological order of faring ill: suffering, sickness, death, failure."[6]

Deasy is convinced that the misfortunes of the Jews are signs of divine wrath. He rationalizes hatred in the name of justice and places it in the grand scheme of God's self-revelation. Not only does he agree with Haines that "history is to blame" (p. 20), but he insists that the events of history are directed according to a supernatural plan. By appealing to the deity, he denies human freedom and abnegates personal responsibility for injustice.

Deasy clings to a primitive philosophy of exclusion. Even the language of his argument is structured by a preconscious terror of defilement, a fear of intermixture and infectious contact. "They sinned against the light, Mr. Deasy said gravely" (p. 34). He denotes the Jews by means of the anonymous, subtly condemnatory pronoun, "they," branding the Hebrew race as irretrievably alien. "They" connotes "otherness"; it refers to "*l'autrui,*" "those who are different from *us.*" The first-person subject, "we," is the direct pronominal opposite of "they." And it is "we" who have the "light," another ambiguous term signifying the truth, mysterious and secret, exclusively possessed by *us.* "Sin" and "light" are words that primitive myth, Greek tragedy, and Christian philosophy have archetypally defined. "Sin" connotes all that is evil; "light," all that is good. Hence the Manichean antithesis that distinguishes "them" from "us," vice from virtue, darkness from light. The Jew today is "*l'autre,*" bound by a two-thousand-year-old transgression so heinous that it continues to defile.

"And you can see the darkness in their eyes," Deasy continues, again appealing to the antinomy between "you" and

45

"they," the unforgettable *otherness* of the scapegoat. Deasy extends his original aphorism by piling up sentence units that substitute conjunctive parallelism for a logical sequence of causes. "You" who have the light can "see" darkness in *their* eyes. Deasy is not cognizant of the physical contradiction in terms: one cannot *see* darkness, a word denoting all that is *not* visible. But the stain of defilement always "dwells in the half-light of a quasi-physical infection."[7] The pedagogue assumes the validity of the second term of his syllogism and hastily rushes on to its conclusion. He triumphantly explains: "And that is why they are wanderers on the earth to this day." "That" includes "all that went before" and vaguely alludes to a rational explanation for Jewish persecution. Deasy attempts to evoke preconscious dread of the exile and fear of contamination. The auditor should infer the antecedent of "that," not through logical deduction, but from the emotional hostility he has supposedly associated with "they."

The first and second persons that constitute the "we" are defined by a process of restriction and alienation. It is precisely this movement of rejection that Deasy depends on for his bigoted harangue. The schoolmaster has turned against the Jewish race a Sartrian *regard,* the "gaze" of petrifaction. In the act of condemnatory judgment, he excludes the Hebrews from the subject-community of the "we" and from the rhythm of humanity. His "Medusa gaze" transfixes his enemy in historical stasis.[8]

Stephen responds to the assertion that "they sinned against the light" by asking the question, "Who has not?" He appeals to a syntactical form of inclusion to make *all* men participants in the scapegoat category. The phrase "Who has not?" implies that "We all have." Stephen invokes the language of confession to raise the notion of defilement to a more generalized concept of universal "sin." Darkness is not a stain imposed by the deity for a particular transgression. It is, in fact, our common experience of limitation, the darkness of fallibility inherent in the human condition. As Stephen declares in "Proteus," "Darkness is in our souls, do you not think? . . . Our souls,

46

shame-wounded by our sins, cling to us yet more, a woman to her lover clinging'' (p. 48). Stephen imagines the soul as a feminine anima embracing the darkness at the center of human life. Because the individual cannot escape the shadowy side of his nature or deny a ''shame-wounded'' condition of animality, he unconsciously ascribes the experience of finitude to some inherent fault. In an Augustinian vision of original sin, Stephen suggests that darkness abides not in the eyes of the Jews, but in the soul of every human being.

Deasy clings so fiercely to the idea of contamination that he feels dumbfounded by the terminology of inclusion. He fails to understand even the basic denotation of Stephen's language and can only query, ''What do you mean?'' ''He came forward a pace and stood by the table. His underjaw fell sideways open uncertainly. Is this old wisdom? He waits to hear from me'' (p. 34). The schoolmaster has been shaken from his original posture of certitude. In his perplexity, he alters his geographical as well as his psychological stance, in order to get a closer look at the enemy. He has begun to wonder if Stephen actually belongs to the first-person elite and can be counted among those blessed with light. Perhaps he is even searching the young man's eyes for signs of hostile darkness.

According to the schema that Joyce sent Carlo Linati, Mr. Deasy supports the ''wisdom of the old world,'' the archaic modes of Western historical thought.[9] Like the taverners in ''Cyclops,'' Deasy insists that the Hebrews must bear their religious burden of guilt. ''They are wanderers on the earth to this day,'' he declares, attempting to justify by false logic the contemporaneity of racial prejudice.

History, moreover, has determined the pedagogue's linguistic attitudes. Deasy spouts meaningless aphorisms like an automaton declaring the content of its memory chamber. He envisions time as a line of points progressing from an initial creation to a distant teleological end. His perspective is Christian, historical, and eschatological—hardly in line with the cyclical philosophy Joyce adopted from Vico. The old ''history,'' like a ball in a hockey game, moves through time toward "one great goal." To Stephen, the linear framework is absurd. "What if the nightmare gave you a back kick" (p. 34) and put the ball back into play? The younger man tries to dissociate the present phenomenon of the moment, an individual instant of time and space, from the vast categorical structures invoked by the schoolmaster. He negates the Western concept of history as an infinite number of points on a line, an unbreakable time-space continuum. History is a pier, a "disappointed bridge": reality is constantly in cyclical flux, thrusting the individual back into the waves of Heraclitean movement.

Because language, too, belongs to history, Stephen must revert to signs, to gestures, to a hand that points toward the phenomenon itself. He "jerked his thumb towards the window," saying, "That is God" (p. 34). God is no longer an atemporal deity inhabiting a noumenal realm. The divinity that the new religion shall worship is the god-like freedom of human consciousness to transcend itself in a moment of epiphany:

> Hooray! Ay! Whrrwhee!
> What? Mr. Deasy asked.
> A shout in the street, Stephen answered, shrugging his shoulders. (P. 34).

The *quidditas* suddenly revealed is the radiance of pure being. By their cries of excitement, the children have achieved a condition of "ecstasy" insofar as the meaning of *ekstasis* is "a distance from self." They momentarily exult in spontaneous existence, the unmediated union of perceiver and object.[10]

As a twentieth-century artist, Stephen realizes that the moment itself constitutes the temporal dimension of psychological freedom: it allows the individual to get beyond the historical axes of time and space. For the modern hero, "the moment is all"—whether it is the moment of vision, of fantasy, or of epiphanic discovery. Spontaneity becomes the temporal mode of revelation. The instant negates linear time and asserts the primacy of perception within the "here and now." As Joyce declares in his essay "James Clarence Mangan," "poetry . . . makes no account of history, which is fabled by the daughters of

48

memory, but sets store by every time less than the pulsation of
an artery, the time in which its intuitions start forth.''[11]

Consciousness may freely create itself by transcending historical stasis and the confines of a self-reflexive past. The artist
becomes god-like in the ecstasy of phenomenal discovery.
Once the mind is liberated from the bonds of historical determinism, it stands open to ''sudden spiritual manifestation.'' It
can unite with the newly formed object of epiphanic vision in an
act of aesthetic ''postcreation.''

Unlike the boys on the playing field, Garrett Deasy has
yielded to the nightmare of viscosity. The fluidity of his consciousness is slowly being sucked into a murky past. Deasy's
thoughts are disordered, his historical data jumbled, and all his
arguments confused. Like a man drowning in quicksand, he is
well on his way to death. Deasy is not an evil person: he has
simply fallen prey to a grandiose myth of history and to the
imperialistic rhetoric that supports it. His life has been
fashioned by forces of the past—by Puritan frugality, evangelical Christianity, and Edwardian xenophobia. Raised on fifty
years of Victoriolatry, he attributes political conflict to unfaithful women, from Eve and Helen to Kitty O'Shea. *Per vias
rectas,* he will travel by the straight roads of narrow-minded-
ness toward the attainment of ''one great goal,'' the
manifestation of God.

Stephen, for his part, refuses to serve the self-revelation of an
''allbright'' deity. He takes refuge in the ''mind's darkness''
that shelters ''a sloth of the underworld, reluctant, shy of
brightness, shifting her dragon scaly folds. Thought is the
thought of thought. . . . Tranquillity sudden, vast, candescent:
form of forms'' (p. 26). Like Christ, like the Hebrew race, like
Averroes and Moses Maimonides, he will join those ''dark men
in mien and movement, flashing in their mocking mirrors the
obscure soul of the world, a darkness shining in brightness
which brightness could not comprehend'' (p. 28).

Stephen aspires to become the god of his own creation,
outside of time, politics, and determinism. He will explore
those imaginative possibilities for which history has no room,

49

and which art alone can actualize. He will draw the past into the present in the mode of creative memory. Stephen intends to break out of the closed chamber of history into the realm of the intellectual imagination. He will become a god unto himself, creating that which "never was" by transforming the nightmare of history into the magical stories of art.

1. According to Aristotle, "time is a derivative (*pathos*) of motion" ("Natural Science," in *Aristotle,* trans. and ed. Philip Wheelwright, p. 50).

2. William Blake, *The Complete Writings of William Blake,* ed. Geoffrey Keynes, pp. 604–5.

3. The "nightmare" that Stephen is trying to escape approximates the complex of ideas and feelings that Jean-Paul Sartre describes by using the word "facticity." The English neologism fails to convey Sartre's precise meaning, since the English word "factitious" has inappropriate and misleading connotations. "Facticity" indicates an amalgam of the individual's present situation and past history, both biographical and social; it constitutes the temporal dimension of "being-in-itself" that restricts consciousness to the static viscosity of the past. "Facticity" is, in effect, the persona that the individual presents both to the self and to the world. It is the social identity contingent on one's situation, accomplishments, failures, and victories—in short, all those things that make up the dead past of experience. According to Sartre, the existential self is "pure possibility," defined entirely by future project and by the ability of consciousness to "nihilate" its past. "Nihilate" is another term coined by Sartre. As Hazel Barnes explains: "Consciousness exists as consciousness by making a nothingness [q.v.] arise between it and the object of which it is consciousness. Thus nihilation is that by which consciousness exists. To nihilate is to encase with a shell of non-being" (Jean-Paul Sartre, *Being and Nothingness,* p. 632, glossary).

4. In his "Natural Science," Aristotle accounts for the eternality of time by the argument that "time can neither exist nor be conceived apart from an actual 'now.' But what we call 'now' is a kind of intermediate state, having the twofold character of a beginning and an end—a beginning, that is to say, of future and an end of past time. Hence . . . it follows that time must necessarily extend backwards from that 'now' as well as forwards from it" ("Natural Science," in Wheelright, *Aristotle,* pp. 49–50).

5. Paul Ricoeur, *The Symbolism of Evil,* p. 155. Deasy invokes a primitive notion of defilement, which "precedes any ethics of the second person and is immersed in the archaic belief in the maleficent virtues of shed blood" (p. 28). As Ricoeur explains, "the representation of defilement dwells in the half-light of a quasi-physical infection that points toward a quasi-moral unworthiness. This ambiguity is not expressed conceptually but is experienced intentionally

in the very quality of the half-physical, half-ethical fear that clings to the representation of the impure" (p. 35).

6. Ibid., p. 27. "Vengeance causes suffering. And thus, through the intermediary of retribution, the whole physical order is taken up into the ethical order; the evil of suffering is linked synthetically with the evil of fault. . . . Suffering evil clings to doing evil as punishment proceeds ineluctably from defilement" (ibid., p. 31).

7. Ibid., p. 35.

8. As Sartre declares in *Being and Nothingness,* the Other tries to confer on the for-itself an identity as "a thing among things. This petrifaction in initself by the Other's look is the profound meaning of the myth of Medusa" (p. 430).

9. The Linati schema and its English translation were first published by Richard Ellmann in *Ulysses on the Liffey.* Ellmann explains: "The famous table of colours, techniques, organs, and other aspects of *Ulysses,* which Gilbert printed in his book, had a predecessor in one which Joyce made for Carlo Linati in September 1920. In the letter accompanying it he remarked, 'My intention is not only to render the myth *sub specie temporis nostri* but also to allow each adventure . . . to condition and even to create its own technique'" (pp. xvi–xvii).

10. According to Sartre, "the For-itself has to be its being ekstatically"; and "change belongs naturally to the for-itself inasmuch as this for-itself is spontaneity" (*Being and Nothingness,* pp. 136, 148). Sartre takes the term *ek-stasis* from Martin Heidegger, who writes in *Being and Time:* "We therefore call the phenomena of the future, the character of having been, and the Present, the '*ecstases*' of temporality. . . . That *Present* which is held in authentic temporality and which thus is *authentic* itself, we call the '*moment of vision*'. This term must be understood in the active sense as an ecstasis. It means . . . a rapture which is *held* in resoluteness" (pp. 377, 387).

11. *The Critical Writings of James Joyce,* ed. Ellsworth Mason and Richard Ellmann, p. 81. Joyce is, of course, adapting Blake to his own purposes. In Virginia Woolf's novel *The Waves,* Bernard declares: "The moment was all; the moment was enough" (*Jacob's Room* and *The Waves,* p. 369).

3

"Proteus": The Art of Perception
"Scylla and Charybdis": The Artist as God

In the ''Proteus episode, Stephen Dedalus rejects the spatial and temporal enclosure of ''Telemachus'' and ''Nestor'' by exposing the conceptual heritage of Western philosophy to a phenomenal *Lebenswelt*. Alone on the beach at Sandymount, he entertains esoteric speculations about the nature of time, space, and reality. He meditates on Gotthold Lessing's definition of time as *nacheinander*—things coming ''one after another'' in a series; and of space as *nebeneinander*—things set ''one beside the other'' on a visible plane. In a skeptical study of perception, he cuts through abstruse layers of epistemology with William of Occam's philosophical razor.[1] Stephen returns to the basic sensory data apprehended by the mind and attempts to judge the first principles of human knowing. He is trying to uncover the pre-linguistic roots of art as image and gesture—the primordial, ''lived experience'' of sight and sound.

Stephen first contemplates the problem of space, which he defines as the ''ineluctable modality of the visible'' and later clarifies as ''what you damn well have to see'' (p. 186). ''Ineluctable modality of the visible: at least that if no more, thought through my eyes. Signatures of all things I am here to read, seaspawn and seawrack, the nearing tide, that rusty boot. Snotgreen, bluesilver, rust: coloured signs. Limits of the diaphane. But he adds: in bodies'' (p. 37). Stephen has gone back to the original ''lived experience in which 'intuition of space' as perception and phantasy takes place.'' Space is, in effect, ''the continuum of the field of vision,''[2] the manner in which objects are given to the mind. The ''nothingness'' of the intellect must necessarily define itself by directing attention toward the external world. Thought originates ''through my eyes,'' through the senses that present objects ''in person'' to consciousness.[3]

If space can be described as the ''ineluctable modality of the visible,'' then time may similarly be defined as a dimension of auditory perception: ''Stephen closed his eyes to hear his boots crush crackling wrack and shells. You are walking through it howsomever. I am, a stride at a time. A very short space of time through very short times of space. Five, six: the *nacheinander*. Exactly: and that is the ineluctable modality of the audible'' (p. 37). Like Gotthold Lessing, Stephen has perceived the serial nature of temporality, and he employs the term *nacheinander* to describe moments following ''one after another.'' He uses an auditory model from an analysis of sound to get beyond ''world time'' to the constitution of internal, ''immanent'' time. Stephen is concerned with the ''generative now'' at the center of primary time-consciousness. Hence his description of time in ever shorter units, ''a very short space of time through very short times of space.'' He is trying to abstract the generative instant from ''the fixed temporal order . . . of an infinite, two-dimensional series.''[4] Time collapses into the present as a ''signature'' of eternity—a sign of time-consciousness detached from linear categories.

Stephen's meditation on the nature of time and space reflects

54

both the philosophical and the aesthetic distinctions posed by Gotthold Lessing in *Laocoön*. According to Lessing:

> . . . Painting employs wholly different signs or means of imitation from poetry,—the one using forms and colors in space, the other articulate sounds in time. . . .
>
> Objects which exist side by side, or whose parts so exist, are called bodies. Consequently bodies with their visible properties are the peculiar subjects of painting.
>
> Objects which succeed each other, or whose parts succeed each other in time, are actions. Consequently actions are the peculiar subjects of poetry.
>
> All bodies, however, exist not only in space, but also in time. . . .[5]

Poetry, unlike the visual arts, communicates itself rhythmically in a temporal medium. In a bit of doggerel verse, Stephen invites "Madeline the mare" to Sandymount. Prior to the jingle, he speaks of "Dominie Deasy"; and the shells, "wild sea money," recall the schoolmaster's coins. Stephen's fragmentary verse is a taunting rejection of Deasy-Nestor and the "nightmare" of history. "Rhythm begins, you see. I hear. A catalectic tetrameter of iambs marching" (p. 37). For the bard, music and poetry become synecdoches for time. Poetic rhythm must be apprehended according to the "ineluctable modality of the audible."

After an amusing reference to Aristotle, the "master of those who know," Stephen proceeds to parody theoretical speculation. His eclectic mind plays with the ponderous wisdom of the past and challenges scholastic precepts to empirical reexamination. Philosophy is grist for the mill of art. *Homo ludens* presides, and a playful creative consciousness pokes fun at the stultified epistemology of Western tradition.

Through the bog of erudite reflections, one can easily miss the humor of "Proteus." The language of the episode is amorphous, allusive, and elusive, as well. Stephen's mode of consciousness is extremely ironic. He constantly satirizes his own tendency toward aesthetic solipsism and Berkeleyan self-enclosure. The Stephen of "Proteus" is the nascent Shem of *Finnegans Wake,* locked in his haunted inkbattlehouse.

Before opening his eyes, Stephen is careful to prolong the "instant" of his reverie. "Open your eyes now. I will. One moment. . . . I will see if I can see." "See now. There all the time without you: and ever shall be, world without end" (p. 37). He "sees" with his eyes and understands with his intellect the falsity of a Berkeleyan universe. All has not vanished. The world has been "there all the time." The experiment reaffirms the independent existence of things-in-themselves. The poet's task is to read the "signatures of all things"—the phenomena as they appear to him in their *quidditas* or absolute self-givenness.

The young artist criticizes his earlier writings as too romantic and amorphous: "Books you were going to write with letters for titles. . . . Remember your epiphanies on green oval leaves" (p. 40). His sketches were as shapeless as the cloud in *Hamlet*: "Ay, very like a whale" (p. 40), or like anything else. Stephen facetiously describes his epiphanies as "deeply deep." Yet the idea of "epiphany" is precisely what he is trying to grasp in "Proteus." The epiphany or "showing forth" is a momentary illumination analogous to Christ's self-revelation to the magi. Any natural object "intensely regarded" can disclose signatures of meaning to the imagination. When a phenomenal object is brought before the focal point of perception, consciousness reflects back upon itself in a moment of discovery. The mind apprehends the thing perceived in "wholeness," "harmony," and "radiance." "Thought is the thought of thought" (p. 26). The divinity revealed is not that of the traditional Christ, but the transcendent power of man "to be God" by fashioning a new reality from the creative union of consciousness and external object.

"Will you be as gods? Gaze in your omphalos. Hello. Kinch here. Put me on to Edenville. Aleph, alpha: nought, nought one" (p. 38). Despite Stephen's satire of "mystic monks," he too is engaged in "navel-gazing." He is trying to explore the reflective potentials of the intellect and to become his own "man-God" through the creative possibilities of art. He wants to be put in touch with "Edenville," but he fears the viscosity of the past. Each man is bound to a trail of navel cords, the "strandentwining cable of all flesh" that leads back to Adam, to paradise, and to original sin. "Spouse and helpmate of Adam Kadmon: Heva, naked Eve. She had no navel. Gaze. Belly without blemish, bulging big, a buckler of taut vellum, no, whiteheaped corn, orient and immortal, standing from everlasting to everlasting. Womb of sin" (p. 38).

Both racial and personal history seemingly constitute an inescapable situation in the world. Stephen thinks with dread of his own consubstantial heritage determined by a moment of "blind rut": "Wombed in sin darkness I was too, made not begotten. By them, the man with my voice and my eyes and a ghostwoman with ashes on her breath. They clasped and sundered, did the coupler's will. From before the ages He willed me and now may not will me away or ever. A *lex eterna* stays about him" (p. 38). Even the Creator is bound by eternal law. He willed the existence of Stephen; and at a particular moment in history, that divine thought had to be realized. The soul was given physical form and cloistered in a stultified world of ludicrous relations. Stephen feels as alien as the mad Swift or the mortified prophet Elisha. "Houses of decay, mine, his and all. . . . Come out of them, Stephen. Beauty is not there" (p. 39).

Stephen's reflections soon expand to other aspects of paralysis—to religion and to Irish nationality. He ironically contemplates the "Isle of saints," a land of empty "human shells." His environment is ominous and deadly, threatening to suck the individual into its bowels and drown him in a sea of lifeless essences. Once again the imagery conveys a nauseous sense of viscosity: "Unwholesome sandflats waited to suck his treading soles, breathing upward sewage breath. He coasted them, walking warily. A porter-bottle stood up, stogged to its waist, in the cakey sand dough. A sentinel: isle of dreadful thirst. Broken hoops on the shore; at the land a maze of dark cunning nets; farther away chalkscrawled backdoors and on

57

the higher beach a dryingline with two crucified shirts'' (p. 41).

Stephen is treading in a grotesque, surrealistic world, where nature takes on life of its own and waits in ambush for its victim. The slimy sandflats become animate predators, greedy to suck in and destroy consciousness. The land exudes a poisonous stench of asphyxiation. A phallic porter-bottle stands as an omen of castrated manhood: in the ''isle of dreadful thirst,'' a slimy ooze has supplanted fluidity. The Irish people, half in love with easeful death, are metaphorically sinking down into matter. They have surrendered the possibilities of fluid self-creation to merge with a paralyzed past. A maze of dark cunning nets strangles creativity. Those who do try to escape risk being crucified on a dryingline, as was Little Chandler in the *Dubliners* story ''A Little Cloud.''

Ireland and its sandflats menace Stephen, but he cannot decide on a second exile. He remembers Paris with a sense of dual identity. That ''other self'' of the Latin Quarter seems to be no more than a fictitious alibi. ''Other fellow did it: other me. Hat, tie, overcoat, nose. *Lui, c'est moi.* You seem to have enjoyed yourself'' (p. 41). Stephen tries to believe that ''*Lui, c'est moi,*'' but he continues to speak in second-person dialogue to his alter-ego. ''You were going to do wonders, what? Missionary to Europe after fiery Columbanus'' (p. 42). In *Portrait,* Stephen figuratively strode across the prostrate body of his mother to fly the nets of tradition. But once in exile, he failed to forge the uncreated conscience of his race. In Paris he found the emasculated remnants of an Irish nation—''rabbit'' Patrice and raving Kevin Egan, ''loveless, landless, wifeless'' (p. 43).

The path of exile is desolate, and Stephen has not yet formed specific plans for escape. Nevertheless, he symbolically chooses rebellion by turning away from the sandflats and mounting a hill of boulders:

> He had come nearer the edge of the sea and wet sand slapped his boots. . . . He stood suddenly, his feet beginning to sink slowly in the quaking soil. Turn back.

58

Turning, he scanned the shore south, his feet sinking again slowly in new sockets. The cold domed room of the tower waits. . . . I will not sleep there when this night comes. A shut door of a silent tower entombing their blind bodies, the panthersahib and his pointer. Call: no answer. He lifted his feet up from the suck and turned back by the mole of boulders. Take all, keep all. (P. 44)

The suck of wet sand is pulling Stephen downward, sinking his feet into muddy sockets that impede forward motion. He realizes that he must flee not only the muddy strand but his entire claustrophobic environment. The pull of the sand evokes his earlier terror of asphyxiation. ''The cold domed room of the tower waits. Through the barbicans the shafts of light are moving ever, slowly ever as my feet are sinking, creeping duskward over the dial floor. . . . In the darkness of the dome they wait'' (p. 44). Stephen will not return to the lair of his enemies, for he recognizes the tower as a tomb that encloses ''blind bodies.'' He must rescue himself from the cakey sand dough and from all the symbols of viscosity that portend annihilation.

The beach speaks a language ''heavy of the past,'' ready to draw willing victims into a Lethean prison. ''These heavy sands are language tide and wind have silted here. And there, stoneheaps of dead builders, a warren of weasel rats. Hide gold there. Try it. You have some. Sands and stones. Heavy of the past. Sir Lout's toys. Mind you don't get one bang on the ear. I'm the bloody well gigant rolls all them bloody well boulders, bones for my steppingstones'' (pp. 44–45). The sands have retained a viscous history, a murky tradition of bloodshed, greed, and power, inimical to the artist. Lochlanns and Danevikings haunt these shores: ''Famine, plague, and slaughters. Their blood is in me, their lusts my waves'' (p. 45).

The sight of a drowned dog and the cries of a live one are confounded in the poet's reveries and evoke his earlier fears of death by water. Stephen is jolted into a sudden awareness of the complex guilt hovering at the surface of his mind. He feels powerless to rescue a drowning man or the Irish nation being engulfed by the ''tide flowing quickly in on all sides'' (p. 45).

The dead dog, the drowned corpse, and the ghost of Mary Dedalus have all been overwhelmed by the waters of "bitter death." The bard protests that he "could not save" his mother by obeying her deathbed commands. Had he yielded to her wishes, he would have been drawn "together down" with her into the ocean's engulfing waves: "Waters: bitter death: lost" (p. 46).

In "Nestor," Stephen mimicked himself in the riddle of a "fox burying his grandmother under a hollybush" (p. 27), trying to dispose of a murdered past. Now he identifies with a live dog on the strand, "looking for something lost in a past life. . . . His hindpaws then scattered sand: then his forepaws dabbled and delved. Something he buried there, his grandmother. He rooted in the sand, dabbling, delving . . . vulturing the dead" (pp. 46–47). Like the dog, Stephen feels compelled to dig up the body he buried. He is obsessed with the need to atone for a murder he did not commit, and he must continually revivify the ghost in order to assure himself of exoneration. His mother's specter merges with the "bloated carcass of a dog" that "lay lolled on bladderwrack." "Dogskull, dogsniff, eyes on the ground, moves to one great goal. Ah, poor dogsbody. Here lies poor dogsbody's body" (p. 46). Death becomes the "one great goal" toward which all human history moves. In a negative epiphany, the "dog-god" of the Black Mass manifests itself as a putrid, inedible Eucharist. A drowned dog lies decaying on the beach, a ludicrous symbol of Nietzsche's murdered deity and a gruesome image of matter devoid of spirit. Mulligan's epithet, "poor dogsbody," has materialized in a grotesque sea carcass, a warning to the poet of the fate that awaits him in Ireland.

The "manifestation of dog" is a revelation of death as the temporal end of life, the ironic culmination of Deasy's linear model of history. But the epiphany of dog and panther simultaneously issues a call to meaning—a call to escape from the nightmare of history into the prolific possibilities of dream: "After he woke me up last night same dream or was it? Wait. Open hallway. Street of harlots. Remember. Haroun al Raschid. I am almosting it. That man led me, spoke. I was not afraid. The melon he had he held against my face. Smiled: creamfruit smell. That was the rule, said. In. Come. Red carpet spread. You will see who'' (p. 47). Stephen turns his attention to the prophecies of an unconscious night world. He imagines an illicit encounter with oriental adventure and with a dark stranger who bears the gift of fruitful creation. The dream serves as an uncanny premonition of his future meeting with Leopold Bloom. The older man will introduce Stephen to the ''melonsmellonous'' hemispheres of Gea-Tellus and to the fertile seeds of human relationship, through which the flesh can become word.

At present, Stephen balances the lascivious gaiety of ''The Rogue's Delight'' against somber ''monkwords'' that condemn sins of ''morose delectation'' (p. 47). After a dream calling him to life, he writes a poem about bloodsucking vampires and the kiss of death. He continues to feel alienated from that ''manshape ineluctable'' which binds him to the physical world. ''His shadow lay over the rocks as he bent, ending. Why not endless till the farthest star? Darkly they are there behind this light, darkness shining in the brightness, delta of Cassiopeia, worlds. Me sits there with his augur's rod of ash, in borrowed sandals, by day beside a livid sea, unbeheld, in violet night walking beneath a reign of uncouth stars. I throw this ended shadow from me, manshape ineluctable, call it back. Endless, would it be mine, form of my form?'' (p. 48).

Stephen never responds to the last question, but his answer is implicit. He has already distinguished between the ''I'' and the ''me''—between a conscious, first-person ego and a physically detached first-person object. ''Me'' becomes a separate, corporeal self, sitting on a rock ''with his augur's rod of ash.'' The subjective ''I'' throws forth a finite shadow from the ''me,'' a ''darkness shining in the brightness,'' created by the material deflection of light. Could Stephen project his shadow ''endless till the farthest star,'' he would become a disembodied spirit. He would relinquish his concrete existence as a ''being in the world'' and forfeit personal identity. The shadow-self reminds

Stephen of the darkness endemic to the soul—the "shame-wound" of original sin that shackles the intellect to a dying animal. But the shadow also affirms a physical presence that can be touched by other human beings and can establish contact with kindred spirits, whose comforting solicitude may reveal the "word known to all men" (p. 49). "Touch me. Soft eyes. Soft soft soft hand. I am lonely here. O, touch me soon, now. . . . I am quiet here alone. Sad too. Touch, touch me" (p. 49). Stephen is isolated and despondent because he cannot yet utter the word of love rooted in the flesh.

As noon approaches, Stephen's shadow grows thinner, and he is momentarily arrested by a blinding light. "I am caught in this burning scene. Pan's hour, the faunal noon. Among gumheavy serpentplants, milkoozing fruits, where on the tawny waters leaves lie wide. Pain is far" (p. 49). The goat-god Pan lulls the bard into a temporary lotus-land of viscous, lethargic ease. Stephen's language is sensuous and highly lyrical. He feels himself sinking into the warm sensuality of Lethean repose. But unlike Leopold Bloom, he is loath to submit to the somnolence of lotus-gazing. Emulating the prudent Ulysses, he overcomes a seductive temptation to lose himself in an embryonic environment and to return to that "great sweet Mother/Mother and lover of men, the sea."

Stephen remains on shore, a safe distance from the ocean. He turns from midday slumber to the "masculine" act of urination. In making water, he creates an artistic "wavespeech," a "flower unfurling" that declines to mingle with the ocean: "Listen: a fourworded wavespeech: seesoo, hrss, rsseeiss, ooos. Vehement breath of waters amid seasnakes, rearing horses, rocks. In cups of rocks it slops: flop, slop, slap: bounded in barrels. And, spent, its speech ceases. It flows purling, widely flowing, floating foampool, flower unfurling" (p. 49).

For Stephen, micturition is analogous to poetic creation. It gives rise to the most lyrical passage in "Proteus," and it undergoes such extravagant cerebration that the physical act is barely recognizable: "Under the upswelling tide he saw the writhing weeds lift languidly and sway reluctant arms, hising up their petticoats, in whispering water swaying and upturning

62

coy silver fronds. . . . To no end gathered: vainly then released, forth flowing, wending back: loom of the moon. Weary too in sight of lovers, lascivious men, a naked woman shining in her courts, she draws a toil of waters'' (pp. 49–50). Stephen depicts the ''writhing weeds'' as female temptresses, barren, and ''womb weary.'' The infertile womb of the siren awaits its fullness, but gathers it placental tissues ''to no end.'' Its menses are ''vainly then released, forth flowing, wending back: loom of the moon.''

Earlier in ''Proteus,'' Stephen associated the moon-drawn tide with the feminine menstrual cycle: ''Tides, myriad-islanded, within her, blood not mine, *oinopa ponton,* a wine-dark sea. Behold the handmaid of the moon. In sleep the wet sign calls her hour, bids her rise. Bridebed, childbed, bed of death'' (pp. 47–48). He now portrays the moon-driven sea as a cunning succubus. The ocean is ''mother of all men,'' anxious to devour her sons and snuff out their independence. A giant female demon, she threatens to murder and castrate those who yield to her power: ''Five fathoms out there. Full fathom five thy father lies. At one he said. Found drowned. High water at Dublin bar. Driving before it a loose drift of rubble, fanshoals of fishes, silly shells. A corpse rising saltwhite from the undertow, bobbing landward. . . . There he is. Hook it quick. Sunk though he be beneath the watery floor'' (p. 50). Stephen's terror of the sea projects itself into the drowned corpse, and his quote from *The Tempest* symbolically identifies the dead man with Simon Dedalus, the bard's ''consubstantial'' father. Simon has been emasculated by maternal Ireland, by Mother Church, and by his dead wife Mary. Like the corpse fished out of the sea, he no longer drives before him an erect phallus. He is enslaved to the ''loose drift of rubble'' in Dublin society, to his wife's ''old feather fans,'' and to the ''silly shells'' of a dead tradition.

Stephen contemplates the corpse in terms of metaphorical castration:

Bag of corpsegas sopping in foul brine. A quiver of minnows, fat of a spongy titbit, flash through the slits of his buttoned trouserfly. God becomes man becomes fish becomes barnacle goose becomes

63

featherbed mountain. Dead breaths I living breathe, tread dead dust, devour a urinous offal from all dead. Hauled stark over the gunwhale he breathes upward the stench of his green grave, his leprous nosehole snoring to the sun.

A seachange this, brown eyes saltblue. Seadeath, mildest of all deaths known to man. Old Father Ocean. . . . Just you give it a fair trial. We enjoyed ourselves immensely. (P. 50)

The man "found drowned" has merged with the "great sweet mother," forfeiting his masculinity. His genitals are "a spongy titbit" for a quiver of minnows, and he himself is an object to be devoured by fishes. Once a "god" in his freedom, the drowned man has been reduced to lifeless rubble.

When Stephen identifies his father with the corpse, he is acting out an Oedipal impulse toward partricide. He sees his progenitor dissolving in a claustrophobic environment. But once drowned, his father joins the forces of destruction and becomes an agent of castration. For the first time in *Ulysses,* the sea is depicted as masculine. "Old Father Ocean" beckons the poet to a luscious "seadeath." "Just you give it a fair trial," the corpse expostulates. "We enjoyed ourselves immensely" (p. 50).

Echoing Christ's words on the cross, Stephen turns away from the suicidal temptation and asks for water in the form of drink: "Come. I thirst. Clouding over. No black clouds anywhere, are there? Thunderstorm. Allbright he falls, proud lightning of the intellect, *Lucifer* . . . No. My cockle hat and staff and his my sandal shoon. Where? To evening lands. . . . Yes, evening will find itself in me, without me" (p. 50).

Stephen refuses to merge with the rising tide, just as he would not rest in the lethargy of "faunal noon." He overcomes the seductions of Lucifer, the "light-bearer," by renouncing "proud lightning of the intellect" for the darker, more profound areas of consciousness. "God becomes man becomes fish becomes barnacle goose becomes featherbed mountain." And since the process must be reversible, man may become a Nietzschean divinity by exploring his own mental and volitional powers. The mind's shadow is "the darkness shining in brightness" that constitutes itself through the luminous objects it beholds.

64

Throughout the "Proteus" episode, Stephen drifts on the tides of language and allows thought to "think itself." His prose celebrates the capaciousness of the human mind and the protean possibilities of free association. Consciousness is god-like in its negativity: it embraces and transforms the whole of literary and philosophical tradition; it perceives, reshapes, and interprets present reality. Once the mind stands open to the phenomenal world, the artist can utter the word known to all men, the primordial "yes" that affirms being and makes creation possible.

As the "Proteus" episode concludes, "toothless Kinch," the "superman" (p. 22), becomes the Christ of a new religion, that of artistic postcreation. Alone, micturating on a rock, Stephen makes water in a symbolic, lyrical stream that will eventually buoy him up above the grasp of "old Father Ocean." Searching for the obscure truths of being, he will safely float on top of the void, brandishing the "crosstrees" of post-Christian belief: "He turned his face over a shoulder, rere regardant. Moving through the air high spars of a threemaster, her sails brailed up on the crosstrees, homing, upstream, silently moving, a silent ship" (p. 51). In "silence, exile, and cunning," Stephen Dedalus moves "homeward" toward the self-proclaimed divinity of an artist-God.

In the "Scylla and Charybdis" episode, Stephen defends and elucidates his hypothesis of artistic postcreation. He offers an aesthetic theory that steers an ingenious course between Plato and Aristotle, between A. E.'s theosophy and Mulligan's materialism.

George Russell insists that "art has to reveal to us ideas, formless spiritual essences" that embody "Plato's world of ideas" (p. 185). In the Platonic Trinity of "Father, Word, and Holy Breath," Jesus Christ becomes "magician of the beautiful, the Logos who suffers in us at every moment" (p. 185). Theosophy implies the immanence of a word longing to be spoken.

Armed with his lessons from "Proteus," Stephen tries to

connect the Logos with life. He believes that art gives voice to the pain of bereavement: suffering constitutes the genesis of lyrical expression. "The life esoteric is not for ordinary person" (p. 185). Nor is it for the artist, whose peripatetic musings cling to the rinds of "this vegetable world." "Hold to the now, the here, through which all future plunges to the past" (p. 186).

Aristotle's "dagger definitions" and the schoolmen's universal categories both give way to the evidence of phenomenal experience: "Horseness is the whatness of allhorse. Streams of tendency and eons they worship. God: noise in the street: very peripatetic. Space: what you damn well have to see" (p. 186). The theosophical whirlpool offers a ludicrous perdition: "Through spaces smaller than red globules of man's blood they creepycrawl after Blake's buttocks into eternity of which this vegetable world is but a shadow" (p. 186). By eulogizing idyllic notions of peasant life and by clutching to "H. P. B.'s elemental," George Russell and his mystical band lose all sense of judgment and discrimination: "This verily is that. I am the fire upon the altar. I am the sacrificial butter" (p. 185). "The faithful hermetists await the light, ripe for chelaship, ringroundabout him. . . . Gulfer of souls, engulfer. Hesouls, shesouls, shoals of souls. Engulfed with wailing creecries, whirled, whirling, they bewail" (pp. 191–92).

Because Stephen eschews the threat of intellectual engulfment, he has already faded into social impalpability among the Dublin literati. He is not invited to an evening party at George Moore's. He is unwelcome at the "Yogibogeybox in Dawson chambers" (p. 191). And he has not been asked to contribute to A. E.'s edition of *New Songs,* which Lyster presently announces: "Mr. Russell, rumour has it, is gathering together a sheaf of our younger poets' verses" (p. 192). Stephen feels like an alien among the Irish intelligentsia. The other men agree that Colum "has that queer thing, genius," and they speculate that "our national epic has yet to be written. . . . Moore is the man for it. A knight of the rueful countenance" (p. 192). They all praise James Stephens for "doing some clever sketches." But Stephen Dedalus is deliberately excluded from the list of

66

those who "are becoming important, it seems" (p. 192). Alone, he identifies with the tragic figure of Cordelia and with her Celtic analogue, "Lir's loneliest daughter" (p. 192). "*Cordoglio,*" he thinks—deepest sorrow.

"Necessity is that in virtue of which it is impossible that one can be otherwise" (p. 192). And only through art can the poet challenge historical necessity. "Here he ponders things that were not: what Caesar would have lived to do had he believed the soothsayer: what might have been: possibilities of the possible as possible: things not known" (p. 193). Stephen, Shakespeare, and Leopold Bloom all find refuge from grief and alienation in the infinite "possibilities" of the artistic imagination.

In "Scylla and Charybdis," Stephen cloaks his personal isolation in the biographical mask of Shakespeare, his dialectical opposite. The French triangle that haunts the Renaissance poet is at all points removed from Stephen's own experience. It signifies traumatic collision with a world of "interindividual" relations, the emotional source of pity, terror, and joy. "That lies in space which I in time must come to ineluctably" (p. 217). In time, Stephen will come through space to the figure of Leopold Bloom, whose life situation inadvertently replicates the figurative wound of Shakespeare's adolescence. Bloom will create from his own life miniature "works of art," compassionate stories that spring from imaginative sympathy. He will serve as a model of negative capability for the young artist who has yet to be tempered by the fires of worldly experience.

Caught between the "Saxon smile and yankee yawp" he faces in "Scylla," Stephen insists that "*Hamlet* is a ghoststory" (p. 187). "What is a ghost? . . . One who has faded into impalpability through death, through absence, through change of manners. Elizabethan London lay as far from Stratford as corrupt Paris lies from virgin Dublin" (p. 188). Like Shakespeare, Stephen is a ghost who returns from the limbo of Paris to a Dublin world that has forgotten him—or perhaps that he, in his coming exile, willfully chooses to forget. He foresees his flight from the virgin city as necessary to future creation. Only through the defloration of his own innocence can the poet aspire to intellectual fertility. As a "ghost" of Dublin through absence, Stephen will become father-creator to the phantom children he engenders in the world of art.

Under "everchanging forms," Stephen maintains his personal identity through a continuous memory that shelters remnants of the past: "But I, entelechy, form of forms, am I by memory," he says. "Molecules all change. I am other I now" (p. 189). Yet he is still the same young man who "sinned and prayed and fasted" at Clongowes Wood school. By accepting responsibility for his debt to A. E., Stephen confirms his identity as bearer of the word. He chooses between "I, I" and "I. I." (p. 190). One arrangement suggests the continuity of the transcendental ego that Stephen acknowledges as his subjective self. The other asserts the "pastness" of that ghost-self that has become "not I" by virtue of its impalpability. Stephen's paradigm "A. E. I. O. U." affirms the existence of a continuous ego and proclaims it guardian of the Logos, bringer of the vowel sounds that structure human language. Although Stephen may wish to discard his earlier resemblance to lapwing Icarus, he defends both himself and Shakespeare when he declares: "A man of genius makes no mistakes. His errors are volitional and are the portals of discovery" (p. 190).

Shakespeare, a "ghost by absence" (p. 189), exults in the ghost children he produces in his dramas. Prince Hamlet replaces Hamnet, the son who died at eleven years of age; and Ann becomes the "guilty queen" Gertrude. So "does the artist weave and unweave his image. And . . . so through the ghost of the unquiet father the image of the unliving son looks forth" (p. 194). The artist, who is a "weaver of the wind," sews his image throughout lyrical tapestries informed by a multitude of personal experiences. He creates worlds from words, microcosms inhabited by aesthetic offspring who reflect their parent immortally. "His own image to a man with that queer thing genius is the standard of all experience, material and moral. . . . The images of other males of his blood will repel him. He will see in them grotesque attempts of nature to foretell or repeat himself" (pp. 195–96). The dramatist gives form to the myth

68

and mystery of consciousness. In his plays, he regenerates himself in the character of a ghost-son, a persona conceived by the union of imagination and experience. "He is in my father. I am in his son" (p. 194).

The theme of paternity pervades the "Scylla and Charybdis" episode, and the almighty Father of Catholicism is present everywhere in the mode of absence. "A father, Stephen said, battling against hopelessness, is a necessary evil. . . . Father-hood, in the sense of conscious begetting, is unknown to man. It is a mystical estate, an apostolic succession, from only begetter to only begotten. . . . Paternity may be a legal fiction. Who is the father of any son that any son should love him or he any son?" (p. 207). Paternity, like the whirlpool Charybdis, is founded "upon the void. Upon incertitude, upon unlikelihood" (p. 207). It is a romantic notion unsubstantiated by the rock-like, "Scyllan" proof of physical motherhood. The artist who is insecure in his sexuality retreats into the isolation of spiritual paternity. As androgynous god of his own creation, he becomes father and mother to the fictional daughter-sons that reflect internal images of himself.

"If Socrates leave his house today he will find the sage seated on his doorstep. If Judas go forth tonight it is to Judas his steps will tend. Every life is many days, day after day. We walk through ourselves, meeting robbers, ghosts, giants, old men, young men, wives, widows, brothers-in-love. But always meeting ourselves" (p. 213). Following the por-nosophical tradition of Frank Harris, Stephen "meets himself" in the character of William Shakespeare. The theory that he proposes is itself a new "work of art," a pseudo-biographical rendering of the impetus of genius. Stephen fashions Shakespeare in the image of aestheticism and post-Victorian sexuality. He projects his own self-doubt onto the Renaissance artist, whose work he attributes to the pangs of erotic betrayal: "There is, I feel in the words, some goad of the flesh driving him into a new passion, a darker shadow of the first, darkening even his own understanding of himself. A like fate awaits him and the two rages commingle in a

whirlpool'' (p. 196; corrected from the 1934 Random House edition).

Stephen mourns the poet's loss of self-confidence, that positive image of virility ''untimely killed'' by the seductress Ann Hathaway. Ann ''hath a way'' into the hay with any lovers that would. If Ann could seduce Will, she might take other lovers after marriage. She wields ''woman's invisible weapon'' and can tempt men to hidden sexual pleasures. Fornication planted in Shakespeare's mind the initial seeds of conjugal mistrust. As Stephen observes, ''a man who holds so tightly to what he calls his rights over what he calls his debts will hold tightly also to what he calls his rights over her whom he calls his wife'' (pp. 205–6).

Agenbite of Inwit was born in a ryefield when Will cried his first ''O!'' of orgasmic rejoicing: ''He was overborne in a cornfield first (ryefield, I should say) and he will never be a victor in his own eyes after nor play victoriously the game of laugh and lie down. Assumed dongiovannism will not save him. No later undoing will undo the first undoing. The tusk of the boar has wounded him there where love lies ableeding'' (p. 196). ''*Re* Joyce,'' the cry of doubt continued as the birth pangs of the artist. The ravished Shakespeare piled up creations ''to hide himself from himself, an old dog licking an old sore. But, because loss is his gain, he passes on towards eternity in undiminished personality, untaught by the wisdom he has written or by the laws he has revealed'' (p. 197). To quote Molly Bloom's malapropism, the ''omissions'' in a poet's life give rise to the ''emissions'' of his imagination. Creation provides orgasmic release in a process analogous to mental onanism.

Like Mallarmé's Hamlet, Stephen's Shakespeare is an ''absent-minded beggar'': ''*il se promène, lisant au livre de lui-même*'' (p. 187). Only through art can the madman give form to the chaos of a wounded psyche. Shakespeare expresses his anger at Ann's supposed infidelity by channeling violence into dramatic conflict. Like Leopold Bloom, he kills his enemies in his head. His art is a constant attempt to gain control over psychological and emotional turbulence.

70

Stephen's Shakespeare has known betrayal by everyone close to him: not only by wife, but by father, son, brothers, and homosexual lover. His belief in a Renaissance world order, with the family at its center, has been traumatically shattered. He can no longer maintain faith in a rational universe hierarchically structured by an omniscient deity. The Catholic Father-God has proved himself a "chewer of corpses," devouring in blood sacrifice the poet's young son. With the loss of Hamnet, Shakespeare was forced to relinquish the illusory hope of tribal immortality contingent on a male heir. To perpetuate his image, he had to give birth to fictional progeny who would spring, fully grown, from his own imagination. When the God-creator failed, the artist himself had to assume the responsibilities of a creator-God.

Through this elaborate interpretive biography, Stephen is groping for a new definition of the artist as hero. The modern poet must arise, Christ-like, from the phoenix flames of suffering. Stephen's theory implies that the artist is set apart from society by his discovery of primordial alienation. He perceives the self as "other," the pathetic butt of a metaphysical jest. Thrown into a world that makes little teleological sense, he responds by detaching himself from absurdity and participating in cosmic laughter. He can reify his apprehension of the universe only by creating a fictional microcosm *ex nihilo* in the present. The poet reconstitutes experience in terms of unique and unprecedented perception. Because loss has stripped him of traditional assumptions, he becomes an anarchist and a maverick. He is free to transcend the *a priori* categories that restrict the vision of common men, and he defies both society and history in a quest for psychological liberation.

According to Stephen, the life of Shakespeare must be interpreted as paradigmatic. Betrayal by a Father-God and by a mother-wife wrenches the artist free from traditional roles. He recognizes that human existence is totally "rootless." And in his isolation, he is forced to become wife and mother, "all in all," unto himself. His fertile consciousness has been impregnated by a fresh encounter with experience: the god "Bringforth" speaks and gives birth to a secondary world, a new aesthetic universe.

The poet's loss in the game of life is his gain in terms of imaginative expression. He knows that "'one life is all" (p. 202) he has for the multiplication of joy and sorrow, of sensuous and emotional experience. Haunted by the specter of mortality, he desperately attempts to propagate eternal images of himself that fulfill the infinite possibilities of consciousness. "He is the ghost and the prince. He is all in all" (p. 212). Shakespeare "'was and felt himself the father of all his race" (p. 208).

> —Himself his own father, Sonmulligan told himself. Wait. I am big with child. I have an unborn child in my brain. Pallas Athena! A play! The play's the thing! Let me parturiate! (P. 208)

"Mr. Mulligan . . . has his theory too of the play and of Shakespeare. All sides of life should be represented" (p. 198). Mulligan, the mocker, offers a ludicrous parody of hermaphroditic creation. The "pseudomalachi" characteristically preaches a gospel of egotistical self-indulgence. He suggests that the process of aesthetic conception involves nothing more than a solipsistic projection of the ego onto fictional characters. In a mock drama of parthenogenesis, he gives birth to a juvenile, masturbatory fantasy:

> *Everyman His own Wife*
> *or*
> *A Honeymoon in the Hand*
> *(a national immorality in three orgasms)*
> (P. 216)

The play, a bawdy perversion of Shakespearean drama, only serves to heighten the impact of Stephen's aesthetic theory.

"After God Shakespeare has created most" (p. 212). But no matter how hard the artist tries to be "all in all" to himself and his creations, he can never compensate for the primal treachery of a God that failed. And so he continues to create worlds. He will utter the "word known to all men," the Logos become

72

flesh through poetry and drama. The word that he speaks is the *Fiat* of the Creator: he proclaims, simply, "Let it be." And through the acquiescence of fictional characters, his mandate will be executed. Like the Miltonic Adam, the poet creates through the original act of "naming" a universe.[6] "He acts and is acted on" (p. 212).

If life is a game that man must invariably lose, then his only recourse is to enjoy the game in process, or to assert the validity and the permanence of the games that he devises through the magic of art. Let those who will play. As Joyce would tell us, "I know it is no more than a game, but it is a game that I have learned to play in my own way. Children may just as well play as not. The ogre will come in any case."[7]

In "Scylla and Charybdis," Stephen Dedalus constructs an elaborate theory of art as psychological compensation. The "poetic word" will allow him to transcend the authority of all the patriarchs who have failed, from the Father-God of Catholicism to the alcoholic progenitor who trudges through *Ulysses* with sentimental gait. In order to give birth to himself as an artist, the writer must first slay the ghosts of his consubstantial parents. Through the agency of Leopold Bloom, Stephen will discover a new, solicitous, non-threatening paternity. He will be introduced to the "world of men" from which poetic wavespeech—lyric, epic, and dramatic—can at last be fashioned.

> *Laud we the gods*
> *And let our crooked smokes climb to their nostrils*
> *From our bless'd altars.*

(P. 218)

By the end of the episode, the artist becomes god of his own creation. There are few traditional deities left for us to praise.

---

1. "Essentia non sunt multiplicanda sine necessitate." Stephen recalls Occam a few moments later in another context: "Dan Occam . . . invincible doctor" (p. 40). See Gifford and Seidman, *Notes for Joyce,* p. 36.

2. Edmund Husserl, *The Phenomenology of Internal Time-Consciousness,* pp. 23–24. As Husserl explains: "Consciousness of space belongs in the sphere of phenomenological givens, i.e., the consciousness of space is the lived experience in which 'intuition of space' as perception and phantasy takes place. . . . If we abstract all transcendental interpretation and reduce perceptual appearance to the primary given content, the latter yields the continuum of the field of vision . . ." (ibid.).

3. According to Sartre, the only valid kind of knowledge is "intuitive," "the presence of the thing (*Sache*) 'in person' to consciousness" (*Being and Nothingness,* p, 172).

4. Husserl, *Internal Time-Consciousness,* p. 29. Like Stephen Dedalus and Gotthold Lessing, Husserl is concerned with "the apprehensions of time, the lived experiences in which the temporal in the Objective sense appears" (p. 24). He, too, bases his investigation on an analysis of sound "purely as a hyletic datum" (p. 44); and he compares time to a melody or tonal process held in retention by consciousness.

5. Gotthold Ephraim Lessing, *Laocoön,* p. 91. Joyce had a copy of *Laocoön* in his Trieste library (Ellmann, *The Consciousness of Joyce,* Appendix, p. 117). In *Stephen Hero,* Stephen seems to disdain such theoretical treatises: "the Laocoön of Lessing irritated him" (*SH* 33).

6. In *Finnegans Wake,* the microcosm of the artist is totally dependent upon the "word" that he utters. Word and world, Logos and realization are contiguous. The writer reveals the mystery of himself through the furniture of language: the cosmos he fashions is a unique "night world," an amalgamation of dream and neologism.

7. Joyce, *Letters,* 3:144.

4

"Calypso": The World of Sensuous Reality
"Lotus-Eaters": The Land of Dreams

Joyce's modern hero, Leopold Bloom, is an apt successor to Ulysses, his epic counterpart. Despite the tendency of critics to describe Bloom as a "common man," he is most uncommon in the fertility of his consciousness, the capaciousness of his imagination, and the scope of his humanitarian sentiments. Like Stephen Dedalus, Bloom is trying to awake from a nightmare history. Although he lacks the younger man's vocabulary and rhetoric, he is just as astute, refined, and penetrating in his apprehension of the world. With little erudition and with less philosophical training, he intuitively searches for a humane solution to the dilemma of personal freedom.

Like Stephen, Bloom tries to suspend *a priori* knowledge and to perceive the universe from a fresh perspective, as though he were the first, primordial observer. He attempts to analyze "lived experience" and constantly challenges the popular myths of unexamined thought. By virtue of his curiosity,

75

Bloom is set apart from the herd of common men. He is, in fact, alienated from the "crowd" because he refuses to accept the dictates of conformist behavior.

In the tripartite structure of *Ulysses,* Joyce seems to be satirizing the model of human nature set forth in Plato's *Republic.* Stephen Dedalus embodies the rational dimension of existence—the "head" that proves woefully inadequate in the face of an absurd, irrational cosmos. Leopold Bloom represents the passionate "spirit," including the feelings and sentiments of the heart. And Molly Bloom gives form to the "concupiscent" desires of the sensuous body, committed to the survival of the species. The flesh that Plato scorned becomes elevated as the "eternal feminine," the unique and mysterious source of hope and fertility responsible for the ongoingness of the race. [1]

Appropriately, "Calypso" begins with a description of Leopold Bloom through his passion for the "inner organs of beasts and fowls," at a time of morning when his thoughts are dominated by fantasies of palatal delight. The narrator tells us that "kidneys were in his mind" (p. 55). The inert organs of excretion seem to occupy all the space in Bloom's psyche. Sexual appetites lurk everywhere in the chapter. The vocabulary describing 7 Eccles Street is rife with bawdy innuendo, from the "humpy tray" to the "spout stuck out" in audacious mockery of Poldy, the servile house-husband.

Language invariably serves as Bloom's springboard for the expansion of consciousness and the enlargement of understanding. The narrative voice of the chapter moves from external description to a *style indirect libre*—a mimetic rendering of Bloom's internal monologue. We are told that "Mr. Bloom watched curiously, kindly, the lithe black form" of the cat (p. 55). And through access to Bloom's thoughts, we begin to understand his compassionate apprehension of the world—his extraordinary power to "feel with" other sensibilities in an act of negative capability. He tries, for instance, to imagine what life would be like experienced from a feline perspective: "Wonder what I look like to her. Height of a tower? No, she can jump me" (p. 55). The example of the cat is somewhat playful, but Bloom will later compare Milly to the same animal. He is evidently trying to comprehend the female sensibility, be it that of his wife, his daughter, or a domestic pet. All embody the femininity that fascinates Bloom, but that somehow eludes and mystifies him.

Bloom thinks in short, epigrammatic phrases telegraphed to his mind from the deep structure of cognition. His perceptions are always keen and imaginative, but their transcription is so laconic that the full scope of his awareness may elude the casual reader. The episode acquaints us with Bloom's mind as it moves from primitive apprehension to active thought. Bloom speculates about the world with relentless curiosity, but only a fragment of his meditation ever reaches the linguistic surface of consciousness. He articulates his musings in verbal shorthand: "Cruel. Her nature. Curious mice never squeal. Seem to like it" (p. 55). Pondering the sadomasochistic relationship of cats and mice, he wonders why "mice never squeal" and "seem to like" their ritual dismemberment. Unconsciously, he may be aware of an analogy with his own dependent role as willing victim, servant, and flunkey to Molly.

[handwritten margin note: mouse = Bloom, dismembered by Molly?]

Bloom rapidly translates his thoughts with syntactic economy, eliminating superfluous words that take their meaning from a verbal environment. He condenses conceptual structures into an abbreviated code, which the reader quickly learns to recognize and to distinguish from the more formal and assertive diction of the narrator. Many of Bloom's phrases are punctuated with the word "perhaps": "They shine in the dark, perhaps, the tips. Or kind of feelers in the dark, perhaps" (p. 56). The qualifying abverb suggests a roving, speculative, inquiring mind. Bloom is unafraid to test out new hypotheses or to revise and expand his theories. His linguistic patterns are those of open-ended discourse, qualified by words like "perhaps," "or," "still," and "on the other hand."[2] His conceptual process invites imaginative possibility and implies a mind open to revelation.

As an amateur scientist, Bloom is able to suspend presuppositions and to examine the world with the naïve curiosity of a primordial observer. The foundations of his "parallactic" vision are linguistically established in the first few pages of "Calypso." Language reveals being, and the seeds of Bloom's personal and emotional growth in the course of *Ulysses* are already present in his morning meditation.

Language, in fact, may expose more about Bloom's psyche than do his actions on the morning of 16 June 1904. At this point in the day, his demeanor is one of uxorious and apologetic timidity. He pauses in front of Molly's bedroom and asks after her pleasure "softly in the bare hall" (p. 56). Bloom feels like an outsider in his own home and seems to be groping in a foreign environment of "gelid light and air" (p. 55), a claustrophobic world of domestic trivia.

The announcement, "I am going round the corner. Be back in a minute" (p. 56), serves both as a communiqué to Molly and as an assertion of personal identity situated in time and space. Bloom wants Molly to acknowledge and to care about his *being-there*. Like Stephen Dedalus, he suffers from a sense of alienation that erupts in schizophrenic self-consciousness: "And when he had heard his voice say it he added: — You don't want anything for breakfast?" (p. 56). Bloom is jolted from private meditation to a sudden recognition of his social ego—the self defined as a being-for-others and contingent on perception by a foreign consciousness.

The subjective "he" feels detached both from its domestic persona and from its more distant fictional persona as "Henry Flower." Bloom has fashioned an alter-ego for the innocuous release of aggressive sexual fantasy. He shares his flirtation with a mute confidant, "Plasto's high grade ha" (p. 56). Furtively peeping inside the hatband, he ascertains the security of a hidden postal slip. The paper is "quite safe," as is Bloom's fictive identity as epistolary Don Juan.

In the "happy warmth" of a June morning, Bloom turns his thoughts to dawn "somewhere in the east" and to an ingenious plan for escaping time's ravages by perpetual travel in front of the sun. "Keep it up for ever never grow a day older technically" (p. 57). In the "Proteus" episode, Stephen Dedalus was preoccupied with the western darkness of ''evening lands'' and the thrust of the mind's negative shadow ''endless till the farthest star,'' ''darkness shining in the brightness'' (p. 48). He was fascinated by the ''nothingness'' of an undefined temporal horizon. In contrast, Bloom looks to a cyclical, prelapsarian dream of youth and idyllic passion. He longs for the light and embryonic warmth of an eastern dawn, of lands that promise continual rebirth.

If Stephen wants to shatter the nightmare of history, Bloom hopes to transcend it by taking refuge in the ''Belacqua bliss'' of a capacious imagination. There is a ''touch of the artist about old Bloom'' (p. 235), and more than a touch of art in his creative fantasy life. He delights in the stories that challenge historical inadequacy and defy the limitations of aging and impotence. Bloom recognizes that his mental ramblings capture the ''kind of stuff you read'' (p. 57); but he is not yet aware that the stuff of dreams may be identical with both the stuff of art and the stuff of human compassion. Artistry is latent in the copious intelligence that tries to imagine how publicans flourish in business, how one might traverse Dublin without passing a pub, or how schoolchildren feel doing ''their joggerfry'' (p. 58).

Nor does Bloom's imagination shirk from the blood and guts that make up the sediment of life. He finds appetitive solace in the ''lukewarm breath of cooked spicy pig's blood'' and in the sight of a kidney oozing ''bloodgouts'' (p. 59). His lascivious appetites are aroused by the proximity of the ''nextdoor girl,'' a well-filled sausage with ''vigorous hips'' and a ''strong pair of arms'' (p. 59). Like the sausages fingered by the ''ferreteyed porkbutcher,'' the young woman with ''new blood'' is ''sausagepink. Sound meat there like a stallfed heifer'' (p. 59). Bloom feels enthralled by the sight of ''her prime sausages,'' thick wrists, and ''moving hams.'' He mentally enacts a drama of pursuit and rejection that culminates in sour grapes, crusted toenails, tattered virginal scapulars, and a muscular lover direct from constabulary duty. At the end of his sadomasochistic reverie, he feels a ''sting of disregard'' glowing ''to weak pleasure within his breast'' (pp. 59–60).

On his matitudinal wanderings, Bloom apprehends the world in rich, sensuous images. His early-morning erotic fantasies display a certain coarseness: they are the Freudian perambulations of a masculine id, unmitigated by the delicacy of romantic love. Denied authority in the cave of Calypso, Bloom compensates by a strongly aggressive fantasy life. He sees women as "prime sausages," to be cuddled and devoured. He feels anxious to "make hay while the sun shines" (p. 59). "Soon I am old" (p. 285). And the thought of aging women haunts him as a symbol of terrifying sterility.

Throughout *Ulysses,* appetites for food and sex conspicuously intertwine—sometimes lyrically, often parodically. Bloom recognizes the physical compulsions at the heart of survival. The beast in each of us abides and must be satisfied. We must kill or be killed: "Eat or be eaten" (p. 170). And in order to eat, we must kill animals or destroy vegetable life. Bloom feels both sexual excitement and profound pity when he thinks of the animals slain to appease human hunger: "A young white heifer. Those mornings in the cattlemarket the beasts lowing in their pens, branded sheep, flop and fall of dung, the breeders in hobnailed boots trudging through the litter, slapping a palm on a ripemeated hindquarter, there's a prime one, unpeeled switches in their hands" (p. 59).

"The model farm at Kinnereth on the lakeshore of Tiberias" (p. 59) may afford a "sanatorium" from the afflictions of a brutal world. Agendath Netaim promises Bloom the Eastern dream of perpetual fertility, "vast sandy tracts," "orange-groves and immense melonfields north of Jaffa" (p. 60). The land yields a harvest of citrus fruits that assure lubricity to the human alimentary system: "olives, oranges, almonds or citrons" (p. 60).

Fertility and fertilization rapidly change name and function in the Freudian unconscious, as do fruit and the female genitalia. Descriptive adjectives take on mutiple associations: "Molly in Citron's basketchair. Nice to hold, cool waxen fruit, hold in the hand, lift it to the nostrils and smell the perfume. Like that, heavy, sweet, wild perfume. Always the same, year after year"

(p. 60). A "perfume of embraces" (p. 168) hangs heavy on the fringes of Bloom's mind, ushering in seductive memories of his wife in rich, "pleasant old times." He mentally applies Moisel's description of the fruit to the younger, flawless Molly, whose path to Ireland shared the same Oriental ports of call: "Must be without a flaw, he said. Coming all that way: Spain, Gibraltar, Mediterranean" (p. 60).

Bloom, however, refuses to yield to the idyllic portrait of "quiet long days" spent in pastoral bliss. The promise of Edenic happiness constitutes a lotus dream that he cannot accept as credible: "Nothing doing. Still an idea behind it" (p. 60). Those who imagine that paradise can be re-created in mundane circumstances, "on earth as it is in heaven" (p. 61), are deluded by self-indulgent fantasy. The "cattle, blurred in silver heat" (p. 60) will be scourged and slaughtered for the satisfaction of carnivorous appetites.

A grey cloud shatters the myth of Eden and brings Bloom back to the edge of the void. Agendath Netaim is a Jewish illusion. In truth, the lotus-land is barren. Only the "grey sunken cunt of the world" awaits the desolate dreamer: "A barren land, bare waste. Vulcanic lake, the dead sea: no fish, weedless, sunk deep in the earth. No wind would lift those waves, grey metal, poisonous foggy waters. . . . A dead sea in a dead land, grey and old. Old now. It bore the oldest, the first race. . . . Now it could bear no more. Dead: an old woman's: the grey sunken cunt of the world" (p. 61).

The dark cloud thrusts Bloom into a fit of morbid depression. His dream of the East as a Jewish homeland has proved deceptive. The mirage passes, exposing a desiccated wasteland. The sight of a "bent hag clutching a noggin bottle" (p. 61) precipitates a negative epiphany. Bloom envisions the death of his race, "the oldest people," exhausted from its wanderings and barren of hope. He is assailed by grotesque intimations of mortality. "Grey horror" sears his flesh in premonition of aging, exhaustion, and sterility. As he hurries homeward to evade the threat, terror pursues him with a physical adumbration of death: "Cold oils slid along his veins, chilling his blood:

age crusting him with a salt cloak'' (p. 61). He identifies with the metallic waves of the dead sea evaporating into a poisonous salt marsh. The epiphany propels him to the edge of the void and forces a momentary confrontation with nonbeing. Like his wandering people, Bloom will grow weary and old. His skin will shrivel to a salt crust, and the cold hand of death will paralyze his body.

Bloom appears to be suffering from hot and cold flashes. If anything threatens his racial continuance, it is Molly's fertile interest in her soon-to-be lover, Blazes Boylan. But the scientific mind can rationalize unreasonable fear: ''Morning mouth bad images. Got up wrong side of the bed. Must begin again those Sandow's exercises'' (p. 61). Pragmatism temporarily rescues Bloom from the abyss: he assures himself that diet, exercise, and sufficient rest will relieve the threat of existential terror.

From false dreams of a home in the lotus-land of the East, and from the reveries of an earlier ripeness in his own life, Bloom turns ''homeward'' to his wife Molly, the Oriental prize of Dublin. As always, he is saved from nihilism by the recollection of her ''warm, fullblooded life'': ''To smell the gentle smoke of tea, fume of the pan, sizzling butter. Be near her ample bedwarmed flesh. Yes, yes'' (p. 61). He eagerly pants the amorous incantation, ''Yes, yes,'' sanctified by Molly on the Hill of Howth in a moment of erotic affirmation. The sun, ''quick and warm,'' runs to meet him, as he runs to the security of Molly's bedwarmed flesh. On a sensual level, he retreats to the oral gratification of a pork kidney and to the sight of his wife's maternal bosom.

Once home, Bloom's ''quick heart'' slows as he recognizes a letter addressed to ''Mrs Marion Bloom'' from Blazes Boylan. Conjugal and paternal loss are both heralded by the morning post. In a note to her father, ''silly Milly'' reveals a flirtatious interest in Bannon, a medical student with a roving eye. Maturity and ''sex breaking out'' have stolen Papli's little girl, now ''quite the belle'' (p. 66) in her lovely new tam. Like ''poor old professor Goodwin,'' Bloom smarts from his daughter's outspokenness when she casually alludes to two different Boylans, the composer and the organizer. In his own dual role as "Poldy" and as "Papli," Bloom must come to terms with the emotional upheavals that the morning mail portends.

For the time being, he takes solace in the amplitude of his wife's maternal figure, "her large soft bubs, sloping within her nightdress like a shegoat's udder. The warmth of her couched body rose on the air, mingling with the fragrance of the tea she poured" (p. 63). Bloom's mammary obsession offers momentary comfort. He hides in the sensuous security of mother-Molly and feels reassured by her imperious commands, uttered from "full lips, drinking," smiling. Wife and daughter may desert him; but the mother figure remains, in all her womanly splendor. Baby-Bloom stands by, fondling the fetishes of erotic obsession—"a leg of her soiled drawers" and "a twisted grey garter looped round a stocking" (p. 63). To one so fearful of aging, infantile regression provides welcome sanctuary.

In this metempsychosis, Molly is the seductive Calypso and "Big Mama" to Ulysses-Bloom. Her role is emblematically reinforced by Ruby, Pride of the Ring, who sprawls against an orange-keyed chamberpot in keeping with the excretory vision of pulp fiction. "Metempsychosis" is Greek to Molly, though she herself serves as a twentieth-century reincarnation of both the goddess Calypso and the mortal Penelope. "That we all lived before on the earth thousands of years ago" (p. 65) is the metaphorical assumption implicit in the Homeric parallels of Joyce's epic. Bloom may seem to be a mousy husband and Molly a frumpy wife. But Joyce's magic has just begun. And things may not be what they seem, either in Shakespeare's drama or in the astonishing world of *Ulysses*.

Leopold Bloom shares with his Homeric predecessor the gift of a shrewd and mocking eye. He is astute enough to recognize the "cruelty behind it all" (p. 64)—whether "it" be Hengler's circus, domestic turbulence, the liaison between "Ruby pride of" and her Italian lover, or the spectacles that excite a blood-thirsty mob. "Break your neck and we'll break our sides" (p. 64). He knows that every individual walks a delicate tightrope of survival in a cruel, sometimes barbarous society. Beneath the thin veneer of civilization, the savage waits. If one cannot "look the other way" (p. 64), he must face the unholy spectacle of violence in the theatre of Darwinian conflict.

The Greeks who believed in mythology understood the unity of the human world with its bestial and vegetative components. "They used to believe you could be changed into an animal or a tree, for instance" (p. 65). Bloom unconsciously reiterates Stephen's earlier parable of Protean transformation: "God becomes man becomes fish becomes barnacle goose" (p. 50). If human beings can change into animals or trees, why not into gods and heroes? Can frumpy Molly become a nymph of nature? Bloom a flurrying stork? The kidney a turtle? The "burnt flesh" of the kidney the living flesh of Bloom? All is alive and changing in Joyce's fictional microcosm.

Change bodes "separation" (p. 66), and perhaps reconciliation, if Stephen is correct in his assertion that there cannot be a reconciliation "if there has not been a sundering" (p. 195). Milly has been separated from Bloom by her oncoming maturity, Rudy by death, and Molly by her imminent infidelity. Rudy is lost, and Bloom's loss of both females is inevitable: "A soft qualm regret, flowed down his backbone, increasing. Will happen, yes. Prevent. Useless: can't move. Girl's sweet light lips. Will happen too. He felt the flowing qualm spread over him. Useless to move now" (p. 67). Regret attacks Bloom physically, freezing him in mental stasis. He knows that it would be "useless" to try to prevent Molly's infidelity. He cannot move because interference with his wife's adultery would require either physical violence or psychological coercion—both of which he disdains.

For almost eleven years, Bloom has been sexually paralyzed by the trauma of Rudy's death. Separation by death eventually precipitates conjugal separation by adultery. Because Bloom cannot move toward his wife in an amorous embrace, he is powerless to prevent Boylan's "moves" on Molly or Molly's move toward her newfound lover. Rudy's death initiated a psychological complex that proscribed venereal contact. Bloom's unique form of *coitus interruptus* (coming on Molly's bottom) precludes further assertion of conjugal rights. Bloom can appreciate "lips kissed, kissing kissed. Full gluey woman's lips" (p. 67). And we learn in "Penelope" that he feels oral attraction to Molly's nether lips. But cunnilingus is as close as he dares come to his wife's sexual organs. He eschews the mysteries of Calypso's cave, and with them, the dangers and disappointments of frustrated parenthood. He dolefully watches Molly's "eyes over the sheet, a yashmak. Find the way in. A cave. No admittance except on business" (p. 281).[3]

Milly is ripening into sexuality. Molly is declining into middle age. Boylan will feast on her over-ripe plums, leaving the "plumstones" to her cuckolded husband. Bloom thinks consciously about Milly, unconsciously about his spouse: "No, nothing has happened. Of course it might. Wait in any case till it does. A wild piece of goods" (p. 66). He refuses to worry before his fears prove justified. He realizes that parents cannot "own" children; and he is groping toward a similar recognition in terms of his adult and adulterous spouse. He must have faith that Milly "knows how to mind herself" (p. 66). And Molly, too.

Bloom's bowels are heavy with "troubled affection" and with digestive waste. *Titbits* and the backyard jakes offer the promise of relief. Theoretically, Bloom knows that "dirty cleans." And he plans to "manure the whole place over" some day. "Still gardens have their drawbacks" (p. 68). All fecundity demands the price of personal commitment. And if the garden should fail? Disappointment has ruptured Bloom's faith in cultivation, as well as in procreation. His soil remains unfertilized, as do the furrows of Molly's womb. He spills both feces and semen on barren ground.

Like a child at the anal stage of sexuality, Bloom delights in the sensual pleasures of defecation. The kinetic art of pulp journalism promises emotional distraction. For his delectation on the jakes, he chooses an appropriately salacious piece of hack writing to move his bowels and to wipe his arse, in quick succession. The latter act offers a fitting comment on the value of *Matcham's Masterstroke.*

Despite his envy of the author, Philip Beaufoy, Bloom approaches a much more personal definition of art when he recalls his own journalistic aspirations. "Might manage a sketch. By Mr and Mrs L. M. [Leopold and Molly] Bloom" (p. 69). He remembers trying to capture a trivial "slice" of domestic life by jotting down notes on his shirt cuff. Now he completes the "history" through reverie, as an embellished story rife with grief and compassion.

Bloom calls to mind the bazaar dance at which Molly first displayed interest in Boylan: "That was the first night. Her head dancing. Her fansticks clicking. Is that Boylan well off? He has money. Why? I noticed he had a good smell off his breath dancing" (p. 69). Bloom's memory is fraught with portents of time and shadow. "Ponchielli's dance of the hours" reminds him of the inevitable progress of life from youth to old age: "morning hours, noon, then evening coming on, then night hours." He thinks: "Evening hours, girls in grey gauze. Night hours then black with daggers and eyemasks. Poetical idea pink, then golden, then grey, then black. Still true to life also. Day, then the night" (p. 69).

From the first moment Bloom perceived Molly's "head dancing" with excitement, he understood the inevitable course of adultery from the dawn of infatuation to the ashes of burnt-out physical passion. With amazing sensitivity, he leaps beyond sexual jealousy to sympathize with his wife's fear of aging and unattractiveness. "The mirror was in shadow. She rubbed her handglass briskly on her woollen vest against her full wagging bub. Peering into it. Lines in her eyes. It wouldn't pan out somehow" (p. 69). "Lines in her eyes" remind Molly of creeping middle age and the loss of youthful beauty. The scene functions as an epiphany for Bloom, whose fertile imagination engenders pity for his spouse. As an artist of compassion, he transmutes the rage of conjugal dispossession into a moving psychodrama. He projects himself into Molly's mind and empathizes with her pain, her anxiety, and her isolation. He knows that Molly's affair with Boylan "won't pan out" emotionally. Although Bloom perceives her "young eyes" still, Boylan may see only the lines and move on to the next prima donna in his

86

company. Adultery may constitute Molly's last fling in her losing battle against the ravages of time.

Molly's monologue in "Penelope" gives ample evidence of the terror she associates with aging and with the loss of sexual charm. She apparently believes that a woman is "all washed up" by the age of thirty-five. Molly expects to be sexually attractive only for a few more years; and even in her private calculations, she cannot admit the proximity of middle age. She thinks of "the 4 years more I have of life up to 35 no Im what am I at all Ill be 33 in September" (p. 751). Actually, Molly is already thirty-three, since she was born on 8 September 1870 (p. 736). At least one of the motives for her adultery seems to be her fear of being "finished out and laid on the shelf" (p. 766). She protests: "I cant help it if Im young still can I its a wonder Im not an old shrivelled hag before my time" (p. 777). According to Molly, "a woman wants to be embraced 20 times a day almost to make her look young no matter by who so long as to be in love or loved by somebody" (p. 777). And perhaps the most cynical comment made in "Penelope" is Molly's remark pertaining to society's double standard of beauty: "its all very fine for them but as for being a woman as soon as youre old they might as well throw you out in the bottom of the ash pit" (p. 759).

Ponchielli's dance of the hours, the dance of life, hurls each of us forward toward those night hours with daggers and eyemasks. "Day, then the night" (p. 69). Leopold Bloom is aware that mortality trivializes most of the petty jealousies of life. Ultimately, all must confront the mirror in shadow. The bells of Saint George's church toll the hour—for Paddy Dignam, for Bloom, for Molly, and for us all.

At the end of "Calypso," Bloom emerges from his jakes purged by both literal and figurative catharsis. Like Shem the Penman, he makes art from the ink of human excrement. And in so doing, he prepares the way for the blossoming of "Henry Flower" from the ritual act of fertilization.

In retreat from the threatening reality of "Calypso," Bloom takes refuge in the perfumed passivity of "Lotus-Eaters." He is fascinated by the various narcotics that people use to assuage the pain of existence: tea and alcohol, religion and opium, sleep, fantasy, and sexuality. Bob Doran, on "one of his periodical bends" (p. 74) drowns his domestic sorrows in Guinness. "Poor Papa" chose aconite. And Bloom himself escapes into voyeurism, fantasy, and epistolary flirtation.

The land of the lotus-eaters is a lethargic world ruled by the "law of falling bodies": "Thirty two feet per second, per second. . . . They all fall to the ground" (p. 72). In this illusory paradise, cuckoldry loses its sting and the British army its menace. The soldiers Bloom spies on a recruiting poster have been hypnotized into rhythmic, syncopated action: "Half baked they look: hypnotised like. Eyes front. Mark time. Table: able. Bed: ed. The King's own" (p. 73). The men have been lulled into the forgetful trance of military group-think.

Bloom's unfortunate double, M'Coy, complains that he is "just keeping alive" in a case of marginal survival. Cabbies enjoy "no will of their own" (p. 77). And their gelded horses, "poor brutes," feed in listless insouciance: "Their Eldorado. . . . Damn all they know or care about anything with their long noses stuck in nosebags." Their genitals have shrunk to "a stump of black guttapercha wagging limp between their haunches" (p. 77). Bloom wonders if the animals "might be happy all the same that way"; and his refusal to attach a linguistic subject to the phrase may indicate an oblique defense of his own impotent, if ungelded, sexuality.

Bloom "might be happy" with voyeurism and the titillations of Martha Clifford's abrasive letter, addressed to "Henry Flower." The epistle is rife with material for sadomasochistic fantasy: "Remember if you do not I will punish you. So now you know what I will do to you, you naughty boy, if you do not write" (p. 78). Martha leaves the specific punishment to Bloom's imagination, and his flowered reverie soon fills in the blanks: "Angry tulips with you darling manflower punish your cactus if you don't please poor forgetmenot" (p. 78). Bloom is evidently well-advised to avoid a meeting with Martha, who may have some "naughty nightstalk" waiting in the wings once her "patience are exhausted" (p. 78). Psychologically at least, Martha wants to punish "his cactus." Like the nymph in "Circe," she may have plans to clip Henry's "darling man-flower" in a vengeful act of castration. Bloom remains at a safe distance. He takes pleasure in arousing Martha's prurient disdain for obscene language, despite the brutality implicit in his lascivious suggestions: "Narcotic. Go further next time. Naughty boy: punish: afraid of words, of course. Brutal, why not? Try it anyhow. A bit at a time" (p. 78). Why not use titillating vocabulary, if the effect produces a sting of sexual arousal? One man's pain may be another man's (or woman's) addiction.

"No roses without thorns" (p. 78). Like Mary in the bawdy rhyme, Bloom seems to have lost the "pin" of his "drawers." He is unable to "keep it up" sexually because conjugal intercourse may bode disappointment. Once Bloom has rejected the thorns of reality, the roses are all in his head.

In his next reverie, Bloom identifies the "Martha" and the "Mary" (Marion) of his own experience with the two Hebrew women in the New Testament parable: "Martha, Mary. I saw that picture somewhere. . . . He is sitting in their house, talking. Mysterious" (p. 79). The busy "working girl," Martha, definitely loses to the recumbent Mary, both in the biblical story and in *Ulysses*. Bloom unwittingly sees himself as a Christ figure, impressing the women with his adventures. He fuses Christ with Ulysses, who at last finds rest in the company of a grateful audience: "Nice kind of evening feeling. No more wandering about. Just loll there: quiet dusk: let everything rip. Forget. Tell about places you have been, strange customs" (p. 79). In Bloom's account of the scene, Christ is a master storyteller who enchants females with his exotic narratives. In turn, Marion charms the speaker, who "confesses" before her seductive gaze: "She listens with big dark soft eyes. Tell her: more and more: all. Then a sigh: silence. Long long long rest" (p. 79). Bloom looks forward to the rest he will find

89

in Molly's "big dark soft eyes" and "smellonous melons" after he has confessed an edited version of his odyssey: "Womb? Weary? / He rests. He has travelled" (p. 737). The large black dot at the end of "Ithaca" prepares us for silence and for "long long rest."

Bloom apparently prefers his own imaginative rendering of Christ to the "Ecce Homo. Crown of thorns and cross" (p. 80) in All Hallows Church. He feels intrigued by the ease and languor of Eastern worship: "Buddha their god lying on his side in the museum. Taking it easy" (p. 80). But he recognizes, as well, the possibilities of addiction to be found in a theology unexamined by its believers: "Confession. Everyone wants to. Then I will tell you all. Penance. Punish me, please. . . . Lovely shame. Pray at an altar. Hail Mary and Holy Mary. Flowers, incense, candles melting. Hide her blushes. . . . Monasteries and convents. . . . Liberty and exaltation of our holy mother the church. The doctors of the church: they mapped out the whole theology of it" (p. 83).

Bloom acknowledges that "there's a big idea behind it, kind of kingdom of God is within you feel" (p. 81). He experiences a tinge of regret that he cannot belong to the confraternity of those safe within the arms of Mother Church:

> Look at them. Now I bet it makes them feel happy. Lollipop. It does. Yes, bread of angels it's called. . . . First communicants. Hokypoky penny a lump. Then feel all like one family party, same in the theatre, all in the same swim. They do. I'm sure of that. Not so lonely. In our confraternity. Then come out a bit spreeish. Lourdes cure, waters of oblivion, and the Knock apparition, statues bleeding. Old fellow asleep near that confession box. Hence those snores. Blind faith. Safe in the arms of kingdom come. Lulls all pain. Wake this time next year. (P. 81; corrected from the 1934 Random House edition.)

Bloom is tempted by the "waters of oblivion." But he knows all too well that the price exacted for "blind faith" is "forgetfulness"—a Lethean loss of autonomy and a voluntary destruction of consciousness. The pious man consigns his lib-

90

erty to the "exaltation of our holy mother the church"; in return, he is rocked safely "in the arms of kingdom come." As a twice-converted Jew, Bloom offers a shrewd critique of Catholicism: "*Corpus*. Body. Corpse. Good idea the Latin. Stupefies them first. Hospice for the dying. They don't seem to chew it; only swallow it down. Rum idea: eating bits of a corpse why the cannibals cotton to it" (p. 80). Like Joyce, Bloom is fascinated by the cannibalistic resonances of eucharistic theology. Lestrygonians stalk through lotus-land under the guise of devout Christians. The communion draught provides "cold comfort" to Bloom, who knows it cannot assuage his own alienation.

Bloom is aware that religion is not the only "opiate of the people." The masses create their own narcotics, and the greatest anodyne is a tenacious adherence to orthodox behavior. Bloom has instinctively guessed what Dostoevsky's Grand Inquisitor articulated in theological allegory: that men, like ants, would rather serve than lead. Human beings long for security and reassurance, for the materialistic substantiation of values provided by the crowd. They compulsively forfeit personal freedom and eschew authentic consciousness. Men desperately attempt to transfer personal responsibility to political, religious, and social institutions. Individuals worship what gods they may: for without deities, whence oblivion?

Most men and women deliberately avoid the risk of freedom and lose themselves in a drugged stupor of compulsory repetition. As Samuel Beckett observes, habit offers a safe retreat from "the perilous zones in the life of the individual, dangerous, precarious, painful, mysterious and fertile, when for a moment the boredom of living is replaced by the suffering of being."[4] Well-socialized individuals take refuge in the safety of automatic action: they rely on rules and rituals, palliatives and panaceas. Only those who foster deviant addictions are forced to acknowledge their own narcosis.

When all else fails, there is always: "Chloroform. Overdose of laudanum. Sleeping draughts. Lovephiltres. Paragoric poppysyrup . . . Poisons the only cures" (p. 84). "Suppose they wouldn't feel anything after. Kind of a placid. No worry. Fall

91

into flesh don't they? Gluttons, tall, long legs. Who knows? Eunuch. One way out of it'' (p. 82). People will choose placidity at any price, so long as they can escape freedom. Dostoevsky's Grand Inquisitor knew, and so does Leopold Bloom. In a lotus-eating world, Christians may become addicted to confession and communion, sadists to punishment, monks to hairshirts and marybeads, eunuchs to oral gratification, alcoholics to liquor, Chinese to opium, masochists to suffering, suicides to death, Boylan to women, Leopold to Molly, and everyone to someone else in the name of sentimental romance.

Leopold Bloom can recognize any addiction but his own. In a world of splendid passivity, he prefers fantasy and voyeurism to the risk of reality, Henry Flower to lionous Leopold. In the "Circe" episode, Lipoti Virag uses the term "amnesia" as a euphemism for sexual impotence. He exhorts his grandson to: "Exercise your mnemotechnic" (p. 514). Lotus-land is characterized by lethargic forgetfulness, a voluntary loss of memory on the part of all the addicts who swim through its murky pages.

At the end of "Lotus-Eaters," Bloom mentally immerses himself in a "womb of warmth," repeating the words of Christ at the eucharistic consecration: "This is my body" ["*Hoc est enim corpus meum*"]. Like an Eastern deity, Bloom contemplates his navel, the "bud of flesh" linking him to his ancestors and a vestigial reminder of embryonic life in the maternal womb. He then turns his attention to the phallus: "the dark tangled curls of his bush floating, floating hair of the stream around the limp father of thousands, a languid floating flower" (p. 86). Bloom regresses to a flaccid, infantile sexuality. The "father of thousands" is impotent and will not actualize all "those Godpossibled souls that we nightly impossibilise" (p. 389). His "bud of flesh,'' however, implies a potential that *will* "bloom" and reach fruition. The amniotic fluid of the bath suggests an imminent birth.

In a chapter dominated by the Orient, we might expect to leave our hero in an Eastern attitude of meditation. Most critics have stressed the phallic failure of Bloom's "languid floating flower.''[5] Few have called attention to his androgynous fusion of navel and phallus, of masculine potential and feminine receptivity. The ethic of the West demands the multiplication of souls to carry out God's plan. Eastern philosophy assumes that the Creator's work is complete: that one's primary duty is to contemplate and to understand the universe. The Occident glorifies the birth of individuals; the Orient stresses the continual rebirth of consciousness in a spiritual ascent to wisdom. It is just such a birth that Leopold Bloom will experience in his revitalization as the mature hero of Joyce's *Ulysses*.[6]

1. In the *Republic,* Plato asks: ''And ought not the rational principle, which is wise, and has the care of the whole soul, to rule, and the passionate or spirited principle to be the subject and ally?'' And furthermore, ''these two, thus nurtured and educated, and having learned truly to know their own functions, will rule over the concupiscent, which in each of us is the largest part of the soul and by nature most insatiable'' (pp. 160–61).

2. I am indebted to Donald Hackling for initially suggesting several of the ideas in this paragraph in an unpublished paper written at Stanford University in 1970. Mr. Hackling first pointed out to me Bloom's linguistic deletion of words that depend for their meaning on a syntactic environment and his use of these particular ''qualifiers'' to establish open-ended discussion.

3. Leopold Bloom suffers from ''secondary impotence,'' defined by psychologists as the inability to complete sexual intercourse for reasons of anxiety or trauma. Since Bloom masturbates to climax in ''Nausicaa,'' he obviously is not afflicted with ''primary impotence,'' the inability to experience erection or ejaculation. In ''Ithaca,'' we learn that his usual sexual practice is to come on Molly's bottom. In discussing Bloom's sexuality, I will use the term ''impotence'' to refer to the secondary syndrome from which Bloom apparently suffers.

4. Samuel Beckett, *Proust,* p. 8.

5. See, for instance, Phillip Herring's essay on ''Lotuseaters'' and Adaline Glasheen's essay on ''Calypso'' in *James Joyce's ''Ulysses'': Critical Essays,* ed. Clive Hart and David Hayman.

6. Joyce's fascination with the Eastern, ''Semitic'' origins of Homer's *Odyssey* is fully explored in Michael Seidel's recent study, *Epic Geography*.

"Hades": The Hibernian Underworld "Aelous" and "Wandering Rocks": The World as Machine

In contrast to Stephen Dedalus, the self-proclaimed exile, Leopold Bloom suffers perpetual ostracism in the heart of Irish society. An outcast and a misfit, he cannot fall complacently into predetermined patterns of conduct. He proceeds "energetically from the known to the unknown through the incertitude of the void" (p. 697). Bloom's Jewishness liberates him from the nets of Irish tradition that constrict the life-world of his companions and bind them to a stultified provincialism. He is the only man truly "alive" in the funeral entourage that accompanies Dignam's corpse.

—Are we all here now? Martin Cunningham asked. Come along, Bloom.

Mr. Bloom entered and sat in the vacant place. He pulled the door to after him and slammed it tight till it shut tight. He passed an arm through the armstrap and looked seriously from the open carriage window at the lowered blinds of the avenue. One dragged

95

aside: an old woman peeping. Nose whiteflattened against the pane. Thanking her stars she was passed over. Extraordinary the interest they take in a corpse. Glad to see us go we give them such trouble coming. Job seems to suit them. Huggermugger in corners. Slop about in slipperslappers for fear he'd wake. Then getting it ready. Laying it out. Molly and Mrs. Fleming making the bed. Pull it more to your side. Our windingsheet. Never know who will touch you dead. Wash and shampoo. I believe they clip the nails and hair. Keep a bit in an envelope. Grow all the same after. Unclean job. (P. 87)

In the drama that opens his epic descent into hell, Leopold Bloom has already begun to suffer the silent inferno of exile. Cunningham's question, "Are we all here now," implicitly excludes Bloom from the intimate social group identified as "we." The invisible Jew hovers like a condemned soul on the edge of the small community. He is the "other," an anonymous hanger-on, invited as an afterthought to "come along" merely to fill up space.

The funeral coach is a symbolic microcosm that reflects the outer metropolitan environment. Like the Martello tower, the carriage is a figure of spiritual asphyxiation. Its door slams shut as tightly as a coffin lid. Bloom has stepped into a mausoleum of Dublin life, a world of mental paralysis that immures the Irish in a common tomb. "The Irishman's house is his coffin" (p. 110).

A morbid lethargy hangs in the air, and matter seems weighed down by sheer inertia. From the carriage window, Bloom stares at "lowered blinds. . . . One dragged aside: an old woman peeping. Nose whiteflattened against the pane" (p. 87). Old age and childhood come full circle in senility. The crone flattens her nose against the window in infant wonder, "thanking her stars she was passed over" (p. 87). She feels childish glee at being spared by death. Like "Old Mother Grogan," the woman has been transfixed in powerless immobility.

"Extraordinary the interest they take in a corpse," Bloom muses. "Glad to see us go we give them such trouble coming" (p. 87). In the course of his thoughts, Bloom shifts the referent

96

of "they" from "old people" to women in general, then to Molly in particular. "We" refers to men, "they" to women. The crone becomes a symbol of feminine vengeance through masculine castration and death. Man dies in expiation for the sin of being born, for the agony suffered by his mother in childbirth. Bloom imagines woman as a ghoulish predator anxious to reduce the male to helpless objectivity.

"We" in the carriage sit undisturbed, awaiting passage to the grave: "All waited. Then wheels were heard in front turning: then nearer: then horses' hoofs. A jolt. Their carriage began to move, creaking and swaying. . . . The blinds on the avenue passed and number nine with its craped knocker, door ajar. At walking pace" (p. 87). A jolting kinetic sensation and the sound of horses' hoofs issue in the conclusion that "their carriage began to move." From within the coach, movement seems to be external. The houses are passing before us, "at walking pace," like scenery on a filmstrip. An act of perception assimilates the various sensations and constitutes the reality of locomotion.

As the carriage begins to go faster, the verbal rhythm quickens, and clipped phrases supplant periodic description. "Tritonville road. Quicker. The wheels rattled rolling over the cobbled causeway" (p. 87). Rapid linguistic movement simulates the sensation of speed, and alliteration and onomatopoeia re-create a jolting progression. The carriage rattles forward, noisily proclaiming its act of public homage.

> Mr. Dedalus nodded, looking out.
> —That's a fine old custom, he said. I am glad to see it has not died out.
> All watched awhile through their windows caps and hats lifted by passers. Respect. (P. 88)

Mr. Dedalus is grateful that the traditional salute has not "died out," but he feels little empathy for Dignam, who *has*. As Hugh Kenner notes in *Dublin's Joyce,* "Simon Dedalus has a sense of style, his world is still in touch with spectral fashionable Dublin."[1] Simon is a sentimental Irishman who clings to the husks of a dead aristocratic tradition. He entertains his companions with satirical wit and delights in nostalgic melodies, social gaiety, and the ironic turn of a phrase. By losing himself in the glories of the past, he remains oblivious of family responsibility. He shows no more concern for his son Stephen than for the corpse of Paddy Dignam.

> Mr. Bloom at gaze saw a lithe young man, clad in mourning, a wide hat.
> —There's a friend of yours gone by, Dedalus, he said.
> —Who is that?
> —Your son and heir.
> —Where is he? Mr. Dedalus said, stretching over across. (P. 88)

Simon attempts to establish his son's identity by finding out *where* he is and placing him in a physical frame of reference. It is Bloom who answers the question of *who* Stephen is, a "friend," a "son and heir." Bloom dignifies the bond of sonship that Simon facetiously degrades. Like Shakespeare's Gobbo, the father is unable to recognize his son as a free and independent agent, an individual who cannot be "placed" in a single, determinate situation.

The elder Dedalus works himself into a rage because Stephen has been seen with a "lowdown" crowd offensive to aristocratic breeding. Like the Citizen in "Cyclops," Simon invokes "God and his blessed mother" to help him wreak revenge. He casts aspersions on Mulligan, "a contaminated bloody doubledyed ruffian by all accounts. His name stinks all over Dublin. . . . I'll make it my business to write a letter one of those days to his mother or his aunt or whatever she is that will open her eye as wide as a gate. I'll tickle his catastrophe, believe you me. . . . I won't have her bastard of a nephew ruin my son" (p. 88). Simon can assert his paternity only in terms of archaic, tribal wrath. He interprets his kinship with Stephen as a primitive bond, a blood oath against defilement. The Dedalus tribe must not be contaminated, lest the father be implicated in filial guilt. And Mulligan is impure, a "bastard of a nephew," twice removed from genuine sonship.

98

Bloom correctly judges Simon as a "noisy selfwilled man." He concludes, however, that the boisterous father is "full of his son" and "is right. Something to hand on. If little Rudy had lived. See him grow up. . . . I could have helped him on in life" (p. 89). Bloom interprets even rude boasts as a manifestation of paternal joy. For him, a son is not only something to "hand on" for tribal perpetuation but a human being to be "helped on" through continuing solicitude.

Like Stephen, Bloom is preoccupied with the moment of conception. But in contrast to the younger man, he attributes procreation to natural circumstances rather than to "eternal law." "Just a chance. Must have been that morning in Raymond terrace she was at the window, watching the two dogs at it. . . . And the sergeant grinning up. . . . Give us a touch, Poldy. God, I'm dying for it. How life begins" (p. 89). Birth and death both result from accidents. Human intercourse can be inspired by canine copulation or by the reminiscence of an earlier attraction. Rudy was conceived because Molly spied two mating dogs and a flirtatious officer who reminded her of Mulvey. The grotesque situation makes life no less sacred at its inception. Bloom recalls with amazement the moment of "blind rut" that ended in paternity.

From a conception associated with bestiality came a birth issuing in death. "From me. Just a chance" (p. 89). Bloom produced the sperm that made his son, a "weak seed" that could not support life outside the womb. The father experienced a form of unconscious castration at his son's demise. As Sheldon Brivic points out, "According to one of the standard formulations of psychoanalysis, an infant may often be a symbol for the phallus. For the already neurotic Bloom, Rudy's death evidently symbolized the destruction of the penis that could be 'put out of sight'."[2] The incident struck a mortal blow to Bloom's potency and left him unable to complete sexual intercourse with his wife: "Could never like it again after Rudy" (p. 168).

Bloom pities the "poor children" who must suffer disease, recalling that Milly "got off lightly with illness compared" (p.

90). His sentence is cut short by a silent comparison of Milly and Rudy, the child who did *not* get off lightly. Rudy's death has intensified the anxiety Bloom associates with women. Only the female, it would seem, has enough strength to sustain ongoing life. She can exist independently because she harbors the source of regeneration. "Molly. Milly. Same thing watered down" (p. 89).

Bloom is trying to come to terms with the indignity of death, which appears to be a "beastly" thing determined by chance. As he scans the obituaries, he finds a clue to the mystery. The prayer to Saint Theresa, "Thanks to the Little Flower," reminds him of his pseudonym, "Henry Flower." And it recalls the life potential suggested at the conclusion of "Lotus-Eaters," when Bloom contemplated his "bud of flesh." The outraged father still carries within himself all the powers of fertile creation. He must turn away from death toward the "flowering" of vitality, despite constant reminders of cuckoldry:

> —Blazes Boylan, Mr. Power said. There he is airing his quiff.
> Just that moment I was thinking.
> Mr. Dedalus bent across to salute. From the door of the Red Bank the white disc of a straw hat flashed reply: passed.
> Mr. Bloom reviewed the nails of his left hand, then those of his right hand. The nails, yes. Is there anything more in him that they she sees? Fascination. Worst man in Dublin. That keeps him alive. They sometimes feel what a person is. Instinct. But a type like that. My nails. I am just looking at them: well pared. And after: thinking alone. Body getting a bit softy. I would notice that from remembering. What causes that I suppose the skin can't contract quickly enough when the flesh falls off. But the shape is there. The shape is there still. Shoulders. Hips. Plump. Night of the dance dressing. Shift stuck between the cheeks behind.
> He clasped his hands between his knees and, satisfied, sent his vacant glance over their faces. (P. 92)

At this point in the episode, Bloom has reached the nadir of his descent into hell. He has met the ghosts of Rudy and of his father. Now he confronts the living specter of Molly's adultery.

100

The other men salute Boylan, a Dublin Casanova reputed for amorous conquests. Like a radiant sun god, the lover flashes his white straw hat, a fetishistic symbol of male prowess. The Red Bank restaurant, here associated with Boylan, will later be identified with another enemy—the one-eyed Citizen who spits a Red Bank oyster "out of his gullet" (p. 331) in "Cyclops."

Bloom "reviews his nails" in a futile attempt to exclude Boylan from physical and mental perspective. The trivial occupation fails to hold his attention. His mind keeps shifting back to Molly's lover: "Is there anything more in him that they she sees?" The double pronoun illustrates Bloom's confusion. He first wonders what women in general ("they") see in Boylan. But before he can articulate the thought, his interest turns to the question of how Molly ("she") can be attracted to such a rogue. Everyone knows that Boylan is a scoundrel, the "worst man in Dublin." Yet Molly has been captivated by his glamor. Bloom's judgment of Blazes is clear: he is all flash and no substance. Boylan appears virile and alive; Leopold seems as impotent as a corpse.

Bloom feels desperately alienated from his spouse. "They sometimes feel what a person is. Instinct. But a type like that" (p. 92). A woman may be capable of recognizing her lover's uniqueness from qualities inaccessible to the common eye. The explanation leads Bloom to compassion for Molly, but he feels that his credulity is being taxed. How could a "type like that" possess redeeming merits? How could Blazes be anything other than what he seems—a cad?

To escape the dilemma, Bloom returns to his fingernails. His psyche has been paralyzed by the confrontation with Boylan, and he is attempting to deaden his sensibilities. Earlier in the chapter, he contemplated the nails of a lifeless body as a scientific "phenomenon": "I believe they clip the nails and the hair. . . . Grow all the same after" (p. 87). Bloom's present investigation of his hands reveals his acute anxiety. After seeing Blazes, he feels like a dead man, and he searches his nails for signs of posthumous growth. "My nails. I am just looking at them." The progressive verb, "am looking," affirms the experience of continuing temporality. Bloom not only studies his fingernails; he makes a deliberate effort to see himself in terms of conscious perception. By constituting the ''I'' as a subjective agent, he asserts a transcendental ego—the self aware of itself in the act of mental reflection.

During the struggle to regain his integrity, Bloom has unconsciously been acting out the drama of Molly's adultery. Earlier, he wondered what his wife could see in her seducer, and he hoped that she would refuse to yield. Now he relinquishes such speculation and resigns himself to the affair. Bloom looks ahead to Molly's post-coital reflections: ''And after: thinking alone. Body getting a bit softy'' (p. 92). Once again, he sympathizes with his spouse by imagining the lonely aftermath of adultery. He thinks of Molly lamenting her flabbiness and facing the terrors of approaching old age. ''But the shape is there. The shape is there still. Shoulders. Hips. Plump'' (p. 92). Bloom feels comforted by the memory of Molly's ''shift stuck between the cheeks behind'' the night of the bazaar dance. In a moment of infantile regression, he seeks embryonic security in the fleshy ''cheeks'' of his wife's maternal haunches. As at the close of ''Ithaca,'' Bloom finds solace in the amplitude of Molly's ''adulterous rump.'' In imitation of the clinging shift, he clasps his hands between his legs and enjoys vicarious satisfaction. He looks up at his companions with the vacant stare of a child, only to be spurned by the aggressive males surrounding him.

Mr. Power asks, ''How is the concert tour getting on, Bloom?'' (p. 92). Power's ironic ''And *Madame*'' sets off reminiscences of Mozart's *Don Giovanni,* the musical motif of Bloom's cuckoldry. The anxious husband merely smiles and ignores the taunt. He even feels pity for Power's frustrated love life, a situation ironically similar to his own: ''Who knows is that true about the woman he keeps? Not pleasant for the wife. Yet they say, who was it told me, there is no carnal. You would imagine that would get played out pretty quick'' (p. 93).

When the Dubliners harangue against Reuben J. Dodd, usurers, and Jews in general, Bloom tries to participate in the joke.

He attempts to mitigate anti-Semitism with humor by moving from the general category of defilement to a particular anecdote about Dodd and his son. Simon's angry curse, "Drown Barabbas!" (p. 94), and his conclusion that Reuben paid "one and eightpence too much" (p. 95) for his son's rescue are both implicit insults to Bloom. Dodd's rebellious offspring was saved after a baptismal "death by water"; Bloom's child "drowned" in infancy, a "Jew's son" whose life was beyond purchase.

A tiny coffin flashes by, and Bloom imagines:

> A dwarf's face mauve and wrinkled like little Rudy's was. Dwarf's body, weak as putty, in a whitelined deal box. . . . Our. Little. Beggar. Baby. Meant nothing. Mistake of nature. If it's healthy it's from the mother. If not the man. Better luck next time. . . .
> —But the worst of all, Mr. Power said, is the man who takes his own life. (P. 96)

The death of little Rudy and the suicide of Rudolph the elder come together in painful coincidence. Bloom pictures the pauper child with a face "mauve and wrinkled" like the skin of an old man. The recollection is so unnerving that his words are halted, punctuated in single syntactical units. "Our" stands alone and designates both the indigent child and his own dead son. Until now, Bloom has been thinking about poor "little Rudy." But the memory has become too agonizing. He cuts the phrase short, comes to a full stop, and substitutes the adjective "beggar" for Rudy's name. By channeling pity toward the tiny pauper, Bloom can look at infant mortality from a stoic perspective. In the cosmic scheme of things, the boy "meant nothing. Mistake of nature. If it's healthy it's from the mother. If not the man." Under the guise of cynicism, Bloom reveals the guilt he associates with Rudy's demise. He has judged himself culpable of the "sin" of impotence, and the conviction has proved a self-fulfilling prophecy. Not only does the world regard him as a defiled Jew, but Bloom considers *himself* defiled by the stigma of paternal failure.

103

Furthermore, Bloom has inherited a sense of inadequacy from the family disgrace of his father's suicide: "They have no mercy on that here or infanticide. Refuse Christian burial. They used to drive a stake of wood through his heart in the grave. As if it wasn't broken already" (p. 96). Bloom alludes to his father's death indirectly, in terms of the vague pronominal referent "that." He associates suicide, the worst of all sins, with infanticide, the crime for which he unconsciously condemns himself. Bloom bears the guilt for nature's "murder" of little Rudy. Like Rudolph the elder, he suffers a "broken heart" and is being punished by a society that shows no mercy to men such as he.

The only person who tries to rescue Bloom from this dark circle of hell is Martin Cunningham. Aware of the family history, Martin insists that "we must take a charitable view" of suicide. To Bloom, he seems to be a temporary redeemer: "Sympathetic human man he is. Intelligent. Like Shakespeare's face. Always a good word to say" (p. 96). Martin can utter a "good word" of sympathy because the "life of the damned" (p. 96) has made him responsive to domestic anguish. Bloom is grateful for the "charitable view" that softens Power's tirade against suicidal cowardice. He describes Cunningham as a "human man," using a redundant phrase to emphasize extraordinary kindness.

Sentiments of good fellowship engender compassion, which in turn gives rise to artistic creation. Bloom attempts to understand and to identify with Cunningham's marital torment by imagining ludicrous scenes of conjugal purgation: "And that awful drunkard of a wife of his. Setting up house for her time after time and then pawning the furniture on him every Saturday almost. Leading him the life of the damned. . . . Lord, she must have looked a sight that night. . . . Drunk about the place and capering with Martin's umbrella" (p. 96).

According to his own definition, Bloom is the most "human" of the citizens attending Dignam's funeral. As a sensitive individual, he offers an ethical model for aesthetic creation. Sympathy leads him to realize an artistic mode of life, inspired

104

by the urge to comprehend the joy and the sorrow of his fellow human beings. Through negative capability, he fashions empathic stories that enable him to dramatize the pain and emotional isolation revealed in the lives of others. His pity for Cunningham unwittingly evokes the mythic situations of Sisyphus and Ixion: "Wear the heart out of a stone, that. Monday morning start afresh. Shoulder to the wheel" (p. 96). Bloom has wandered through Hades for so long that he can clearly recognize human misery. As in the case of Stephen's Shakespeare, his loss proves to be another's gain.

The men in the carriage discuss the Gordon Bennett Race as their coach gallops toward the cemetery. The Dubliners are unaware that they too are engaged in the "great race" of life, a contest whose goal is death. Dignam, like Homer's Elpenor, has already won this round and gotten there before them. Only Bloom seems aware of their destiny. He associates "my house down there" with the "ward for incurables there. Very encouraging. Our Lady's Hospice for the dying. Deadhouse handy underneath" (p. 97). Bloom ranks himself among the "dying" by his juxtaposition of 7 Eccles Street and Our Lady's Hospice. Both, in fact, appear to occupy the same adverbial place "there." An "incurable" Jew, cuckold, and mortal, Bloom continues to burn in his private hell.

As cattle pass in front of the carriage, he thinks of death in terms of its lowest denominator—animal slaughter and degustation of the corpse. "Tomorrow is killing day. . . . Roast beef for old England" (p. 97). He suggests two inventions: a tramline to the cattle market and "municipal funeral trams." The projects are ironically similar. Trams would convey cattle to the slaughter and human corpses to the cemetery. In both cases, the end is cold meat.

Like Mulligan, Bloom recognizes death as a physiological phenomenon. But in contrast to Buck, he refuses to consider it "a beastly thing and nothing else" (p. 8). The tragedy of death lies precisely in the interdependence of physical existence and spiritual consciousness. Death reduces the man-god to a "dog"-corpse. Bloom muses: "Simnel cakes those are . . .

cakes for the dead. Dogbiscuits. Who ate them? Mourners coming out'' (p. 100). As if to assure themselves of continuing vitality, the living feast on food that the deceased can no longer enjoy. Their primitive wake rite is but one step removed from tribal cannibalism, a theme portrayed in *Finnegans Wake* when the body of HCE becomes food for Shem and Shaun.

Dead men are ''shades'' in human memory; only the living have substance and participate in authentic existence. Bloom laments that Queen Victoria wasted her energies mourning all ''for a shadow. . . . Her son was the substance. Something new to hope for not like the past she wanted back, waiting. It never comes'' (p. 102). Human life involves a constant process of becoming, of self-projection toward ''something new to hope for.'' The son is physically consubstantial with the father and perpetuates the ''substance'' when his progenitor dies.

In opposition to the sentimental Dubliners, Bloom faces the reality of death as a mechanical breakdown:

> Mr. Kernan said with solemnity:
> —*I am the resurrection and the life.* That touches a man's inmost heart.
> —It does, Mr. Bloom said.
> Your heart perhaps but what price the fellow in the six feet by two with his toes to the daisies? No touching that. Seat of the affections. Broken heart. A pump after all, pumping thousands of gallons of blood every day. One fine day it gets bunged up and there you are. Lots of them lying around here: lungs, hearts, livers. Old rusty pumps: damn the thing else. The resurrection and the life. Once you are dead you are dead. (P. 105)

While Kernan is engrossed in funeral rites, Bloom goes to the heart of the matter: the dead man's heart cannot be ''touched,'' no matter how moving the ceremony. The sentimental Irishman demands consolation from a ''heart-rending'' service. Bloom shows greater compassion for the deceased by recognizing that Dignam's heart is beyond mending. The Jewish mind portrays Christian resurrection in terms of a comic vision: ''Last day! Then every fellow mousing around for his liver and his lights and the rest of his traps'' (p. 106). Death reduces the individual

106

to a "pennyweight of powder in a skull," with no possibility of resuscitation.

Even the story of Mulcahy and the drunks adds to the irony of man's concept of immortality. The drunkard remarks in front of Christ's statue: "*Not a bloody bit like the man. . . . That's not Mulcahy, . . . whoever done it*" (p. 107). The religious figure perpetuates the human vanity of survival through stone memorials. A statue cannot replace Mulcahy, no matter how much reverence one ascribes to it. The effigy is "not a bloody bit like the man" because it fails to possess flesh-and-blood vitality. The stone savior cannot endow Mulcahy's corpse with the faculty of human consciousness.

For Bloom, a physical life-death cycle constitutes the only valid myth of rebirth. He contemplates the "new life" that issues from the cemetery through the caretaker and his wife: "It might thrill her first. Courting death. . . . Love among the tombstones. Romeo. Spice of pleasure. In the midst of death we are in life. Both ends meet. Tantalising for the poor dead. Smell of grilled beefsteaks to the starving gnawing their vitals" (p. 108; corrected from the 1934 Random House edition). But the dead, by very definition, *have* no vitals. They themselves have disintegrated into rotting meat; they resemble "grilled beefsteaks," "roast beef for old England."

In examining death, Bloom unconsciously traces ritual murder back to its origin in ancient fertility rites of vegetation and growth. "It's the blood sinking in the earth gives new life. Same idea those jews they said killed the christian boy" (p. 108). The "same idea" of rejuvenation through sacrifice underlies the archaic ritual of Dionysus; the crucifixion of Christ; and the slaughter of Hugh of Lincoln, the "christian boy" murdered by the Jews. Resurrection myths historically take root in primitive fertility cycles. The boy-god dies, and a flower rises up in his stead.[3] Bloom suggests an ingenious extension of the vegetation ritual: the use of human corpses to fertilize a garden. "Every man his price. Well preserved fat corpse gentleman, epicure, invaluable for fruit garden" (p. 108). His suggestion prefigures the implications of Joyce's neologism "cropse" in *Finnegans Wake*.

The bodily decomposition that Bloom imagines is anything but idyllic: "I daresay the soil would be quite fat with corpse manure, bones, flesh, nails, charnelhouses. Dreadful. Turning green and pink, decomposing. Rot quick in damp earth. . . . Then a kind of a tallowy kind of cheesy. Then begin to get black, treacle oozing out of them. . . . Of course the cells or whatever they are go on living. Changing about. Live for ever practically" (p. 108). Bloom confuses "cells" and atoms, but his conclusion is accurate. The primordial units of chemical matter "live forever." Physiological death is both vegetative and bestial. As for man, "once you're dead, you're dead." Paddy "doesn't know who is here nor care" (p. 109).

In both the Linati and the Gilbert schemata, Joyce designated the heart as the thematic organ of "Hades." Bloom is moving from a strictly mechanical denotation of "heart" to figurative language descriptive of the human condition. He has defined death as a physical breakdown of the center of circulation; the heart becomes "an old rusty pump." But because death annihilates conciousness, it sheds light in a negative way on the "human heart" as the source of emotion. The caretaker enjoys "cracking his jokes too: warms the cockles of his heart" (p. 109). Bloom has begun to speak in analogical terms, and he uses a figure of speech to describe the feeling of good cheer. "Gravediggers in *Hamlet*. Shows the profound knowledge of the human heart. Daren't joke about the dead for two years at least" (p. 109).

Burial is the one service for which an individual must depend on others: "A fellow could live on his lonesome all his life. Yes, he could. Still he'd have to get someone to sod him after he died though he could dig his own grave. We all do. Only man buries. . . . Say Robinson Crusoe was true to life. Well then Friday buried him. Every Friday buries a Thursday if you come to look at it" (p. 109). Death acknowledges the individual as a member of a universal community. By the phrase "We all do," Bloom indicates that each person must recognize his social inclusion at the moment of death, even though he may have denied it during life. At the same time, burial relates directly to those who survive the corpse. "Bury the dead" is the "first thing" that "strikes anybody" (p. 109). By disposing of the dead, the survivor recognizes the human body as an object to be returned to the earth and solidified as physical matter. In the act of burial, he affirms his own transcendent consciousness: he refuses to identify with the death process of absorption into an alien environment.

"Every Friday buries a Thursday." The funeral rite illustrates man's need to transcend his solidified past. The living must project themselves forward into the future. Those who insist on looking back "dig their own graves." Like Lot's wife, they will be petrified into stone, paralyzed by the stasis of history. The individual must constantly bury his past and choose himself anew. Precisely because the Irish have abjured freedom, they are being buried alive by archaic traditions. Joyce's Ireland is a nation of living corpses who turn away from authentic creativity.

Unlike the Dublin mourners, Bloom realizes that death ceases to be a human phenomenon once life has been extinguished. The corpse is a static object that can feel no more, and Bloom directs his pity toward the painful struggle that precedes the end of consciousness. He imagines the sensations of terror, surprise, and incredulity experienced by the dying man: "It's the moment you feel. Must be damned unpleasant. Can't believe it at first. Mistake must be: someone else. Try the house opposite. Wait, I wanted to. I haven't yet. Then darkened deathchamber" (p. 110). The brevity of the scene heightens its macabre accuracy. Bloom contemplates the feeling of impotence with which a modern Everyman must confront his final agony. "Whispering around you. Would you like to see a priest? Then rambling and wandering. Delirium all you hid all your life. The death struggle" (p. 110). The psychodrama of pain and isolation expresses much the same tension as that portrayed in Tolstoy's "Death of Ivan Ilych":

Ivan Ilych saw that he was dying, and he was in continual despair. . . .

> The syllogism he had learnt from Kiezewetter's Logic: "Caius is a man, men are mortal, therefore Caius is mortal," had always seemed to him correct as applied to Caius, but certainly not as applied to himself. That Caius—man in the abstract—was mortal, was perfectly correct, but he was not Caius, not an abstract man, but a creature quite, quite separate from all the others.[4]

The individual tries desperately to escape the reality of personal extinction. He consoles himself by adopting the inauthentic position of the "crowd," by regarding death as a characteristic of the anonymous "One."[5] Death can be comprehended only in terms of others, as an event *pour autrui*. Human consciousness cannot conceive of total annihilation. Since the mind is pure "nothingness," it is able to envision nonbeing only as the corresponding destruction of a personal life-world.

At the end of *Finnegans Wake,* Anna Livia murmurs as she flows toward death: "And let her rain now if she likes . . . for my time is come. I done me best when I was let. Thinking always if I go all goes. A hundred cares, a tithe of troubles and is there one who understands me?" (*FW* 627). Because the individual comprehends his existence through phenomena outside himself, he thinks of death in terms of a universe that continues to exist despite the absence of his *being-there.* But once the mind posits a world, it simultaneously affirms a "transcendental consciousness" aware of death as a phenomenon extrinsic to itself. Hence the illusion of immortality: the transcendental ego refuses to recognize the annihilation of personal identity.[6]

Unwittingly, Bloom applies to the burial rites images from the crucifixion and resurrection of Jesus: "They ought to have some law to pierce the heart and make sure. . . . Flag of distress. Three days" (p. 111). The Jew Leopold is precluding the possibility of a Christian Messiah. If Christ rose after three days, he was never dead; if his heart were indeed pierced by a soldier who "made sure" of death, then Jesus could not have risen from the tomb. Joe Hynes asks Bloom, "What is your Christian name? I'm not sure" (p. 111). Possibly the reporter is not certain about the Jew's "Christianity." Bloom

110

hesitates, then gives the initial "L" before stating his given name.

When Joe Hynes suggests a visit to the "chief's grave," the men pay homage to Charles Stewart Parnell, a half-mythic political leader who legend predicts will "one day come again." In their tribute to Parnell, the Dubliners move toward public ritual and social integration. Bloom, as always, remains an outsider: "Mr. Bloom walked unheeded along his grove by saddened angels, crosses, broken pillars, family vaults, stone hopes praying with upcast eyes, old Ireland's hearts and hands" (p. 113). Bloom traverses a wasteland that neither Jesus nor Parnell could redeem. "Old Ireland's hearts and hands" are dismembered and incapable of action. The hopes of the living have turned cold. The nation has become a degenerate graveyard, a barren Garden of Eden glittering with illusory metal flowers.

"How many! All these here once walked round Dublin. Faithful departed. As you are now so once were we" (p. 113). But the citizens who "walk round Dublin" are already dead. Bloom earlier observed: "Dead side of the street this. Dull business by day . . . the industrious blind. . . . Chummies and slaveys. Under the patronage of the late Father Mathew. Foundation stone for Parnell. Breakdown. Heart" (p. 95). The whole city suffers from a breakdown of the heart, a loss of compassionate vitality. In *Portrait,* Simon Dedalus declared that "the priests and the priests' pawns broke Parnell's heart and hounded him into his grave (*PA* 33–34). Just as Parnell died of a broken heart when spurned by his countrymen, so the Dubliners now offer their liberator a foundation stone crumbling for dearth of political sympathy. The Irish are embedded in blind tradition. Their hearts have been "enchanted to a stone," solidified like the statue of the Sacred Heart, Ireland's Catholic patron.

Like the genteel play-actors of Yeats's poem "Easter, 1916," the Dubliners utter "polite meaningless words" of sympathy for Paddy Dignam. But their concern goes no further than an aristocratic funeral rite that carefully honors tradition.

"Pray for the repose of the soul of. Does anybody really? Plant him and have done with him. Like down a coalshoot" (p. 113). In contrast to the citizens, Bloom scrutinizes death with meticulous realism:

> An obese grey rat toddled along the side of the crypt, moving the pebbles. An old stager: greatgrandfather: he knows the ropes. . . .
> One of those chaps would make short work of a fellow. Pick the bones clean no matter who it was. Ordinary meat for them. A corpse is meat gone bad. . . . Ashes to ashes. Or bury at sea. . . . Earth, fire, water. Drowning they say is the pleasantest. See your whole life in a flash. But being brought back to life no. (P. 114)

The sight of an obese grey rat leads Bloom to a scientific analysis of death as a beastly phenomenon. The well-fed rodent has fattened himself on corpses; he is an "old stager: great-grandfather." A few moments earlier, Bloom had suggested putting "a gramophone in every grave. . . . Put on poor old greatgrandfather Kraahraark!" (p. 114). The verbal repetition intentionally deflates Bloom's scheme: "greatgrandfather" has disappeared into the digestive tract of a rat. Death has reduced the body to "meat gone bad"—food for flies, maggots, and rodents. "Regular square feed for them" (p. 114). The corpse has returned to the soil and become part of the elemental substances of earth, fire, and water. "Drowning they say is the pleasantest," Bloom muses, echoing Stephen's temptation to lose himself in a seachange. "Just you give it a fair trial. We enjoyed ourselves immensely" (p. 50). Yet even "death by water" offers no hope of resurrection, and Bloom is not deluded. "See your whole life in a flash. But being brought back to life no" (p. 114).

Both Stephen and Bloom contemplate a material corpse, and both arrive at similar conclusions. Stephen imagines the drowned man as a "bag of corpsegas sopping in foul brine. A quiver of minnows, fat of a spongy titbit, flash through the slits of his buttoned trouserfly. . . . Dead breaths I living breathe, tread dead dust, devour a urinous offal from all dead" (p. 50).

112

The drowned body has become a delectable morsel for fishes and is being absorbed into the waters of bitter death. The living consume "a urinous offal from all dead" in a process of molecular cannibalism. Human bodies fertilize vegetation and feed fishes that will later nourish men. Every corpse becomes a "cropse," to be eaten by its survivors.

Like Stephen, Bloom recognizes the corpse as meat to be devoured by scavengers. He depicts the dead man as food for human consumption, describing the body in gustatory images: "Saltwhite crumbling mush of corpse: smell, taste like raw white turnips" (p. 114). With the verbal technique used by Mulligan, Bloom portrays death in terms of palatal sensations. He is sufficiently repulsed by his own description of the corpse, however, to reject the land of the dead. "Back to the world again. Enough of this place" (p. 114).

For Joyce, reification, not resurrection, lies at the end of Christian eschatology. Consciousness, aware of its eventual extinction, must repudiate the grave and turn "back to the world again. . . . My ghost will haunt you after death. There is another world after death named hell. I do not like that other world she wrote. No more do I. Plenty to see and hear and feel yet. Feel live warm beings near you. Let them sleep in their maggoty beds. They are not going to get me this innings. Warm beds: warm fullblooded life" (pp. 114–15).

Bloom adamantly challenges the phantoms that haunt him. He "does not like that other world" called hell, nor the ghosts that arise from its depths. He has descended into Hades and seen the true nature of infernal torment. Those who cling to moribund traditions have been cut off from creative vitality. Like the characters in Sartre's *Huis Clos*, they are trapped in a solidified past: life is *déjà fait*. Hell reveals itself as "hemiplegia of the will"—a state of complete paralysis that destroys the possibility of growth, relationship, or a change of heart.

Bloom consciously chooses the upper air, then enumerates his senses like a wondrous child: "Plenty to see and hear and feel yet. Feel live warm beings near you." He rejects the "maggoty beds" of the dead and prefers the "warm fullblooded life'' of his wife Molly. On the primitive level of sense experience, he is working toward an ethic of love, compassion, and charity. Bloom delights in social contact, and he intuitively believes that salvation might be found through the physical and spiritual ''warmth'' of other human beings. He is beginning to articulate the philosophy of *caritas* that he later will preach in ''Cyclops'' and will embrace in ''Ithaca,'' along with equanimity.

Bloom refuses to be numbered among the Dublin corpses, whether they lie in the cemetery or walk the city streets. John Henry Menton, with ''oyster eyes,'' is one of the city's living dead. He gazes backward to the time years ago when he took a ''rooted dislike'' to Bloom over a petty bowling game. The paralyzed Dubliner was ''mortified'' by ''hate at first sight'' (p. 115). Now he snubs Bloom's sincere attempt to be gracious. Unlike his Jewish adversary, Menton is immersed in his own grave: he has become enslaved to the grudge he bears and to a spiritual breakdown of the heart.

Up to this point in the novel, Joyce's use of indirect free style has given us the illusion of unmediated access to the minds of Stephen and Bloom. Joyce as ''incarnate author'' has functioned as the voiceless presence behind and above and beyond the text—present in the mode of absence, but never intrusive as narrator. After the ''Hades'' episode, we become increasingly aware of a narrative voice independent of the characters—a fictional persona whose role in the novel approximates that of the traditional omniscient author.

In a work that makes extensive use of interior monologue, the reader holds intervention suspect. Narrative mediation never seems fully trustworthy, since it threatens our unobstructed access to psychological revelation. We have learned to believe the characters themselves, though they falter in their perceptions or stumble into bogs of scientific misinformation. The presence of a narrator banishes us to an external perspective. We must infer the thoughts and feelings attached to emotional states through the indirect evidence of symbolic activity.

In the first six episodes of *Ulysses,* the narrator remains mockingly sober.[7] With "Aeolus," he begins to disrupt our complacent sense of intimate knowledge. Joyce may have added the Aeolian headlines as an afterthought, but their presence entirely changes the character of the narrative. Typographical intrusion alienates us from the mimetic realism of the text. We are forced to realize that Joyce has created a self-contained universe. Visitors are welcome, so long as they keep in mind that the work of fiction is autotelic and self-referential.

The implicit narrator of "Aeolus" is an agent of mechanical perverseness. As *homo ludens,* he delights in experimental games—catalogues, parodies, word plays, verbal distortions, and neologisms. He tries to persuade us that life is a "beastly thing and nothing else" (p. 8). He insists that language involves only game and linguistic play, stripped of moral or metaphysical significance. His voice often resembles those of the principal characters; but his perspective is obliquely slanted, making it virtually impossible for us to establish a firm center of consciousness. Whenever the narrator usurps center stage, he exposes the paralytic emptiness of Dublin life.

The newspaper episode bombards us with windy rhetoric and a journalistic view of "DEAR DIRTY DUBLIN" (p. 145). All the characters in the chapter are determined to "raise the wind" (p. 147). They are convinced that language is a tool of manipulation. Words are "things" that conceal, rather than reveal, subjective consciousness. As Professor MacHugh prudently warns, "We mustn't be led away by words, by sounds of words" (p. 131). In the game of life, language functions as a primary tool of psychological manipulation.

The newspaper manipulates the attention of the crowd, just as newspaper headlines focus our attention on the trivia of Dublin life. Stephen takes on the persona of a punster and satirizes Ireland's political apathy in a bawdy parable of national seduction. The young man amuses his compatriots; but like Antisthenes, he becomes a pawn of his own acerbity. He prostitutes the cold steelpen of his wit to the demands of a debased, journalistic mentality.

115

The rhetoric of "Doughy Daw" or of John F. Taylor is windy enough to blow the Irish populace into a heat of Celtic ardor. The Old Testament offers a theocratic model for a modern Irish state, ruled by a corrupt clergy that bargains with England and betrays its believers for scraps of political power. The Irish nationalists are automatons set in motion by stirring polemic and by chauvinistic wind.

Even Leopold Bloom is blown in and out of the episode, for once a puppet of the trade he follows. In the newspaper office, he contemplates the obituary of Paddy Dignam, that "MOST RESPECTED DUBLIN BURGESS" (p. 118) whose heart-machine "got bunged up." "This morning the remains of the late Mr. Patrick Dignam. Machines. Smash a man to atoms if they got him caught. Rule the world today. His machineries are pegging away too. Like these, got out of hand: fermenting. Working away, tearing away. And that old grey rat tearing to get in" (p. 118). Bloom is threatened by the industrial technocracy of "Aeolus"; and he associates his fear of getting smashed "to atoms" with Dignam's corpse, now disintegrating into random atomic particles that fertilize the earth or feed the bowels of a rat.

The newspaper world is a microcosm of paralysis and of mechanical aggression: "The machines clanked in threefour time. Thump, thump, thump. Now if he got paralysed there and no one knew how to stop them they'd clank on and on the same, print it over and over and up and back. Monkeydoodle the whole thing. Want a cool head" (p. 119). The men in the office "clank on and on" in machine-like volubility. Sometimes the frightening engines seem more personal than the staff who operate them: "Sllt. Almost human the way it sllt to call attention. Doing its level best to speak. . . . Everything speaks in its own way" (p. 121).

Bloom's job as ad-canvasser makes him into a polite, ingratiating machine. His work is often demeaning. He must toady to the editor, Myles Crawford, in an attempt to arbitrate the demands of a client, Alexander Keyes. Crawford's insult, "K. M. R. I. A.," prefigures the brutal invective of the Citizen

116

in "Cyclops." "He can kiss my royal Irish arse, Myles Crawford cried loudly over his shoulder. Any time he likes, tell him" (p. 147). Crawford facetiously demands a "royal" prerogative in his scatological retort—a comment that exposes the ironic contradiction between the editor's democratic ideology and his debased, aristocratic demeanor.

Ireland is itself a "house of bondage," spiritually bankrupt and enthralled by English domination. Bloom's theological meditation offers a scathing critique of Irish biblical rhetoric: "All that long business about that brought us out of the land of Egypt and into the house of bondage *alleluia*. . . . Justice it means but it's everybody eating everyone else. That's what life is after all" (p. 122).

Stephen's "Parable of the Plums" makes a witty and ribald statement about "everybody eating everyone else" in terms of voracious imperialism. The Dublin vestals unconsciously worship Nelson, a "one-handled adulterer" perched atop his phallic column in the heart of the Hibernian metropolis. They honor a British hero guilty of the same scandalous "crimes" that rendered Parnell unfit to lead the Irish Catholic nation to home rule. England gets the plums, Ireland the plumstones. The Dublin virgins, barren and womb weary, unwittingly prostitute themselves to the titillating conqueror. "THOSE SLIGHTLY RAMBUNCTIOUS FEMALES" (p. 148) pay ludicrous homage to the scattered seed of England's adultery. Imperial Britain seduces Ireland, sucks the life out of her economy and her government, and finally betrays "Old Mother Grogan" to fatuous senility. The symbolism of Stephen's anecdote hints at both sexual and excretory release. "DIMINISHED DIGITS PROVE TOO TITILLATING FOR FRISKY FRUMPS. ANNE WIMBLES, FLO WANGLES" (p. 150), and both facilitate the pollution of their Hibernian capital. Like Moses on Mount Pisgah, the Dublin dames survey a desiccated wasteland that seems far from political redemption. Neither woman will realize the promise of national independence in her lifetime. The landscape is church-dominated, and the shadow of the "one-handled adulterer" casts its pall everywhere, like an

117

ominous sundial stretched out against the sky and challenging the power of the heavens.

Later, in "Wandering Rocks," the narrator presents us with another bird's-eye view of Dublin, a city dominated by clerical and viceregal power. The art of the chapter is "mechanics," the technique "labyrinthine." Stephen and Bloom are reduced to impersonal forms in the maze of Irish society.[8] The city is rendered through a kaleidoscopic set of distorted perspectives, and interpolation in each cameo section suggests the prominence of authorial manipulation. The formal disjunction of language and perception challenges our notion of serial temporality. As we learned in "Proteus," literature is an art that unfolds in time. We expect things to follow "one after another." And when they emulate the shape of cubist painting, distorted to collapse our certitudes about time and space, we feel the impact of narrative intervention.

Taken together, the vignettes in "Wandering Rocks" form a mosaic portrait of Irish paralysis. Each section might be construed as a rough sketch for a tale that could have been included in *Dubliners*. Many of the brief scenes evoke a "negative epiphany"—the sudden spiritual manifestation of matter devoid of spirit. The *quidditas* revealed is that of a heartless, mechanical cosmos. The bits of interior monologue to be found in the chapter respond, with fear or with fascination, to the threat of individual engulfment.

Bloom, the "cultured allround man" (p. 235) wallows in a whirlpool of morose delectation as he peruses a pornographic bookstall. Despite the salacious humor of the scene, implications of impersonal sex come close to sensual obsession. Birth, love, and death are yoked together in a grotesque bond of comic violence. The plates of "Aristotle's *Masterpiece*" depict gestation as sordid and bestial: "infants cuddled in a ball in bloodred wombs like livers of slaughtered cows" (p. 235).[9] In the works of James Lovebirch and of Leopold von Sacher-Masoch, coition is a sadomasochistic rite of torturous debasement. *Sweets of Sin* evokes for Bloom a synesthetic fantasy that previews the eroticism of Nighttown: "Warmth showered gently over him, cowing his flesh. Flesh yielded amid rumpled clothes. Whites of eyes swooning up. His nostrils arched themselves for prey. Melting breast ointments (*for him! For Raoul!*). Armpits' oniony sweat. Fishgluey slime (*her heaving embonpoint!*). Feel! Press! Crushed! Sulphur dung of lions!'' (p. 236). We are not far from the sensuous world of "Circe," where human beings are metamorphosed into slaves of sexual compulsion.

Stephen, too, yields to the thrill of amorous fantasy. He thinks of his lapidary prose inspired by gems "born all in the dark wormy earth, cold specks of fire, evil lights shining in the darkness" (p. 241). "And you who wrest old images from the burial earth! The brainsick words of sophists" (p. 242). From these inert minerals, he fashions a kinetic figure of sensual desire—a bejeweled belly-dancer performing before the lurid glare of a sailor: "She dances in a foul gloom where gum burns with garlic. A sailorman, rustbearded, sips from a beaker rum and eyes her. A long and seafed silent rut" (p. 241). Bloom is entranced by the pornography he reads; Stephen is fascinated by his own creation of lascivious art. In both cases, sex is imagined as a mechanical act of frictional excitation. The titillations of erotic dream demand phallic conquest and female violation.

Stephen has strayed far from the path of Aquinas Tunbelly. He feels trapped in a world that he perceives as heartless. The dynamos from a nearby powerhouse give rise to an epiphany of terrifying contingency: "Beingless beings. Stop! Throb always without you and the throb always within. Your heart you sing of. I between them. Where? Between two roaring worlds where they swirl, I. Shatter them, one and both. But stun myself too in the blow" (p. 242). For once, Stephen loses intellectual control. He experiences a visceral horror of personal annihilation and a searing comprehension of mortality. He realizes the futility of artistic song in terms of cosmic engulfment. The poet sings of his own heart, a throbbing pump that will eventually break down. The shadow of death mocks the permanence of aesthetic creation.

Stephen is aware of the transcendental ego, the subjective "I" that confirms individual uniqueness. But he feels terrified by the recognition of his own being as a "nothingness"—as pure potential, mediating between an internal, biological microcosm and an external, perceptual macrocosm. Human consciousness must be constituted negatively, by a definition of that which it is *not*—the physical body it inhabits or the material universe it "nihilates." The "I," that elusive "ego," hovers "between two roaring worlds where they swirl." It can be identified with neither; yet, paradoxically, it is contingent on both.

The horror of mechanical determinism prompts Stephen to flirt briefly with suicide. But he shuns the temptation of a *dio boia* visible in the chaotic Irish metropolis. Like Bloom, he snaps back defiantly: "Shatter me you who can. Bawd and butcher, were the words. I say! Not yet awhile. A look around" (p. 242). He turns to the reality of external phenomena to escape self-indulgent morbidity. Artifoni was right: if Stephen perceives the world as *una bestia,* he only sacrifices himself (p. 228).

In a mechanistic universe, the heart is nothing but a "wonderful" timepiece ticking off the seconds of mortality. "Heroes' hearts" throb strongly in the breasts of heavyweight boxers who celebrate violence and virility. Love is defined as sensual excitement, evoked by the witchery of an aphrodisiac charm: *"nebrakada femininum! Amor me solo!"* (p. 242).

Dilly Dedalus, starved for food and for knowledge, will need more than a magic formula to relieve her desperation. The sight of Dilly casts a shadow over Stephen's mind and gives rise to Agenbite of Inwit: "She is drowning. Agenbite. Save her. Agenbite. All against us. She will drown me with her, eyes and hair. Lank coils of seaweed hair around me, my heart, my soul. Salt green death" (p. 243). These thoughts may be somewhat melodramatic, but Dilly functions as an awful reminder that loyalty to his "consubstantial" family will drag Stephen down into the engulfing waters of Irish oblivion.

In "Aeolus" and in "Wandering Rocks," Stephen and Bloom are threatened by spiritual paralysis and by hemiplegia of the will. In the heart of the Hibernian metropolis, they

120

discover the other side of Hades—a world of automation and will-lessness that sanctions death-in-life. Above and beyond the Dublin scene stands the omniscient narrator, a hangman god who relates the tale of "things as they are" and gleefully satirizes the myopia of human society.

1. Hugh Kenner, *Dublin's Joyce,* p. 22.

2. Sheldon R. Brivic, "James Joyce: From Stephen to Bloom," p. 157.

3. Sir James Frazer describes the earlier Greek legend: "Like the other gods of vegetation . . . Dionysus was believed to have died a violent death, but to have been brought to life again; and his sufferings, death, and resurrection were enacted in his sacred rites. . . . Pomegranates were supposed to have sprung from the blood of Dionysus, as anemones from the blood of Adonis and violets from the blood of Attis. . . . Where the resurrection formed part of the myth, it also was acted at the rites, and it even appears that a general doctrine of resurrection, or at least immortality, was inculcated on the worshippers" (*The New Golden Bough,* p. 200).

4. Leo Tolstoy, *"The Death of Ivan Ilych" and Other Stories,* pp. 131–32.

5. As Martin Heidegger explains, "The analysis of the phrase 'one dies' reveals unambiguously the kind of Being which belongs to everyday Being-towards-death. In such a way of talking, death is understood as an indefinite something which, above all, must duly arrive from somewhere or other, but which is proximally *not yet present-at-hand for one-self,* and is therefore no threat. . . . In Dasein's public way of interpreting, it is said that 'one dies,' because everyone else and oneself can talk himself into saying that 'in no case is it I myself,' for this 'one' is *the 'nobody.'* . . . Dying, which is essentially mine in such a way that no one can be my representative, is perverted into an event of public occurrence which the 'they' encounters. . . . *The 'they' does not permit us the courage for anxiety in the face of death"* (*Being and Time,* pp. 297–98).

6. In Sartre's short story "The Wall," one of the condemned prisoners declares: "I tell myself there will be nothing afterwards. But I don't understand what it means. . . . I see my corpse; that's not hard but *I'm* the one who sees it, with *my* eyes. I've got to think . . . think that I won't see anything anymore and the world will go on for the others" (*Intimacy,* pp. 20–21).

7. Marilyn French points out in *The Book as World* that Joyce wrote these chapters in what he called the "initial style," a stream-of-consciousness form that establishes the "decorum" of the novel and "has three main strands: interior monologue, third person description of action and exteriors, and naturalistic dialogue" (*The Book as World: James Joyce's "Ulysses,"* p. 54). According to French, these chapters make us so thoroughly sympathetic

to Stephen and to Bloom that we later choose sentiment and human emotion over the cold, mockingly rational world of the scientific, experimental narrator.

8. Bloom, for instance, is described as a "darkbacked figure under Merchants' arch" (p. 227). Clive Hart suggests that in "Wandering Rocks," the author adopts "the persona of a harsh and awkward narrator whose difficult personality is the most salient thing about the chapter." According to Hart, the narrative consciousness of the episode functions as the *spiritus loci* "of Dublin itself, and the spirit is endowed with a distinctive personality. . . . But the objectivity is a disingenuous fraud, a deliberate trap." "This narrator is omnipresent, and very much in charge. He is remote, 'behind or beyond' his handiwork, but by no means indifferent. He reports, but rarely condescends to explain, conceals and reveals according to whim, and both we and the characters suffer from his totalitarian dominance" (Clive Hart, "Wandering Rocks," in *James Joyce's "Ulysses,"* ed. Clive Hart and David Hayman, pp. 186, 189, 190)

9. *Aristotle's Masterpiece* (1694) was, in fact, a pseudonymous work sold as a titillating sex manual throughout the eighteenth and nineteenth centuries. Molly later thinks about the same book in "Penelope," and her comment is relevant, despite its malapropism: "like those babies in the Aristocrats Masterpiece he brought me another time as if we hadnt enough of that in real life without some old Aristocrat or whatever his name is disgusting you more with those rotten pictures children with two heads and no legs thats the kind of villainy theyre always dreaming about with not another thing in their empty heads" (p. 772). Molly condemns males for lewd-mindedness and for obsessive absorption in sexual fantasy—precisely those charges which critics have leveled against Molly Bloom, and which each sex has perennially brought against the other, "the pan calling the kettle blackbottom" (p.767).

122

**"Lestrygonians" and "Sirens":
Food for Men and Gods**

At the end of "Hades," Leopold Bloom renounces the spirit-world of sentimental religion and heart-rending grief. He casts a cold eye on the corpse of Paddy Dignam and decides to "pass by" the grave this inning. The stark reality of death as a physical phenomenon forces Bloom back to warm, sensuous life. He eschews that "other world" of lifeless essences and the ghosts that cling to its shadows. Bloom prefers to take his chances in dear dirty Dublin, a city that is "beastly alive" and offers sensual delights to eye and palate. His thoughts turn to alimentary satisfaction in "Lestrygonians" and later in "Sirens"—chapters that describe a godly and an earthly meal that intersect in notable parallax.

The "Lestrygonians" episode is one of Joyce's more successful examples of aesthetic integration of organ and technique. Combining symbolist metaphor with realistic detail, Joyce is keenly aware of the basic interdependence of soma

123

and psyche. In a world of symbolic analogies, the most obvious correspondences take root in primal interaction between mind and body: the hour before lunch is "the very worst hour of the day. Vitality. Dull, gloomy: hate this hour. Feel as if I had been eaten and spewed" (p. 164). With an empty stomach, Bloom begins to feed on himself. "Nature abhors a vacuum" (p. 164). Internal space leads him to the brink of the void and gives rise to gaping terrors of annihilation: "Never know anything about it. Waste of time. Gasballs spinning about, crossing each other, passing. Same old dingdong always. Gas, then solid, then world, then cold, then dead shell drifting around, frozen rock like that pineapple rock" (p. 167). Bloom imagines a post-apocalyptic earthball winding down to a cold, barren, inhuman landscape—a vision of lifeless frigidity inspired by Laplace's nebular hypothesis of "universal cooling."

In peristaltic fluctuation, Bloom readily succumbs to erotic fantasy engendered by the rich, synesthetic beauty of Grafton Street: "A warm human plumpness settled down on his brain. His brain yielded. Perfume of embraces all him assailed. With hungered flesh obscurely, he mutely craved to adore" (p. 168). Physical hunger mingles with lascivious desire, olfactory pleasure with kinesthetic satisfaction. But Bloom suffers a rude awakening at the door of the Burton restaurant:

Stink gripped his trembling breath: pungent meatjuice, slop of greens. See the animals feed.

Men, men, men.

Perched on high stools by the bar, hats shoved back, at the tables calling for more bread no charge, swilling, wolfing gobfuls of sloppy food, their eyes bulging, wiping wetted moustaches. . . . A man spitting back on his plate: halfmasticated gristle: no teeth to chewchewchew it. . . . Bolting to get it over. . . . Am I like that? See ourselves as others see us. Hungry man is an angry man. . . .

Smells of men. His gorge rose. Spaton sawdust, sweetish warmish cigarette smoke, reek of plug, spilt beer, men's beery piss, the stale of ferment.

Couldn't eat a morsel here. . . . Get out of this. (P. 169)

124

Bloom has left lotus-land for the masculine, predatory arena of Darwinian struggle. This is Mulligan's Dublin, where human beings devour food in unthinking herds and feed on one another for want of better sustenance. "Hungry man is an angry man." Deprivation precludes communal solicitude: men are driven by a megalomanic rage to stuff their gullets and to fill the angry void inside. "Peace and war depend on some fellow's digestion" (p. 172). Bloom unwittingly recognizes a Marxist economic base at the heart of political conflict: "Every fellow for his own, tooth and nail. . . . Eat or be eaten. Kill! Kill!" (p. 170). Human beings murder one another and cannibalize themselves in a frustrated, aggressive environment: "Suppose that communal kitchen years to come perhaps. . . . Have rows all the same. All for number one. Children fighting for the scrapings of the pot. Want a soup pot big as the Phoenix Park. Harpooning flitches and hindquarters out of it. Hate people all round you" (p. 170). "Justice it means but it's everybody eating everyone else" (p. 122) in a crude ritual of competitive cannibalism.

Men and women are "piled up in cities," unable to escape the claustrophobic pressures of futility and anonymity in the industrial megalopolis. People feel alienated from their work and from themselves: "Houses, lines of houses, streets, miles of pavements, piledup bricks, stones. . . . Piled up in cities, worn away age after age. Pyramids in sand. Built on bread and onions. . . . No one is anything" (p. 164).

Hungry and skeptical, Bloom suffers from a depressed and melancholic vision of reality. He perceives a society in which males victimize one another; and females are condemned to live as broodmares, sentenced to "life with hard labor": "Poor Mrs. Purefoy! Methodist husband. Method in his madness. . . . Hardy annuals he presents her with. . . . Selfish those t.t's are" (p. 161). Mina Purefoy's plight assaults Bloom's compassion: "Three days imagine groaning on a bed with a vinegared handkerchief round her forehead, her belly swollen out! Phew! Dreadful simply! Child's head too big: forceps. Doubled up inside her trying to butt its way out blindly, groping

125

for the way out. Kill me that would" (p. 161). Mrs. Purefoy's Methodist husband masticates saffron bun and soda while his wife groans in labor. Safe within a Dickensian view of paternal righteousness, "Dear Doady" escapes the pain of delivery to wallow in the satisfactions of fatherhood.

Leopold Bloom empathizes with suffering men and women enslaved to the exigencies of bed, board, and breeding. As victim and underdog, he feels genuine compassion for individuals battling the forces of social and historical circumstance. In his own private world, Bloom feels like a scapegoat in the most primitive sense of the term. Thoughts of cannibalism torment his consciousness:

> *There was a right royal old nigger*
> *Who ate the balls of Mr. MacTrigger*
> *His five hundred wives*
> *Had the time of their lives*
> *It grew bigger and bigger and bigger.* [1]

Bloom cannot remember all of the limerick, which parabolically associates food and sexuality, cannibalism and eroticism. His mental block is understandable. In "Hades," he imagined himself sexually dead. Now he feels as if his genitals are figuratively being consumed by Boylan, whose womanizing prowess will be enhanced by the titillations of adultery. Bloom refuses to adopt the predatory ethic of kill or be killed, "eat or be eaten" (p. 170). The injunction to violence and retribution is precisely the urge he finds so appalling in the society around him. He will not adopt a masculine, aggressive ethic or attempt to dispatch the suitors of Penelope.

Bloom the victim barely allows fear to take shape on the surface of his mind. In clipped, abbreviated phrases, he thinks of Molly's flirtation with Boylan twelve days before: "He other side of her. Elbow, arm. He. Glowworm's la-amp is gleaming, love. Touch. Fingers. Asking. Answer. Yes" (p. 167). Bloom has societal approbation to try to "stop" his wife's infidelity; but instead, he chooses to stop himself from thinking about a moment that already belongs to the stasis of the past: "Stop.

126

Stop. If it was it was. Must'' (p. 167). Bloom cannot suppress the physical symptoms of acute anxiety: he breathes quickly; his heart palpitates; and his mental telegrams become laconic, almost indecipherable. He responds like a condemned man to the threat of cuckoldry: adultery *must* occur as punishment for his sins of conjugal neglect. Old MacTrigger faces the stew pot with resignation. The natives will dance in erotic glee at his wake. Like Finn MacCool, Bloom-MacTrigger is the potted meat on the menu.

Bloom's attitude is more than sheer fatalism. In terms of personal relations, it is admirable, even heroic. Bloom can neither change the past nor close off the future. The past is unalterable: "If it was it was." It is part of a given situation that he must assimilate into consciousness and handle as an existential reality. Nor can he limit the horizons of the future. He must prevent himself from circumscribing his wife's independence. What good is fidelity if it is forced? Bloom recognizes Molly's freedom and accedes to the priority of individual choice.

Leopold Bloom is one of the few heroes in literature to acknowledge that the beloved "object" is *not* an object at all but a subjective individual capable of independence, change, and self-transcendence. He may not dictate or control conduct, even when social approval or a marital contract sanctions the attempt to do so. Consciousness cannot be appropriated—either in the name of love, or by the Medusa gaze of hatred. "The lover does not desire to possess the beloved as one possesses a thing."[2] Bloom eschews the double standard and goes beyond a proprietary notion of conjugal relations. He sees Molly not as a "wife-possession-object" but as a unique, autonomous individual. He avoids that "avarice of the emotions" described by Stephen in "Scylla and Charybdis": "a man who holds so tightly to what he calls his rights over what he calls his debts will hold tightly also to what he calls his rights over her whom he calls his wife" (pp. 205–6). If human life is indeed defined by "freedom"; if choice and volition are the primary faculties of reason; then the greatest tribute of love must be a mutual recognition of personal liberty.

Bloom situates himself in the "stream of life" and acknowledges the mutability of human existence: "How can you own water really? It's always flowing in a stream, never the same, which in the stream of life we trace. Because life is a stream" (p. 153). One cannot solidify the "motion of matter" nor truly *own* anything. Life is ever changing, and time moves forward ineluctably. Bloom cannot help being preoccupied with the minutes rushing ahead: "Six, six. Time will be gone then. She . . ." (p. 174). After Molly's tryst with Boylan, there will be no "time" left for lamentations.

Love as an existential task is difficult. The past, with its memories of youth and romance, offers a seductive dream of escape into a time when love came easily. Bloom recalls his early days of marriage to Molly before Rudy was born: "I was happier then. Or was that I? Or am I now I? . . . Would you go back to then?" (p. 168). He never answers the question, "Would you go back to then?", for he knows that it is entirely rhetorical. Such a choice is not within the scope of his liberty. His past is the "dead" part of himself beyond control, and he can alter only the phenomena accessible to future project. He cannot reverse life's forward-moving stream.

In Davy Byrne's pub, Bloom again encounters threats of sentimental nostalgia. But recollection is carefully restricted to the frame of positive memory, rather than the lure of futile reminiscence. Bloom is learning to use the past supportively by drawing it into the present as an artistic mode of self-discovery. Imagination and memory expand the horizons of sympathetic experience and enlarge the possibilities of conscious creation.

After a meal of wine and cheese, physical satiety inspires lyrical contemplation. In a Proustian moment of bodily remembrance, Bloom's meal is sanctified by a spiritual love-communion with Molly:

> Stuck on the pane two flies buzzed, stuck.
> Glowing wine on his palate lingered swallowed. . . . Sun's heat it is. Seems to a secret touch telling me memory. Touched his sense moistened remembered. Hidden under wild ferns on Howth. Below us bay sleeping sky. No sound. . . . Pillowed on my coat

128

she had her hair, earwigs in the heather scrub my hand under her
nape, you'll toss me all. O wonder! . . . Ravished over her I lay,
full lips full open, kissed her mouth. Yum. Softly she gave me in
my mouth the seedcake warm and chewed. Mawkish pulp her
mouth had mumbled sweet and sour with spittle. Joy: I ate it: joy.
Young life, her lips that gave me pouting. Soft, warm, sticky
gumjelly lips. Flowers her eyes were, take me, willing eyes. . . .
Wildly I lay on her, kissed her; eyes, her lips, her stretched neck,
beating, woman's breasts full in her blouse of nun's veiling, fat
nipples upright. Hot I tongued her. She kissed me. I was kissed. All
yielding she tossed my hair. Kissed, she kissed me.
    Me. and me now.
    Stuck, the flies buzzed. (Pp. 175–76)

The "big memory" of consummated love is punctuated by
two copulating flies. A frame of animal sensuality sets off an
extremely humane recollection of sensuous communion.
Bloom's androgynous reverie connects food with sexual excitement, masculine passivity with feminine nurturance, and physical desire with lyrical transcendence. In a symbolic seed exchange, Leopold, the lover and son-husband, transmits the
seminal gift of himself to his mother-wife. Molly, in turn,
nourishes Bloom with predigested food in an act of amorous,
maternal solicitude. Out of their union will come new life, the
life of Milly Bloom. But Leopold focuses on communion rather
than on conception. He celebrates a eucharistic hymn of
metaphysical delight. There is "a touch of the artist about old
Bloom" (p. 235); and nowhere is his gift more apparent than in
this rhapsodic description of sexuality. Love makes poets of us
all: in the act of procreation, the mind transcends itself.
Bloom's lyrical paean to love provides emotional justification
for his continued fidelity to Molly. It offers a key to the
resolution of his cuckoldry by defining conjugal affection in
terms of agape as well as Eros.
    After such ecstasy, Bloom can leave to the gods a diet of
ambrosia and nectar. He implicitly rejects the cold, immortal
beauty of ideal Platonic forms: "Lovely forms of woman
sculped Junonian. Immortal lovely" (p. 176). Bloom is not, nor
does he wish to be, a member of the Olympian community that

eats electric light. He prefers seedcake from the mouth of a woman, the seeds of that "penny pippin" offered to Adam by our mother Eve. He chooses the "warm, fullblooded life" of Molly over "shapely goddesses, Venus, Juno: curves the world admires" (p. 176). Once again, the memory of Molly saves him from despair and self-pity.

Bloom's epic battle with jealousy, possessiveness, and anger has only begun. In the "Sirens" episode later that afternoon, he suffers still another trial of rationality and compassion. Joyce deliberately conflates Ulysses-Bloom with "betrayed" lovers of operatic melodrama and martyr-heroes of Ireland. Grief and loss strike the dominant chords of the chapter's musical overture: "All is lost now. . . . All gone. All fallen. . . . Last rose Castille" (pp. 256–57). The Sirens tempt us to pity and pray for that "last sardine of summer. Bloom alone" (p. 289).

At no other point in his odyssey does Bloom suffer such anguish. Molly's adultery is imminent. Boylan sets off for his rendezvous, and the "jingle-jaunty" of his cab resonates in Bloom's psyche like the metronome of fate. The chorus wends its way toward 7 Eccles Street with the "ineluctable modality" of audible catastrophe. Bloom gnashes his teeth on liver and bacon, but he refuses to yield to the siren-song that entices him to self-pity. Pathos surrounds his futile attempts at mental diversion. Like many gourmands, Bloom responds to severe anxiety by recourse to oral gratification. He forfeits his noon-time vegetarian diet and primes himself for battle by consuming a carnivorous meal of the "inner organs of beasts." Food offers sensual compensation for sexual loss, but Bloom feasts distractedly and with little relish. He tries a menu of "sauce for the gander" and soon grows bored with his letter to Martha Clifford. He listens to the sentimental lyrics of "M'appari" wafted his way from the adjacent bar room, and he quickly discovers the dangers of maudlin art.

Though Bloom may be sorely tempted to pursue Boylan and to catch Molly "in the act" of adultery, he realizes just how disastrous such a decision would be. In the next episode, "Cyclops," he expresses his opinion of the use of force—whether

130

in marriage, politics, or religion. Bloom's later diatribe against violence offers an *ex post facto* defense of his present refusal to resort to physical constraint. What would be the point of waylaying Boylan or of chaperoning Molly's rehearsal? Bloom cannot incarcerate his wife, like the fantasy Princess Selene, in purdah forever. Imprisonment in a compound, veils and yashmaks have all given way in the West to the more humane restrictions of religious taboo and societal disapproval. The cuckolded husband is lashed to the mast. In a moment of Freudian amnesia, he has conveniently forgotten his house key, thus precluding the possibility of a surprise return. With such defective mnemotechnic, Bloom could hardly intrude on the lovers.

The two barmaids, Lydia Douce and Mina Kennedy, are Platonic sirens who lure to fantasy rather than to violence. They tempt their victims to the fatal "Dublin disease" of sentimentality. Simon Dedalus complains that his "dancing days are through," though his singing days are not. In "Hades," he mourned the wife he drove to the grave: "Wore out his wife: now sings" (p. 274). Ben Dollard longs for the "good old days" of fun and frolic, when he was sober enough to get singing engagements. And "Father" Bob Cowley dreams of a pastoral time when the roof was safe overhead, and both wolf and landlord kept away from the door. All three men idealize "those dear dead days beyond recall." Like Kevin Egan, they are "loveless, landless, wifeless" (p. 43). They survive on songs, nostalgia, alcohol, and pathos.

Once again, Bloom confronts the whirlpool. Frustrated and helpless, he clutches at sentimental reminiscence, only to recognize its futility: "Golden ship. Erin. The harp that once or twice. Cool hands. Ben Howth, the rhododendrons. We are their harps. I. He. Old. Young" (p. 271). Unlike the barflies, he apprehends the irrevocable cleavage between past and present identities. A gulf of time separates the third-person, objective self from the first-person subject, "I." Bloom's earlier "self" has joined the ranks of the dead and cannot be brought back to life. The subjective "I" has no retreat from age and no recourse from the chaotic flux of phenomenal reality.

Bloom's reverie painfully acknowledges the "givenness" of human freedom. An air from Bellini's opera *La Somnambula* reinforces the feeling that "all is lost": "Yes, I remember. Lovely air. In sleep she went to him. Innocence in the moon. Still hold her back. Brave, don't know their danger. Call name. Touch water. Jingle jaunty. Too late. She longed to go. That's why. Woman. As easy stop the sea. Yes: all is lost" (pp. 272–73). Bloom might still attempt to "hold Molly back," but to what end? The effort would be as futile as cupping water in his hands. He can no more curb the moon-drawn tides of female desire than "stop the sea" or possess the ocean. Molly is fluid, fertile, overwhelming; she contains multitudes, but she cannot herself be contained. Bloom gnashes his teeth, but lashes himself to the mast. Like the prudent Ulysses, he knows that the siren-call to conjugal mastery is senseless and naive.

"Hate. Love. Those are names" (p. 285). Bloom is far more concerned with the phenomenon, the "thing in itself" behind the name. He bears no hate toward his spouse. And he even considers the possibility of marital reconciliation. In a moment of "conversion," he turns from fatalistic despair to authentic, forward vision: "I too, last my race. Milly young student. Well, my fault perhaps. No son. Rudy. Too late now. Or if not? If still?" (p. 285).[3] Bloom suddenly escapes self-pity by projecting himself into an ecstatic dimension of the future, beyond the whirlpool of guilt and helplessness. If Molly is free, then so is Leopold. He is at liberty to plan, to hope, and to consider change as a genuine possibility. Within the boundaries of physical necessity, the future stands open to human potential. Bloom transcends the Dublin world of psychic paralysis and the death-grip of a solidified past. He does not submit to the final cry of the dying soul, "too late now." He rejects the siren-lure of closed horizons and chooses, instead, the subjunctive aspiration, "If still?"

"Under the sandwichbell lay on a bier of bread one last, one lonely, last sardine of summer. Bloom alone" (p. 289). Leopold has cause for severe depression. He feels alienated

132

from the Dubliners in the Ormond and from Molly, the last seat of affection to whom he can turn in search of approval:

> Thou lost one. All songs on that theme. Yet more Bloom stretched his string. Cruel it seems. Let people get fond of each other: lure them on. Then tear asunder. Death. Explos. Knock on the head. . . . And one day she with. Leave her: get tired. Suffer then. Snivel. Big Spanishy eyes goggling at nothing. . . .
> Yet too much happy bores. He stretched more, more. Are you not happy in your? Twang. It snapped. (P. 277)

Once again, Bloom "snaps back" from sentimental reverie to the phenomenal world present at hand. He escapes the siren temptations of grief, vengeance, and despair. "All is lost" only if Bloom projects his entire self-worth into the issue of Molly's fidelity. Possession is a necessary prerequistite for loss.[4]

As Joyce declares in *Exiles*, thieves cannot steal what one refuses to appropriate. Richard Rowan, the protagonist of Joyce's Ibsenian drama, expresses a rationale that elucidates not only his own conduct but that of Leopold Bloom in response to Molly's infidelity. Richard thus explains the politics of non-ownership to his son Archie:

> Richard: Do you understand what it is to give a thing?
> Archie: To give? Yes.
> Richard: While you have a thing it can be taken from you.
> Archie: By robbers? No?
> Richard: But when you give it, you have given it. No
> robber can take it from you. . . . It is yours then
> for ever when you have given it. It will be yours
> always. That is to give.[5]

Both in *Exiles* and in *Ulysses*, Joyce seems to imply that the most harmful aspect of adultery is the outmoded aura of social and cultural taboo associated with the name. "Hate" and "love" are "names." And so are "cuckold" and "adulteress." Leopold and Molly will both challenge the totemic assumptions of twentieth-century society: Bloom by his cosmic perspective on human interaction, and Molly by her insistence that sex is "only natural."

In the "Sirens" episode, Bloom is sorely tempted to yield to tears and self-pity in the melodramatic role of cuckold. He is too perceptive, however, not to recognize the destructive lure of comfortable helplessness in "Bloom, soft Bloom, I feel so lonely Bloom" (p. 287). He knows that pathos is ultimately a disguise for romantic self-indulgence: "Thrill now. Pity they feel. To wipe away a tear for martyrs. For all things dying, want to, dying to, die. For that all things born. Poor Mrs. Purefoy. Hope she's over" (p. 286). Bloom's genuine compassion for Mina Purefoy sharply contrasts with the false pity mustered by the Dubliners for the croppy boy.

The barflies illustrate Stephen's plagiarized definition of "sentimentality": *"The sentimentalist is he who would enjoy without incurring the immense debtorship for a thing done"* (p. 199). They live in a world that lauds the past and feels betrayed by the present. Like the men in Kiernan's pub, they get a sadistic thrill from singing about the croppy boy's innocence and execution. They enjoy "shedding a tear" for the young man who lost his life for the glory of Ireland. These citizens respond eagerly to cathartic sentimentality, but their patriotism is confined to bold rhetoric. Song is more soothing than action. They prefer to sing about nationalism than to sacrifice life, comfort, or alcohol. The young croppy serves as an excellent surrogate for their own heroic fantasies: the martyr has paid the "immense debtorship" of Irish republican sentiment. The ballad of the "Croppy Boy" evokes kinetic emotions of pity and terror hardly akin to Joyce's ideal of static art: "And deepmoved all, Simon trumping compassion from foghorn nose, all laughing, they brought him forth" (p. 287). What have these men to do with the croppy boy, or he with them?

"Love and war, Ben, Mr. Dedalus said. God be with old times" (p. 268). The barflies are "dying" men who "want to," are "dying to, die" (p. 286). Life is more easily lived when one is spiritually dead. These men have transferred the immense debtorship of personal responsibility to the melodramatic Lionel of Von Flotows's opera and to the patriotic croppy of the Irish ballad. Buffered from the realities of existence, they

134

inhabit a microcosm of vicarious pleasure and secondhand pain. Their backward glance to a world of nostalgia is a death-trap from which Bloom is dying to escape.

Up to this point in "Sirens," Bloom has been acting like a cuckold facing martyrdom. He has harbored the thoughts and the mind-set of a prisoner about to be executed. Now he applies the same words to the croppy boy's death and to Molly's adultery: "The chords consented. Very sad thing. But had to be" (p. 286). The chords consent to the croppy's execution, but Bloom refuses to identify with the patriotic scapegoat. As in "Hades," he flees from the land of the dead in an act of self-preservation: "Get out before the end. Thanks, that was heavenly" (p. 286).

The siren-song may be "heavenly," but Bloom has more mundane concerns. Recalling the last words of another Irish hero, he releases an audible comment on sentimental patriotism. Robert Emmet's speech is counterpointed by the noise of Bloom's body letting off gas. The synchronized fart is a scatological satire on Irish Republican fervor. At the conclusion of the episode, the gas is "done"; and so are Molly's seduction and Emmet's epitaph. No "wonderworker" in the world will undo the past or reclaim those "dear dead days" lost beyond recall.

1. The limerick has been reconstructed from Bloom's fragmentary recollections. Parts are quoted on pp. 171–72 of *Ulysses* and elsewhere in "Lestrygonians."

2. Sartre, *Being and Nothingness,* p. 367.

3. Bloom insists that he is the "last of his race," even though his daughter, as child to two half-Jewish parents, is just as Hebraic as he. Milly bears Leopold's surname, but her flirtation with a "young student" may change this. Most critics who discuss *Ulysses* in terms of a quest for paternity ignore the fact that Bloom is *already* a father. Leopold seems convinced that by not fathering a life-sustaining male child, he has failed to prove his manhood. These self-indulgent tendencies may, however, constitute one of the neuroses Bloom must overcome.

4. Bloom's meal in "Sirens" is fully orchestrated by music from comic operas whose theme is the apparent, rather than the actual, loss of love and

fidelity. All may *seem* lost to the operatic heroes, who are disabused by the last act of the drama. Simon Dedalus sings a popular rendition of "M'appari" from Von Flotow's *Martha* and reminds Bloom of the first time he saw the "form endearing" of Molly. Leopold identifies with the melancholic hero, Lionel, who temporarily loses mental balance over the loss of his beloved Martha and sings: "Not a ray of hope remains. / Come thou lost one / Come thou dear one." In "Sirens," Bloom is similarly tempted to abandon reason over his wife's infidelity; his equanimity is not restored until after he has confronted the specters of his terror in Nighttown.

When Richie Goulding whistles a tune from Bellini's *La Somnambula,* Bloom internalizes the despair of Amina's lover, Elvino, who proclaims: "All is lost now, / By all hope and joy / I am forsaken. / Nevermore can love awaken." Yet Elvino's loss, like Bloom's, is apparent rather than actual. His grief is based on circumstantial evidence, and all is righted in the end. Amina, the sleepwalker, innocently assures her fiancé that "Thou alone hast all my heart," just as Molly Bloom implicitly assures Leopold of her own spiritual fidelity by the end of the "Penelope" episode.

(I am indebted to Gifford and Seidman's *Notes for Joyce* for the identification of many of the fragmentary operatic lyrics alluded to in "Sirens.")

5. James Joyce, *Exiles,* pp. 46–47. Stephen Dedalus declares in *Stephen Hero:* "Love . . . is a name, if you like, for something inexpressible. . . . When we love, we give" (p. 175).

7

"Cyclops": Giant and Jew

Although Leopold Bloom has escaped the embrace of sentimental patriotism, he soon encounters more bellicose representatives of the Dublin dead. In the "Cyclops" episode, Joyce applies the technique of "gigantism" or mechanical inflation to the content of Irish life. The Rabelaisian style serves as an appropriate vehicle for moral and political satire. The Dubliners fight a boring, inauthentic existence with the weapon of exaggeration. They use language that distorts reality, fantasize on insignificant events, and rely on gigantism to fashion illusory self-esteem.[1]

The narrator and his peers resemble one-eyed giants limited to the monoscopic horizons of brutality. Violence magnifies trivia. For the listless barflies in Kiernan's pub, time is something that must be "passed." Idleness breeds boredom, and the minutes hang heavy on the slow-moving hands of the clock. All the Dubliners feel weighed down by pressures of the past. Time has assumed the density of automatic action, and the citizens have frequent recourse to whisky and gossip to survive a tedious day.

As in "Sirens," a narrative overture sets forth the principal themes of the "Cyclops" episode. We are told that old Troy "was in the force," and a pun introduces the motif of force, the central issue of Bloom's debate with the taverners. The speaker tells Joe Hynes that "a bloody big foxy thief . . . lifted any God's quantity of tea and sugar . . . off a hop of my thumb by the name of Moses Herzog" (p. 292). "Circumcised!" exclaims Joe, sounding the pervasive note of anti-Semitism. Sympathies are with Geraghty rather than with his victim, even though the "plumber" is reputed "the most notorious bloody robber you'd meet in a day's walk." "Jesus, I had to laugh at the little jewy getting his shirt out. *He drink me my teas. He eat me my sugars. Because he no pay me my moneys?"* (p. 292). The debt-collector sees Herzog as a "little jewy," a kind of midget in a Brobdingnagian world. He mimics the victim's muddled speech, a language that actually communicates more than either realizes. By interposing the indirect object "me" before oddly pluralized nouns, Herzog frantically points to the reality of his persecution. Geraghty is usurping the "substance" of the unlicensed vendor. He is eating up the Jew's tea and sugar, commodities that Herzog regards as palpable extensions of himself. The Jewish merchant feels as if he is literally being "eaten" and "drunk" by his unscrupulous opponent. Sacrificed on the altar of commerce, Herzog has become the food of a mercantile Eucharist.[2]

The caustic dialogue gives way to further gigantism, expressed by a second narrative voice naïvely mimicking the traditional omniscient author. The "interpolator" or parodist embellishes his environment with fabulous tales of glory and adventure. If the debt-collector has access to the worst side of Dublin life, the parodist sees only the best. He celebrates the most heroic dimensions of Irish culture. His Cyclopian voice describes the region of Inisfail as "the land of holy Michan.

. . . There sleep the mighty dead as in life they slept, warriors and princes of high renown'' (p. 293). "Michan," Kiernan's parish, has proved in actuality to be an "aqueous kingdom" whose inhabitants drink like fish and drown themselves in a sea of inauthenticity. The dead rest "as in life they slept." The ironic phrase suggests that the warriors "slept" through life, paralyzed by an alcoholic trance.

The next interpolation describes a living giant, the Citizen in the tavern "doing the rapparee and Rory of the hill" (p. 295). The portrait reflects the Citizen's self-image: he imaginatively compares himself to the mythic giants of Irish history. In his mind, he identifies with Rory, the last king of Eire, and with the Rapparees who harassed the English army after the Battle of the Boyne.[3] The Citizen envisions himself as a rock of patriotism and a mountain of strength, metaphors that satirically depict a "hard-headed" and a "stony-hearted" Cyclops. The Rabelaisian eulogy glorifies the Fenian in mock-heroic terms. The epic hero is a collage of vegetable and mineral characteristics, so Irish that he belongs to the country's landscape. The giant's "rocklike mountainous knees were covered . . . with a strong growth of tawny prickly hair in hue and toughness similar to the mountain gorse." In his bristly nostrils, "the fieldlark might easily have lodged her nest." And his eyes "were of the dimensions of a goodsized cauliflower" (p. 296).

Like Garrett Deasy, the Citizen is a rabid anti-Semite who has plunged into history and has been paralyzed by its grasp. A nationalistic robot, he spouts chauvinistic rhetoric and acts with mechanical certitude. Petrified by patriotic fanaticism, he is transfixed in a single, unalterable frame of mind. The passionate Fenian wants to be "massive and impenetrable," to escape the dominance of reason, and to elude personal change. He is frozen in a predetermined stance, as lifeless as a rock or a mountain.[4]

The patriot identifies with all the legendary "Irish heroes and heroines of antiquity," including Goliath, Patrick W. Shakespeare, and Adam and Eve. But the following interpolation designates the true man of heroic stature: "Who comes through

Michan's land, bedight in sable armour? O'Bloom, the son of Rory: it is he. Impervious to fear is Rory's son: he of the prudent soul'' (p. 297). The prudent Ulysses, Leopold Bloom, sports brains rather than brawn. O'Bloom is the genuine ''son of Rory,'' the true liberator opposed to the fraudulent aggressor.

When Bloom enters the pub, Joe Hynes is reading a letter from the hangman, H. Rumbold: *"Honoured sir i beg to offer my services in the above-mentioned painful case"* (p. 303). The barflies express disgust at Rumbold's ''dirty scrawl,'' but they are entranced by his black humor. They read the letter with sadistic fascination and graphically discuss the hanging:

> So they started talking about capital punishment and of course Bloom comes out with the why and the wherefore and all the codology of the business. . . .
> —There's one thing it hasn't a deterrent effect on, says Alf.
> —What's that? says Joe.
> —The poor bugger's tool that's being hanged, says Alf.
> —That so? says Joe.
> —God's truth, says Alf. I heard that from the head warder that was in Kilmainham when they hanged Joe Brady, the invincible. He told me when they cut him down after the drop it was standing up in their faces like a poker.
> —Ruling passion strong in death, says Joe, as someone said.
> —That can be explained by science, says Bloom. It's only a natural phenomenon, don't you see, because on account of the
> . . .
> And then he starts with his jawbreakers about phenomenon and science and this phenomenon and the other phenomenon. (P. 304)

Joe Hynes concocts a dramatic explanation for the hanged man's erection, a theory far more appealing than Bloom's medical analysis. The taverners refuse to face reality or to hear ''jawbreakers about phenomenon and science.'' Enslaved to categorical thinking, they cannot recognize a three-dimensional world. Of the men in Kiernan's pub, Bloom is the only person not trapped in a grid of emotional prejudice. The term ''parallax,'' which has haunted him throughout the day, now becomes associated with stereoscopic perspective. ''Bloom with his *but don't you see?* and *but on the other hand"* (p. 306) is striving for clear intellectual vision, a broadminded analysis of the objects given to consciousness. Unlike the one-eyed Dubliners, he looks at *both* sides of the issue: he examines "this phenomenon and the other phenomenon" to constitute the depth of three-dimensional perception.

In contrast to Bloom, the taverners respond automatically to emotional stimuli: "So of course the citizen was only waiting for the wink of the word and he starts gassing out of him about the invincibles" (p. 305). Bloom's rhetoric mechanically prompts an angry response, first from the Citizen, then from the narrator: "Bloom of course, with his knockmedown cigar putting on swank with his lardy face. Phenomenon!"(p. 305). The debt-collector is enraged by the word "phenomenon," which he does not understand and keeps repeating with disgust. He considers the term pretentious jargon, a scientific coinage of Greek, non-Celtic origin. He vents his anger by slandering Bloom's wife; and he facetiously compares the full, round "o" sounds in the word to Molly's voluptuous bottom: "The fat heap he married is a nice old phenomenon with a back on her like a ballalley" (p. 305).[5]

The Citizen is more vocal in his retort: " —*Sinn Fein!* says the citizen. *Sinn fein amhain!* The friends we love are by our side and the foes we hate before us" (p. 306). By screaming the Irish revolutionary slogan, "We ourselves! . . . We ourselves alone!", the Fenian indicts Bloom as a stranger and an enemy. He invokes the sacrosanct category of the "we" against third-person outsiders, and he blatantly challenges Bloom as a defiled scapegoat who does not belong "among us." Of the twenty words the patriot utters, six comprise Gaelic and English variations of the first-person-plural pronoun. Like Garrett Deasy, the Citizen exhorts his peers to antagonism through emotional hostility towards the "other." Bloom is "*l'autre,*" different from "us."

The charges against the innocent Jew continue to pile up. He sold illegal lottery tickets for the "royal and privileged Hungarian robbery" (p. 313). He would "have a soft hand under a hen" (p. 315), despite his present attempt to help Mrs. Dignam procure insurance money. Bloom is judged unpatriotic for defending English lawn tennis; and as penance, he must listen to the taverners discuss Boylan's "organization" both of Myler Keogh and of Molly Bloom.

Because of his Jewishness, Bloom inhabits a world in which every action is culpable. Even his compassion for Mrs. Breen incites the patriot's anger: "Pity about her, says the citizen. Or any other woman marries a half and half. . . . A fellow that's neither fish nor flesh. . . . A pishogue, if you know what that is" (p. 321). The Fenian implicitly condemns Bloom for racial intermixture—for being neither "fish nor flesh," Christian nor Jew. Bloom's Gentile heritage has been contaminated by alien blood. Like the crucified man-God, he feels "despised and rejected of men," but continues to turn the other cheek.

The Citizen vilifies not only Bloom but James Wought, Reuben J. Dodd, and all the other members of the "bottlenosed fraternity": "Those are nice things, says the citizen, coming over here to Ireland filling the country with bugs. . . . Swindling the peasants . . . and the poor of Ireland. We want no more strangers in our house" (p. 323). The rabid patriot quotes a line from Yeats's 1902 play *Kathleen ni Houlihan* and gives to the word "strangers" the connotation of both Saxons and Jews.[6] Like Garrett Deasy, he is obsessed with history, adultery, and anti-Semitism. He almost mimics the schoolmaster's speech by insisting that "the adulteress and her paramour brought the Saxon robbers here. . . . A dishonoured wife, . . . that's what's the cause of all our misfortunes" (p. 324). The religion of nationalism demands its myth of a fall and a regeneration. The "adulteress" is analogous to a Christian Eve or a Greek Pandora. She is responsible for breach of fidelity, the sin that transformed prelapsarian Ireland from a paradise to an inferno. Her treason delivered the kingdom over to "his Satanic Majesty" and the Sassenach brigade (p. 330).

Only Bloom, the outsider, sees irony in the Citizen's crude political philosophy of "might makes right." "We'll put force

142

against force, says the citizen" (p. 329). According to Fenian logic, force is outrageous on the part of the British, but valorous when used by the Irish. The word "force" takes on a double connotation. It may be laudable or abhorrent, according to the situation.

"But, says Bloom, . . . wouldn't it be the same here if you put force against force?" (p. 329). Bloom is trying to grasp the meaning of force apart from *a priori* categories. He refuses to interpret English force as reprehensible and Irish force as praiseworthy.[7] Bloom fervidly tries to point to the real issue: both British tyranny and Fenian violence are manifestations of national hatred. "Some people, says Bloom, can see the mote in the others' eyes but they can't see the beam in their own" (p. 326). He quotes the New Testament in support of his thesis, but the Dubliners have no desire to hear the truth. They resent a non-Christian for preaching the gospel message "that ye love one another."

When Bloom tries to expose the brutality of "national hatred," his companions demand a categorical definition of "nation":

> —Persecution, says he, all the history of the world is full of it. Perpetuating national hatred among nations.
> —But do you know what a nation means? says John Wyse.
> —Yes, says Bloom.
> —What is it? says John Wyse.
> —A nation? says Bloom. A nation is the same people living in the same place.
> —By God, then, says Ned, laughing, if that's so I'm a nation for I'm living in the same place for the past five years.
> So of course everyone had a laugh at Bloom. (P. 331)

The taverners have unwittingly defined racial persecution as psychological coercion forcing an individual to inhabit the same historical "place" ascribed to his ancestors. Nationalism requires its scapegoat as well as its myth of original sin. Leopold Bloom becomes the new paschal lamb to be sacrificed on the altar of history. He is condemned by his companions on the basis of arbitrary racial contingencies. Fettered to two thousand years of defilement, Bloom is branded as impure and forced into social exile.

Bloom has been indicted by a primitive ethic of contamination and inherited guilt. His chief accuser, the Citizen, is bound to a pre-logical notion of alienation. He maligns his enemy as a "foreigner," despite Bloom's declaration of allegiance to Ireland:

> —What is your nation if I may ask, says the citizen.
> —Ireland, says Bloom. I was born here. Ireland.
> The citizen said nothing only cleared the spit out of his gullet and, gob, he spat a Red bank oyster out of him right in the corner. (P. 331).

Symbolically "spat upon," Bloom resembles another "outspoken Jew" vilified by the populace. Bloom is not disturbed that the Jews were *once* scorned by mankind, or that they have *always* been scapegoats. He is enraged by *present* persecution—by the world's persistent denial of "selfhood" to the Jewish stereotype:

> —And I belong to a race too, says Bloom, that is hated and persecuted. Also now. This very moment. This very instant. . . .
> —Are you talking about the new Jerusalem? says the citizen.
> —I'm talking about injustice, says Bloom. (P. 332)

The modern prophet will not reduce his perceptions to abstract biblical metaphor. He insists on condemning racial hatred, and he preaches justice in *this* world rather than paradise in the next.

Bloom is keenly aware that, for the citizens, "Jewish" and "British" constitute equally despised categories of alienation. But whereas the British imperialists cannot be daunted, the Jews are fair game for political persecution. The Irish complain of being English scapegoats, then vent their anger on the scapegoat Jews. In *Dubliners,* Joyce portrays a similar case of aggression-frustration displacement. The alcoholic protagonist of "Counterparts" slinks home to beat his son after being harassed at work for incompetence. The injured victim strikes the weaker until all have been demoralized: "it's everybody eating everyone else" (p. 122).

Bloom decries the fact that Jews have been perpetually treated as things to be mocked and tormented or sold on the open market: "Robbed, says he. Plundered. Insulted. Persecuted. Taking what belongs to us by right. At this very moment, says he, putting up his fist, sold by auction off in Morocco like slaves or cattles" (p. 332). In "Hades," Bloom felt pity for cattle being driven to market and compared the dead in the cemetery to "roast beef for old England." Now his compassion is transferred by analogy to the suffering Hebrew race. The plural of "cattle" recalls the archaic word "chattels," or "goods." The full purport of Bloom's argument derives from his funeral experiences: to the anti-Semites, Jews are cattle predestined for slaughter. They are lifeless objects frozen in historical stasis.

Bloom is so enraged that, for the first time, he abandons his earlier meekness and becomes revolutionary. He identifies with the Jewish people who have been "Robbed. . . . Plundered. Insulted. Persecuted." Asserting his own Hebraic origins, Bloom recognizes the devastating indignity of discrimination. He voluntarily affirms his racial allegiance, not to prophesy a "new Jerusalem," but to "talk about injustice." Bloom acknowledges the formal category of "Jew" only to refuse categorical reduction. He situates himself in alienation in order to proclaim that race "is purely and simply a collective fiction, that only individuals exist."[8]

The Dubliners reveal that they have missed the point of Bloom's impassioned sermon when they exhort him to "stand up to it then with force": "That's an almanac picture for you. . . . Old lardyface standing up to the business end of a gun. Gob, he'd adorn a sweepingbrush. . . . And then he collapses all of a sudden, . . . as limp as a wet rag" (p. 333). For the Irish mob, force constitutes the only solution to injustice, despite its self-defeating nature. Once the oppressed take up arms, they themselves become oppressors. The obtuse narrator interprets Bloom's pacifism as cowardice. He considers

145

Leopold an effeminate Jew, and his images suggest sexual as well as political impotence: "old lardyface" backs down and "collapses like a wet rag" whenever his manliness is called into question.

The taverners have forgotten the words of an earlier pacifist who proclaimed that "not by the sword shall ye conquer." Bloom finds himself pinned against a wall. He must reiterate his philosophy of *caritas* in terms intelligible to the vulgar, unconverted laity:

> —But it's no use, says he. Force, hatred, history, all that. That's not life for men and women, insult and hatred. And everybody knows that it's the very opposite of that that is really life.
> —What? says Alf.
> —Love, says Bloom. I mean the opposite of hatred. I must go now, says he to John Wyse. Just around to the court a moment to see if Martin is there. If he comes just say I'll be back in a second. Just a moment. (P. 333)

Bloom attempts to convey his message by declaring what individual consciousness is *not*—"force, hatred, history . . . insult." He is trying to abstract human personality from the bondage of traditional categories, whether of language or perception. His description of love as "the opposite of hatred" recalls Stephen's earlier assertion that "love . . . is a name, if you like, for something inexpressible. . . . When we love, we give" (*SH* 175). The Christian ethic of "charity" provides a grasping, halted definition of sympathetic understanding. Bloom is talking about a humanistic philosophy that acknowledges the sanctity of personal consciousness. Like Stephen Dedalus, he is preaching liberation from historical bondage. He points to the present instant, as well as to the unique human being. And he proposes to supplant the *mythos* of history with a contemporary recognition of individual dignity.

> —A new apostle to the gentiles, says the citizen. Universal love. . . .
> Love loves to love love. . . . Constable 14A loves Mary Kelly. Gerty MacDowell loves the boy that has the bicycle. M. B. loves a fair gentleman. . . . You love a certain person. And this person

loves that other person because everybody loves somebody but God loves everybody. (P. 333)

The romantic interpolation takes off from the Citizen's elephantine brain and elaborates on all the sloppiest aspects of sentimentality. The catalogue describes love in terms of effusive emotion, as the brawny Titan conceives of it. The Fenian regards all love as a synonym for weakness, whether it be the adolescent fantasies of Gerty MacDowell or the religious piety of Father Conmee. The Citizen would never understand Bloom's definition of universal love apart from Gerty or Gerty's God. Bloom has tried to imply that the phenomenon of "love" is something that "everybody knows" from examining life as it really is: "love" is "that word known to all men" who are willing to explore the horizons of negative capability. Bloom wants to emphasize the fact that we *all* belong to the subject-community of "everybody": we must become "god-like" by extending our concern beyond erotic interest in one particular "somebody" to an all-encompassing ethic of charity. Bloom preaches the social inclusion of universal love, based on the uniqueness and sanctity of the conscious life-world of every individual.

For the men in the tavern, "God loves everybody" has degenerated into a useless platitude. The Dubliners continue to mouth religious phrases and to precede every drink with "the blessing of God and Mary and Patrick." But the Christian injunction to charity is as meaningless to them as Joyce's parodic hagiography. The barflies interpret "universal love" in terms of its historical debasement: "sanctimonious Cromwell" murdered women and children "with the bible text *God is love* pasted round the mouth of his cannon" (p. 334). The British tame docile Africans with a sword and a bible, converting to Christianity from motives of economic exploitation.

The taverners are scandalized by Belgian treatment of the Congolese: "Raping the women and girls and flogging the natives on the belly to squeeze all the red rubber they can out of them" (p. 335). They are repelled by the thought of Africans

147

made into rubber-producing objects, but they fail to see the resemblance between such horrors and their own bigoted conduct.

In the midst of J. J. O'Molloy's account of Congolese atrocities, Lenehan first accuses Bloom: "I know where he's gone. . . . He had a few bob on *Throwaway* and he's gone to gather in the shekels" (p. 335). Within a few moments, the Dubliners indict their victim on charges of conspiracy and avarice. They judge him on "circumstantial" evidence, having already condemned him in their minds. In the pub watercloset, the narrator ponders the case between asides on urination. He concludes that Bloom's actions must have been slyly calculated, "all of a plan so he could vamoose with the pool if he won" (p. 335). The phrase "trading without a license" recalls the Jewish merchant Herzog. The debt-collector assumes that one can "never be up to those bloody . . . Jerusalem . . . cuckoos" (p. 335), and the conversation in the tavern makes it clear that Bloom is on trial for nothing less than his racial heritage:

—And after all, says John Wyse, why can't a jew love his country like the next fellow?
—Why not? says J. J., when he's quite sure which country it is.
—Is he a jew or a gentile or a holy Roman or a swaddler or what the hell is he? says Ned. Or who is he? (P. 337)

"—That's the new Messiah for Ireland! says the citizen" (p. 337). The Dubliners are unaware that Bloom is, in fact, a "new Messiah" insofar as he preaches a gospel of Christian charity and universal love. The narrator admits that "there's many a true word spoken in jest," but he fails to recognize the truth of the Fenian's mocking appellation. Both the Jews and the Irish are "still waiting for their redeemer"; and both perpetually err in assuming that they will be liberated by force. Bloom teaches the doctrine of salvation, but he is despised for his Messianic tidings. Bloom-Christ-Ulysses proclaims the spirit of humanism to a dumbfounded populace. Like Christ, "sheepfaced" Leopold becomes a victim to be sacrificed for the sins of

148

mankind. He is vilified by a crowd of bigots for the alleged transgressions of his Jewish ancestors—crimes of meekness, miserliness, and sexual masochism.

The enraged barflies suggest that Bloom lacks the phallic force to do a "man's job." They express vituperation by publicly casting aspersions on Bloom's sexual prowess:

> —Do you call that a man? says the citizen.
> —I wonder did he ever put it out of sight, says Joe.
> —Well, there were two children born anyhow, says Jack Power.
> —And who does he suspect? says the citizen.
> Gob. . . . One of those mixed middlings he is. Lying up in the hotel Pisser was telling me once a month with headache like a totty with her courses. Do you know what I'm telling you? It'd be an act of God to take a hold of a fellow the like of that and throw him in the bloody sea. Justifiable homicide, so it would. Then sloping off with his five quid without putting up a pint of stuff like a man. (P. 338)

The Dubliners suggest that "old lardyface" is too sheepish to prove his manhood by treating drinks or by putting his male organ "out of sight" and into a woman. The "new womanly man" is a "mixed middling" who ought to be crucified for the common good.

Bloom's mock trial and condemnation on charges of Semitic stinginess provides illusory meaning for the otherwise trivial lives of the citizens. The taverners survive on alcohol and acerbity. They are men "drowned in the crowd, and the ways of thinking and reacting of the group are of a purely primitive type."[9] Feeling that they have been denied free drinks, they exclude Bloom from tribal solidarity and blame him for the aggregate of Irish woes. Not daring to revolt against the British, they make Bloom their political, social, and sexual scapegoat.

Bloom's metaphorical crucifixion is prefigured by the parodic execution of an Irish martyr-hero. The hanging is described as a "genuinely instructive treat," reported in a journalistic style that reduces death to social entertainment. Joyce explodes the pretensions of bourgeois culture: every lady is given a "tasteful souvenir" of the event, as the entrails of the disemboweled hero are carted off to the local animal shelter.

Political rhetoric proves one-sided and deceptive in "Cyclops." It detaches language from meaning, feeds on chauvinistic cliché, and desensitizes its audience to horrors committed in the name of the state. The "common welfare" sanctions brutal atrocities. Liberally seasoned with violence, "love and war" are both crowd-pleasers. Political language makes murder palatable and aggression acceptable.[10]

The boasting Fenian of "Cyclops" is at heart a coward who must "murder" his victim in effigy with an empty biscuit tin. "There's a Jew for you! All for number one. Cute as a shithouse rat" (p. 341). The Citizen maligns Bloom as a petrified racial object, and Joyce's rat simile recalls the corpse-fed rodent in "Hades." The maniacal patriot has consigned Bloom to the land of the dead and is determined to carry out his sentence: "By Jesus, says he, I'll brain that bloody jewman for using the holy name. By Jesus, I'll crucify him so I will" (p. 342).

Bloom responds to the attack by screaming that: "Christ was a jew like me" (p. 342). Both he and Jesus are "mixed middlings," not wholly of Hebrew origin. And both insist on transcending the object-category of Jewishness to proclaim the value and dignity of individual existence. Bloom is figuratively crucified by the Citizen, and the event precipitates an earth-shattering apocalypse: "And they beheld Him even Him, ben Bloom Elijah, amid clouds of angels ascend to the glory of the brightness at an angle of fortyfive degrees over Donohoe's in Little Green Street like a shot off a shovel" (p. 345). Could this be the new Messiah for Ireland?

1. From the standpoint of political, social, and cultural satire, the "Cyclops" episode resembles Joyce's earlier work, *Dubliners*. Joyce wrote to Constantine Curran in 1904: "I call the series *Dubliners* to betray the soul of that hemiplegia or paralysis which many consider a city." Trying to persuade Grant Richards to publish the collection, Joyce declared in 1906: "I believe that in composing my chapter of moral history in exactly the way I have composed it I have taken the first step towards the spiritual liberation of my country. . . . It is not my fault that the odour of ashpits and old weeds and

150

offal hangs round my stories. I seriously believe that you will retard the course of civilisation in Ireland by preventing the Irish people from having one good look at themselves in my nicely polished looking-glass'' (*Letters,* 1:55, 62–64).

2. Sartre points out that the French expression *manger du Juif* indicates an anti-Semitic desire to exterminate the Jew. (*Réflexions sur la question juive,* p. 63) This notation is omitted from the English translation.

3. Weldon Thornton, *Allusions in "Ulysses,"* pp. 259, 266.

4. Jean-Paul Sartre, in *Anti-Semite and Jew,* describes the attitude of men who are attracted by the ''durability of stone'': ''They wish to be massive and impenetrable; they wish not to change. Where, indeed, would change take them? We have here a basic fear of oneself and of truth. . . . It is as if their own existence were in continual suspension. . . . Only a strong emotional bias can give a lightninglike certainty; . . . it alone can remain impervious to experience and last for a whole lifetime'' (pp. 18–19).

5. If we accept Helmut Bonheim's theory of the ''os'' motif in *Ulysses,* then the word ''phenomenon'' links Bloom with Molly, since the female organs are ''explicitly referred to as yonic (referring to 0 or zero),'' and the ''round o'' sound evokes the ''mystery of female hollowness'' (*Joyce's Benefictions,* pp. 32–35).

6. In Yeats's play, the Old Woman who represents Ireland declares that she was put astray by ''too many strangers in the house,'' and she now clings to ''the hope of putting the strangers out of my house'' (W. B. Yeats, *Selected Plays,* pp. 250, 253).

7. In 1898, Joyce wrote ''that all subjugation by force, if carried out and prosecuted by force is only so far successful in breaking men's spirits and aspirations. Also that it is, in the extreme, productive of ill-will and rebellion, that it is, again, from its beginning in unholy war, stamped with the stamp of ultimate conflict'' (''Force'' in *Critical Writings,* p. 17).

8. Sartre, *Being and Nothingness,* p. 524.

9. Sartre, *Anti-Semite,* p. 30. As Sartre points out, ''The anti-Semite . . . is a man who is afraid. Not of the Jews, to be sure, but of himself, of his own consciousness, of his liberty, of his instincts, of his responsibilities, of solitariness, of change, of society, and of the world—of everything except the Jews. He is a coward who does not want to admit his cowardice to himself; a murderer who represses and censures his tendency to murder without being able to hold it back, yet who dares to kill only in effigy or protected by the anonymity of the mob; a malcontent who dares not revolt from fear of the consequences of his rebellion'' (ibid., p. 53).

10. It is possible that while composing ''Cyclops,'' Joyce may have had in mind the pacifism of his friend Francis Sheehy-Skeffington. In an ''Open Letter to Thomas MacDonagh,'' published in the ''Irish Citizen,'' 22 May 1915 (p. 4, cols. 2-3), Skeffington expressed his abhorrence of ''militarism . . . organised to kill'':

. . . In the "Irish Volunteer" last issued, I find mimic war extolled as "the greatest game on earth," "the noblest game any Irishman can play." Are not the bulk of the Irish Volunteers animated by the old, bad tradition that war is a glorious thing, that there is something "manly" about going out prepared to kill your fellowman? . . .

I advocate no mere servile lazy acquiescence in injustice. . . . But I want to see the age-long fight against injustice clothe itself in new forms, suited to a new age. I want to see the manhood of Ireland no longer hypnotised by the glamour of "the glory of arms," no longer blind to the horrors of organised murder. . . .

We are on the threshold of a new era in human history. . . . The foundations of all things must be re-examined.

"Nausicaa": Romantic Fantasy
"Oxen of the Sun": Procreative Reality

At the end of the "Cyclops" episode, Leopold Bloom triumphantly defeats the one-eyed Citizen and rises as prophet of a new humanism, proposing a gospel of love for the twentieth century. Bloom's heroism may seem shamefully deflated by the "fall" that occurs in "Nausicaa." On Sandymount strand, Bloom masturbates to the tune of church bells and the noise of fireworks. Critics who interpret *Ulysses* as a mock-heroic novel often cite "Nausicaa" as prime evidence of Joyce's satirical purpose. But in a world of natural phenomena, Bloom's erotic stimulation is just as understandable as that of Rumbold's hanged man. Masturbation is a physical, unromantic response to Gerty MacDowell's flirtation—a seduction inspired by the florid prose of Dublin ladies' magazines.

Gerty springs, like a "smiling soubrette," from the fashion pages of the *Lady's Pictorial,* from the pulp fiction of the "Princess novelette," and from the advertising columns of the

Irish Times. Her embarrassing proximity to the females of popular literature may account for the fact that she is frequently dismissed by readers as a sugary and ephemeral caricature.

Much of the serious criticism devoted to "Nausicaa" centers on Gerty's erotic culpability. Should we consider the young woman a seductive "nymph" or a virginal "nun"? Fritz Senn describes her as an "avatar of the temptress."[1] Mark Shechner suggests that Gerty represents "the narcissistic phase of Irish Catholic adolescence whose primary role in Joyce's life and fantasies was to provoke desire and deny fulfillment. . . . If Gerty is a joke, she is nevertheless the *reductio ad absurdum* of a long line of virginal villains who are implied in her portrait."[2] Are we to believe that Gerty willfully seduces Leopold Bloom? Or is she the naive object of Bloom's sexual exploitation, a woman more sinned against than sinning?

According to Fritz Senn, Gerty MacDowell may be Joyce's autobiographical persona filtered through an ironic sex-role reversal. Senn points out that Gerty seems to possess all the sentimental, languishing, romantic tendencies that Joyce himself exhibited in his epistolary affair with Martha Fleischmann. Reportedly, Joyce once sent Martha a postcard "addressed from 'Odysseus' to 'Nausicaa.'"[3] Does the author want us to empathize with his fictional Nausicaa? Or is he using her satirically to exorcise the ludicrous traits of his own personality?[4]

The answer to such speculation is necessarily ambivalent. Despite her narcissism and her vanity, Gerty MacDowell remains a sympathetic figure. Joyce parodies her willful self-deception; but he understands her foibles, and he respects her relentless compulsion to fictionalize experience. Like Leopold Bloom, and like Stephen's Shakespeare, Gerty creates from the pain of personal loss. She consciously refashions her life in the mode of popular romance. She shares with Bloom a distaste for the brutal "world of men," and she uses art to mitigate a reality that otherwise might prove intolerable.

To shield her wounded sensibilities, Gerty has withdrawn to the comforting shelter of feminine imagination. She is desperately trying to like herself; and in an effort to mold a positive self-image, she compensates for bodily deformity by heightened pride in physical attractiveness. What initially appears to be narcissism may also be interpreted as a bold defiance of isolation. Once we learn of Gerty's lameness, we have to admire the bravado of her self-assertion in the competitive sexual market of 1904. In her heart, Gerty harbors a royal, fairy-tale personality: "Had kind fate but willed her to be born a gentlewoman of high degree in her own right and had she only received the benefit of a good education Gerty MacDowell might easily have held her own beside any lady in the land" (p. 348). Fate has cast a wicked spell on her frame. Only love can release her by revealing the innate spiritual refinement that will make Gerty desirable "for herself alone" (p. 358).

The poignant, satirical jest of "Nausicaa" is directed not against Gerty, but against the manipulative society of which she is a victim. The episode offers a striking parody of female socialization in the modern world. Joyce's portrait of Gerty MacDowell, composed over fifty years ago, provides an incisive criticism of a media-controlled self-image.

Gerty has been reared on sentimental journalese, and her mind has been shaped by the clichéd rhetoric of Dublin fashion magazines: "It was Madame Vera Verity, directress of the Woman Beautiful page of the Princess novelette, who had first advised her to try eyebrowleine which gave that haunting expression to the eyes, so becoming in leaders of fashion, and she had never regretted it" (p. 349). The aim of Madame Verity's commercial art is not "truth," as her name would imply, but a simpering obfuscation of reality. Gerty has been sucked into a whirlpool of commercial fantasy that promises instant panacea. Relief is just a swallow (or a touch) away.

Had Gerty consulted the *Irish Times* on 16 June 1904, she would have been offered the wonders of "Beecham's Pills," a medicine "specially suitable for females of all ages" and a mandatory prescription for "every woman who values health." She might have been allured by the more dazzling advertisement for "Carter's Little Liver Pills," guaranteed to cure "biliousness, sick headaches, torpid liver, indigestion, constipation, sallow skin, dizziness, and furred tongue." Or she could have been seduced by a simple panacea such as "Mother Seigel's Syrup," a mixture promising relief from any troubling symptom.[5] It is ironically appropriate that Gerty should be attracted to Leopold Bloom, whose career as an ad canvasser depends on public gullibility. The twentieth-century media provide opiates for the masses. Commercial art deceives, manipulates, and ultimately paralyzes.

Subjected to a daily bombardment by countless promises of feminine fulfillment, Gerty longs for the miracle drug or elixir that will transform her into Cinderella. She helplessly pines for the beautiful Prince Charming who will waken her from adolescent obscurity. Gerty feels convinced that if she religiously makes use of all the products offered by Madame Verity and Woman Beautiful, she will surely succeed in attracting the man of her dreams, in achieving upward social mobility, and in gaining a vicarious identity through masculine approval.

Needless to say, Gerty MacDowell is male-identified. And the paucity of masculine affirmation in her life intensifies her alienation. Her father is an alcoholic; Father Conroy a celibate; and Reggy Wylie has exhibited little affection since his days in short pants. In a society where males are enervated, impotent, or simply uninterested, male-identification may be disastrous.

Gerty's monologue springs from the sentimental view of love parodied in "Cyclops": Nausicaa "loves to love love" and is convinced that "this person loves that other person because everybody loves somebody but God loves everybody" (p. 333). Joyce described "Nausicaa" to Frank Budgen as an episode "written in a namby-pamby jammy marmalady drawersy (alto la!) style with effects of incense, mariolatry, masturbation, stewed cockles, painters' palette, chitchat, circumlocutions, etc., etc."[6] Gerty not only speaks, but *thinks,* in a "namby-pamby jammy marmalady drawersy" style.

She perceives herself as a woman of "innate refinement"and "queenly *hauteur,*" "a fair specimen of winsome Irish girlhood. . . . She was pronounced beautiful by all who knew her

156

. . . Her figure was slight and graceful, inclining even to fragility but those iron jelloids she had been taking of late had done her a world of good much better than the Widow Welch's female pills and she was much better of those discharges she used to get and that tired feeling. The waxen pallor of her face was almost spiritual in its ivorylike purity . . ." (p. 348). Colorless and anemic, Gerty has the waxen pallor of a Greek nymph, a plaster saint, or the Catholic Virgin, "Tower of Ivory." She dresses in "electric blue," reminiscent of Mary and of the gods who drink electric light.

Gerty scorns the body, disdains eating in public, and would prefer a more lyrical diet: "she didn't like the eating part when there were any people that made her shy and often she wondered why you couldn't eat something poetical like violets or roses" (p. 352). Gerty bears a striking resemblance to the spiritualized nymph of "Calypso," who protests in "Circe": "We immortals, as you saw today, have not such a place and no hair there either. We are stonecold and pure" (p. 551). The nymph promises Bloom a respite from desire: "Only the ethereal. Where dreamy creamy gull waves o'er the waters dull' (p. 552). Such languid virtue is contingent on sexual repression. Once threatened, the nymph draws a poniard and tries to dispatch Bloom. The plaster saint cracks, emitting a cloud of stench from her private parts. She proves to be the Janus-image of Bella Cohen, "mutton dressed as lamb" (p. 554). Similarly, the lamb-like Gerty can break out of her reverie to express envy, cattiness, or sheer ill temper. Erotic desire smolders beneath the surface of her romantic musings and finally explodes in pyrotechnic fury. Like Leopold Bloom, Gerty sustains herself through the copious creations of a fertile imagination. Bloom dreams of erotic titillation; Gerty yearns for spiritual passion. Both share a pathetic isolation from consummated physical love.

Caught in a trap of self-deception, Gerty MacDowell places naive faith in all the opiates her society has to offer: religion and poetry, eyebrowleine and romantic myth. In a "toilettable" drawer, she has stashed "her girlish treasures trove, the tortoiseshell combs, her child of Mary badge, the whiterose scent,

157

the eyebrowleine, her alabaster pouncetbox'' and her confession album with ''some beautiful thoughts written in it in violet ink that she bought in Hely's of Dame Street'' (p. 364). Like Mary Dedalus, the young girl collects trinkets and relics of a paralyzed past. She regards religion as a kind of cosmetic that assuages the harshness of reality. As a ''child of Mary'' sodalist, she is eligible to participate in the Lotus-rite earlier observed by Bloom in All Hallows Church: ''Something going on: some sodality. Pity so empty. Nice discreet place to be next some girl. . . . Good idea the Latin. Stupefies them first'' (p. 80). Popular culture and popular religion both offer ''one way out'' for a society that demands narcotic forgetfulness. Myth consumes the spirit and lays the weary heart to rest in a heavenly ideal. ''It would be like heaven. For such a one she yearns this balm summer eve'' (p. 352). The metaphysical power of that final, consummating kiss can never be described in words. The ecstasy of love, like divine beatitude, is ineffable. As the media assure Gerty, romance is the ''one great goal'' of every young girl's existence.

Brainwashed by popular literature, the ingenue is convinced that love should be ''a woman's birthright,'' her chief preoccupation, and her final happiness. Hence Gerty's frustration at the difficulty of claiming a matrimonial heritage. She feels like a disinherited female, but she continues ''hoping against hope'' (p. 351). She pathetically makes use of the least sign of interest or affection to fire her romantic dreams: ''Gerty MacDowell yearns in vain. Yes, she had known from the first that her daydream of a marriage . . . was not to be. He was too young to understand. He would not believe in love, a woman's birthright. The night of the party long ago in Stoers' (he was still in short trousers) when they were alone and he stole an arm round her waist . . . and snatched a half kiss (the first!) but it was only the end of her nose'' (p. 351). Hence the source of Gerty's elaborate dreams of ''weddingbells ringing for Mrs Reggy Wylie T. C. D.''; of ''expensive blue fox''; of love and marriage; of husband, home, and morning ''brekky.'' That memory of Reggy's juvenile kiss seems to be one of the few

158

treasures in Gerty's barren hope-chest. Like the Citizen in "Cyclops," she fosters an inflated, romanticized perception of herself. She constructs "worlds" from words, gestures, a peck on the nose, and a vacation postcard. As Bloom later remarks: "She must have been thinking of someone else all the time. What harm? Must since she came to the use of reason, he, he and he. First kiss does the trick. The propitious moment. Something inside them goes pop. Mushy like, tell by their eye, on the sly. First thoughts are best. Remember that till their dying day" (p. 371).

Rejected by Reggy, the child-lover who has ceased to ride his bicycle in front of her window, Gerty yearns for an older man who will offer her both passion and compassionate understanding: "No prince charming is her beau ideal to lay a rare and wondrous love at her feet but rather a manly man with a strong quiet face who had not found his ideal, perhaps his hair slightly flecked with grey, and who would understand, take her in his sheltering arms, strain her to him in all the strength of his deep passionate nature and comfort her with a long long kiss" (pp. 351–52).

Like Stephen Dedalus, Gerty MacDowell has been deserted by an alcoholic "consubstantial" father. God, Leopold Bloom, and Father Conroy ("tree of forbidden priest" [p. 375]) all seem promising surrogates. She considers, but rejects, the carbuncly gentleman strolling along the beach: "She would not like him for a father because he was too old or something or on account of his face (it was a palpable case of doctor Fell) or his carbuncly nose with the pimples on it" (p. 354). Out of her own sense of isolation, Gerty turns to the dark stranger roaming the strand: "He was in deep mourning, she could see that, and the story of a haunting sorrow was written on his face" (p 357). With surprising accuracy, Gerty identifies Bloom as a grass widower. She intuits more about his mental state than even he will acknowledge. Gerty sympathizes with Bloom's melancholy because she feels his pain. She is "heartbroken about her best boy throwing her over. . . . She had loved him better than he knew. Lighthearted deceiver and fickle like all his sex he would never understand what he had meant to her'' (p. 362). Gerty insists that she is ''not a one to be lightly trifled with. As for Mr Reggy with his swank and his bit of money she could just chuck him aside as if he was so much filth and never again would she cast as much as a second thought on him and tear his silly postcard into a dozen pieces'' (p. 362). Gerty unwittingly projects her own sense of rejection onto her ''new conquest'': ''Perhaps it was an old flame he was in mourning for from the days beyond recall. She thought she understood'' (p. 364). As Bloom remarks, ''When you feel like that you often meet what you feel'' (p. 369).

Ironically, Gerty *does* understand the pathos of Bloom's state of mind, though she misinterprets the circumstances of his grief: ''the face that met her gaze there in the twilight, wan and strangely drawn, seemed to her the saddest she had ever seen'' (p. 356). The additional presence of baby Boardman, a ''picture of health,'' eleven months old and shrieking syllables that approximate ''papa,'' may serve to remind Bloom of still another loss suffered eleven years earlier.

Gerty is one of the few characters in the novel who accepts Bloom as he is. She remains entirely oblivious of his Jewishness. Gerty speculates about his nose, ''aqiline' or 'slightly *retroussé*,'' but she never associates it with the ''bottlenosed'' breed scorned by the Citizen. She elevates Bloom to the sublime status of ''her dreamhusband, because she knew on the instant it was him. . . . She was a womanly woman . . . and she just yearned to know all, to forgive all if she could make him fall in love with her, make him forget the memory of the past. Then mayhap he would embrace her gently, like a real man, crushing her soft body to him, and love her, his ownest girlie, for herself alone'' (p. 358).

Gerty turns to Bloom for both amorous approval and paternal solicitude. Safe in the ''sheltering arms'' (p. 351) of her father-love, she no longer need fear rejection for ''that one shortcoming'' (p. 364). Intuitively, Gerty knows that no cosmetic will ever sufficiently compensate for her lameness or give her an equal chance on the marriage market. Physical deformity has

160

jeopardized her amorous "birthright." As she struggles to emulate the ideal "womanly woman," Gerty must assure herself that "love laughs at locksmiths" (p. 364). Nothing is impossible in the realm of true romance. Surely a magical dreamhusband will unbind her from the chastity belt of lameness.

Gerty MacDowell takes refuge in the "dreamy, creamy" Platonic sphere of adolescent fantasy. Joyce tempts us to think of her as a virginal nymphette, a sweet young Lolita barely out of undies: "As for undies they were Gerty's chief care and who that knows the fluttering hopes and fears of sweet seventeen . . ." (p. 350). But Gerty is no longer an adolescent. We are prepared to accept her as a starry-eyed teenager. Joyce teases us, then deflates our expectations by adding, "though Gerty would never see seventeen again" (p. 350). She will be "twenty-two in November" (p. 352), the same age as Stephen Dedalus. Gerty has reached her majority. She should be "womanly wise," but is not. In Dublin of 1904, Gerty MacDowell is fast on the decline toward old maidenhood. Despite elaborate dreams of matrimony, she is still unkissed (or half so), unwedded, and unbedded.

Occasionally, grouchy and vindictive "spinster-like" traits break through Gerty's romantic façade and reveal another side of her personality. The young woman thinks of the "exasperating little brats of twins" as "little monkeys common as ditchwater. Someone ought to take them and give them a good hiding for themselves to keep them in their places" (p. 359). She envies Cissy, who runs with "long gandery strides": "It would have served her just right if she had tripped up over something accidentally on purpose with her high crooked French heels on her to make her look tall and got a fine tumble" (p. 359). Gerty dismisses Edy Boardman as an "irritable little gnat . . . poking her nose into what was no concern of hers" (p. 360), "like the confounded little cat she was" (p. 362). "Sister souls showing their teeth at one another" (p. 369), Bloom observes.

With intermittent sadistic lapses, Gerty retreats to a spiritualized notion of her "beau ideal." *"Art thou real, my ideal?"* asks "that poem that appealed to her so deeply that she had copied out of the newspaper she found one evening round the potherbs" (p. 364). The reader is led to suspect that very few of Gerty's romantic ideals approach reality. Considering the paucity of her amorous experiences in the past (a peck on the nose and a sign from a bicyclist), one can assume that 16 June 1904 will be a landmark in her imagination. She has proved, perhaps for the first time, that she can attract and arouse male sexual interest: "And while she gazed her heart went pitapat. Yes, it was her he was looking at and there was meaning in his look. His eyes burned into her" (p. 357). Gerty's heightened emotion corresponds to Bloom's tumescence. She palpitates with excitement, then imaginatively elaborates on the scene. Gerty is so starved for love that several fantasies crowd in at once. She regards the stranger as a devil whose eyes burn into her: he spiritually seduces and scorches her with his gaze. He resembles a matinee idol and a foreigner. And his "pale intellectual face" (p. 357) may suggest the conquering "pale Galilean" of Swinburne's verse. Like Christ, "he had suffered, more sinned against than sinning" (p. 358). Gerty, the Blessed Virgin Nausicaa, star of the sea and refuge of sinners, longs to take him to her bosom in a sympathetic embrace. She recalls Father Conroy's confessional forgiveness, and she wants to forgive Bloom; but she cannot pardon the "exasperating little brats of twins" for noisily quarreling.

Gerty has so confused religious and erotic sentiment that choir music from the Catholic benediction service provides a fitting background for her titillating striptease: "The choir began to sing *Tantum ergo* and she just swung her foot in and out in time as the music rose and fell" (p. 360). As the music rises, so does Bloom; and so do Gerty's skirts. Her foot simulates the piston and cylinder movement of the sexual act, and the young seductress takes vicarious pleasure in Bloom's agitation. The two reenact the primal temptation between Eve and the Serpent in the Garden of Eden: "He was eyeing her as a snake eyes its prey. Her woman's instinct told her that she had raised

162

the devil in him'' (p. 360). Gerty innocently blushes at the euphemistic reference to Bloom's erection. But she quickly sublimates physiological fact to allegorical interpretation: "His dark eyes fixed themselves on her again drinking in her every contour, literally worshipping at her shrine" (p. 361). In her mind, she is not Eve but the Virgin Mary receiving adoration.

Gerty, however, is less innocent than she will admit: ''because she knew about the passion of men like that, hot-blooded, because Bertha Supple told her once in dead secret and made her swear she'd never about the gentleman lodger that was staying with them out of the Congested Districts Board that had pictures cut out of papers of those skirtdancers and highkickers and she said he used to do something not very nice that you could imagine sometimes in the bed. But this was altogether different from a thing like that because there was all the difference because she could almost feel him draw her face to his and the first quick hot touch of his handsome lips'' (pp. 365–66).

The ingenue deliberately exposes herself and takes pleasure in Bloom's arousal. Good Catholic that she is, Gerty recognizes her ''sin'' and absolves herself in advance: ''Besides there was absolution so long as you didn't do the other thing before being married . . . and besides it was on account of that other thing coming on'' (p. 366). With a voice sounding suspiciously like Molly Bloom's, Gerty argues that all sins can be forgiven in confession; and besides, it's ''only natural'' to feel sexual desire at the time of menstruation. Bloom seems to share Gerty's opinion: ''Near her monthlies, I expect, makes them feel ticklish'' (p. 368). ''Devils they are when that's coming on them. Dark devilish appearance'' (p. 369). And he realizes that Gerty is fully aware of his excitation: ''Did she know what I? Course. Like a cat sitting beyond a dog's jump'' (p. 371).

Our heroine is determined to preserve her chastity and not to ''do the other thing before being married.'' She feels nothing but contempt for prostitutes and ''fallen women'': ''From everything in the least indelicate her finebred nature instinctively recoiled. She loathed that sort of person, the fallen women off the accommodation walk beside the Dodder that went with the soldiers and coarse men, with no respect for a girl's honor, degrading the sex'' (p. 364). Gerty wants a Platonic relationship, free of physical contact, and her wishes are granted. This "fair, unsullied soul" shares Bloom's passion, but she preserves her virginity intact. Spiritual masturbation may be as close as Gerty ever comes to sexual expression. Beneath her romantic dream of matrimony lies a virginal terror of the sexual act: "No, no: not that. They would be just good friends like a big brother and sister without all that other in spite of the conventions of Society with a big ess'' (p. 364).

Leopold Bloom is still an "unconquered hero," "a sterling man, a man of inflexible honour to his fingertips" (p. 365).He has proved to be Gerty's ideal, "her all in all, the only man in all the world for her for love was the master guide" (p. 365). Bloom assures the young girl of her sexual attraction, but he makes no physical demands. He "knows what a woman is" and respects the privacy of her solipsistic dreamworld.

Bloom is the perfect Platonic lover: like a chaste courtier, he pierces his lady with nothing more dangerous than a burning gaze. In fact, he resembles the Renaissance lover depicted in an almanac picture that Gerty has tacked up on the wall of an unmentionable place: "the picture of halcyon days where a young gentleman in the costume they used to wear then with a three-cornered hat was offering a bunch of flowers to his ladylove with oldtime chivalry through her lattice window. You could see there was a story behind it" (p. 355). Gerty's image of perfect devotion is "oldtime chivalry," a gesture of sacerdotal obeisance that sublimates erotic aggression. The "ladylove" is tucked safely behind a lattice window: she symbolically accepts flowers, but not defloration. The courtier submits to the spiritual reign of his beloved, to whom he offers the ideal praise of asexual devotion.

In actuality, Gerty's dreams of feminine power and masculine docility are controverted everywhere in the Dublin environment of 1904. Irish society assures power to males from infancy to old age. In a culture that tacitly approves of masculine aggression, "boys will be boys" (p. 347). The golden rule

164

of male permissiveness forces girls and women to be "feminine" and constantly to mollify incipient violence. Tommy and Jacky Caffrey mimic war games and play raucously on the shore. Whether the "apple of discord" be a sand castle or a rubber ball, females must arbitrate disputes and minimize the destructive effects of anger. The woman's role is to smooth over "life's tiny troubles," to kiss away "the hurtness" (p. 347), and to assuage the unpleasantness of castor oil with a placating gift of syrup and brown bread. When male violence is sanctioned, the female must assume the complementary role of eternal placebo. ("Of course they understand birds, animals, babies. In their line" [p. 371]). Tommy Caffrey displays his burgeoning manhood by throwing a temper tantrum and appropriating a rubber ball: "The temper of him! O, he was a man already was little Tommy Caffrey since he was out of pinnies" (p. 353). Like a miniature war general, Tommy "wins the day" by bullying Cissy into snatching the toy from baby Boardman. "Anything for a quiet life" (p. 353), Cissy explains. She tries to restore "halcyon days" at whatever price.

Even the "young heathen," baby Boardman, has already learned the power of intimidation. His "infant majesty" is "most obstreperous" (p. 357) and can be appeased only by a surrogate female teat from a suckingbottle. This "perfect little bunch of love . . . would certainly turn out to be something great, they said" (p. 357). But no such promises of grandeur await Cissy Caffrey, Edy Boardman, or Gerty MacDowell. Cissy sometimes rebels against her female role by acting the part of a tomboy or playing transvestite games. The only alternative she can envision is that of a masculine woman who usurps phallic power, complete with burned cork moustache, cigarette, and the sadistic right to flagellate the effeminate. Prefiguring Bella Cohen, "Madcap Ciss" expresses a desire to spank the "gentleman opposite" on the "beetoteetom": "Give it to him too on the same place as quick as I'd look at him" (p. 353).

Gerty, in contrast, would never be sufficiently brazen to challenge male authority. Only once does the source of her "pentup feelings" reveal itself. Conscious of the men's temperance retreat concluding nearby, Gerty muses that her home life might have been different "had her father only avoided the clutches of the demon drink, by taking the pledge or those powders the drink habit cured in Pearson's Weekly" (p. 354). Gerty sublimates the hostility she feels toward her father by lamenting the ravages of alcohol, "that vile decoction which has ruined so many hearths and homes. . . . Nay, she had even witnessed in the home circle deeds of violence caused by intemperance and had seen her own father, a prey to the fumes of intoxication, forget himself completely for if there was one thing of all things that Gerty knew it was the man who lifts his hand to a woman save in the way of kindness deserves to be branded as the lowest of the low" (p. 354). The young girl witnesses her father's acts of domestic violence and recoils at the spectacle of masculine brutality. She retreats into the sentimental rhetoric of domestic virtue: "Poor father! With all his faults she loved him still" (p. 354). But she has few compunctions about looking elsewhere for a surrogate to replace her inebriate Oedipal figure.

Gerty offers herself on the altar of amorous devotion as a compensatory gift to her new father-lover, Leopold Bloom. Scornful and defiant of her physical progenitor, of Reggy Wylie, and even of her lifelong religious training, she becomes the holocaust burnt as a priapic offering during the pyrotechnic festival of heat and light. "She would make the great sacrifice. . . . Come what might she would be wild, untrammelled, free" (pp. 364–65). Gerty suppresses shame and modesty in order to share the "wonderment" of physical intimacy with Bloom: "Whitehot passion was in that face, passion silent as the grave, and it had made her his. . . . His hands and face were working and a tremor went over her. She leaned back far to look up where the fireworks were and she caught her knee in her hands so as not to fall back looking up and there was no one to see only him and her when she revealed all her graceful beautifully shaped legs . . . and she seemed to hear the panting of his heart" (p. 365). The young girl feels herself "trembling in

166

every limb from being bent so far back he had a full view high up above the knee no-one ever not even on the swing or wading and she wasn't ashamed and he wasn't either to look in that immodest way like that because he couldn't resist the sight of the wondrous revealment half offered'' (p. 366).

Both Bloom and Gerty seem to experience erotic fulfillment, though Gerty's spiritual orgasm may be a wishful projection of the male authorial imagination: ''She would fain have cried to him chokingly, held out her snowy slender arms to him to come, to feel his lips laid on her white brow the cry of a young girl's love, a little strangled cry, wrung from her, that cry that has rung through the ages. And then a rocket sprang and bang shot blind and O! then the Roman candle burst and it was like a sigh of O! and everyone cried O! O! in raptures and it gushed out of it a stream of rain gold hair threads'' (pp. 366–67). ''My fireworks,'' thinks Bloom. ''Up like a rocket, down like a stick'' (p. 371).

Joyce is obviously satirizing the disjunction between Bloom's highly physical response to the scene and Gerty's religious interpretation. As ''Nausicaa'' shifts its parallactic perspective, Bloom is chided by an inflated narrative voice attuned to the parodic excesses of ''Cyclops'': ''What a brute he had been! At it again? A fair unsullied soul had called to him and, wretch that he was, how had he answered? An utter cad he had been. He of all men!'' (p. 367). But such outworn, sentimental ethics are no longer appropriate to the mores of contemporary society. Bloom's reaction to Gerty's deformity may be self-indulgent, but it is far from callous: ''Jilted beauty. A defect is ten times worse in a woman. But makes them polite. Glad I didn't know it when she was on show. Hot little devil all the same. . . . Anyhow I got the best of that'' (p. 368). Bloom's thoughts correspond to physical detumescence, and they expose uncensored layers of postorgasmic reflection. Unlike Gerty MacDowell, Bloom does not confuse compassion with passion. He knows that the two are separate, discrete emotions, conflated in popular ''soap opera'' journalism, but distinct in real life. ''See her as she is spoil all. Must have

167

the stage setting, the rouge, costume, position, music'' (p. 370).

Masturbation may be a ''Mulligan'' solution to sexual frustration. Yet Bloom's ''bird in hand'' has harmed no one; nor has he violated his own humanitarian ethic of love, the ''opposite of hatred.'' Bloom pities Gerty as she limps away: ''Poor girl! That's why she's left on the shelf and the others did a sprint'' (pp. 367–68). And he realizes that some kind of personal communication has taken place in their erotic encounter: ''Still it was a kind of language between us'' (p. 372). Like Gerty, Bloom perceives a redemptive mutuality in the experience, despite his smug feeling that he has gotten the best of the bargain: ''Cheap too. Yours for the asking. Because they want it themselves. Their natural craving'' (p. 368). Both Bloom the ''seducer'' and Gerty the ''temptress'' have shared a brief moment of intimacy that allows temporary escape from sexual isolation.

In the ''Circe'' episode, Gerty limps forward onto the stage, displaying ''*coyly her bloodied clout*.'' She accuses Bloom of a perverse act of psychological defloration: ''You did that. . . . When you saw all the secrets of my bottom drawer. . . . Dirty married man!'' (p. 442). The assertion involves a pun on Gerty's underwear and reminds us of the sacramental ''toilettable drawer'' stuffed with adolescent mementoes. But Gerty adds candidly: ''I love you for doing that to me'' (p. 442). The young girl's unconscious admits what her waking mind would never acknowledge. She has experienced an initiation into womanhood, and she feels grateful to her voyeuristic lover for untying the knot of virginity. Bloom fancifully speculates: ''Virgins go mad in the end I suppose'' (p. 368).

Both participants in the afternoon drama are ''thankful for small mercies'' (p. 368). Bloom feels flattered that Gerty ''saw something in him,'' though he cannot imagine what. ''Sooner have me as I am than some poet chap with bearsgrease, plastery hair lovelock over his dexter optic'' (p. 369). He senses the young woman's need for tenderness and privacy: ''Gently does it. Dislike rough and tumble. Kiss in the dark and never tell'' (p.

168

369). Gerty is attracted to Bloom for much the same reason that Molly found him handsome years earlier: "Why me? Because you were so foreign from the others" (p. 380).

In *Joyce in Nighttown,* Mark Shechner culls from "a number of sly, circumstantial hints" that Gerty's cameo appearance in "Circe" might label her a professional prostitute.[7] The theory is playful, but unfounded in the text. Gerty MacDowell is no more (and no less) a whore than Molly Bloom, Josie Breen, or the Princess Selene—all of whom arise as specters in Nighttown. Leopold Bloom has mentally deflowered the nymph of his fantasy, and his psyche registers the impact. Gerty accuses him of voyeuristic rape, but she delights in her erotic victory over the dark, enchanting stranger. Bloom's id may label Gerty a prostitute and Lipoti Virag a pimp; but one is a technical virgin and the other is dead. Neither phantasm has a "real" identity in the Dublin night world.

Gerty MacDowell is far more than a pornographic pin-up for Leopold Bloom. In "Nausicaa," Gerty soars to ecstasy with the rockets and with Bloom. She proves that she can arouse, titillate, and satisfy masculine desire. As the new "blessed virgin" and votary of Dame Fashion, Gerty shows mercy to an impotent gentleman who worships at her shrine. She is paid the final tribute of Bloom's silent ejaculation: "For this relief much thanks" (p. 372).

At the end of the episode, Bloom is still uncertain about his male ego, and he fails to go beyond the vapid assertion of "I. . . . Am. A" (p. 381) to an affirmation of personal identity. Once again, Joyce challenges us to fill in the blank: "I am a man?" "A lover?" "A human being?" "A fool?" Fritz Senn points out that there is "a faint adumbration of a Jehovean I AM THAT I AM" and reminds us that AMA is one form of the Latin verb, "to love."[8] But as we later learn in "Ithaca," Bloom, like Ulysses, is "Everyman" and "Noman." In the role of "Everyman," he can be every ghost lover that has haunted the dreams of Gerty MacDowell. Because he is "Noman," Bloom offers an erotic *tabula rasa* on which the fantasies of love and romance can be etched by Gerty's fictional imagination.

Bloom has given pleasure both to Gerty and to himself. As Richard Ellmann declares, "masturbation enables him to return to his usual solicitude for other creatures. . . . For the first time in literature masturbation becomes heroic. It is a way of joining ideal and real, and while simplistic or vulgar, it is not negligible. It brings Bloom back to goodwill and away from indifference. He leaves behind Narcissus drowned in the pool."[9]

The act of onanism releases Bloom from a prison of sexual frustration. It provides physical relief, as well as psychological compensation. By some cosmic coincidence of gravitational fields, Molly's magnetic attraction to Boylan has interrupted the mechanism of Bloom's watch: "Very strange about my watch. Wristwatches are always going wrong. Wonder is there any magnetic influence between the person because that was about the time he. Yes, I suppose at once. Cat's away the mice will play. . . . Back of everything magnetism" (pp. 373–74). Time has stopped at half past four, "half past kissing time," as a mocking reminder to Bloom that "his waterworks were out of order" (p. 361). Cissy's pun reflects the dysfunction of both timepiece and codpiece. "Was that just when he, she?" Bloom wonders (p. 370). The coincidence of the watch ushers in the shock of recognition that Bloom has so carefully been holding at bay: "O, he did. Into her. She did. Done" (p. 370). The staccato rhythm of his prose simulates rapid sexual excitement, and the climactic finality of the word "done" seals Bloom's fate as a cuckold. But it also reminds us of the end of "Sirens" and the association of "done" with the release of digestive gas. Here Bloom achieves another kind of relief. Unconscious repression of Molly's adultery has weighed on his psyche like a knot of uncomfortable gas. In a flash of recognition, Bloom imagines the act of copulation, digests the information, and acknowledges Molly's infidelity. Psychic pressure explodes in a moment of personal honesty that lifts the burden of emotional denial. Masturbation has given Bloom the courage to imagine Boylan and Molly "doing it," and voyeurism offers a key to understanding. "Aftereffect not pleasant. Still you have to get rid of it someway. . . . The strength it gives a man. That's the

170

secret of it'' (p. 370). "Back of everything magnetism. . . . Tip. Woman and man that is. Fork and steel. Molly, he. . . . Tip. Have to let fly" (p. 374). Bloom's searing candor becomes more poignant later in the episode, when he thinks: "I am a fool perhaps. He gets the plums and I the plumstones" (p. 377). "Eating off his cold plate" (p. 370). Masturbation, an apparent escape from anxiety, has brought Bloom back to a recognition of conjugal inadequacy: "Think you're escaping and run into yourself. Longest way round is the shortest way home. . . . The young are old. His gun rusty from the dew" (p. 377).

In his meditation on time, space, and magnetism, Bloom thinks of time in Aristotelian terms as the "motion of matter": "Earth for instance pulling this and being pulled. That causes movement. And time? Well that's the time the movement takes" (p. 374). He confronts the paradox of cyclical temporality and linear age: nature repeats itself, but the youth of the individual slips away ineluctably. The stream of life moves onward as "the year returns. History repeats itself. . . . Life, love, voyage round your own little world" (p. 377). Attempts to recapture the past are necessarily doomed to futility: "Tired I feel now. . . . My youth. Never again. Only once it comes. . . . Returning not the same. . . . The new I want. Nothing new under the sun" (p. 377). "Love, lie and be handsome for tomorrow we die" (p. 381).

There is little question that Bloom's escapade has restored his humanitarian sentiment. "Goodbye, dear. Thanks. Made me feel so young" (p. 382). His reminiscences of his daughter are tender, loving, solicitous, and calm—though they seem to be suffused with grim thoughts about nausea, death, and children getting lost. "Don't know what death is at that age. . . . But being lost they fear" (p. 379). Bloom is magnanimous in his attitude toward the brawling Citizen: "Suppose he hit me. Look at it other way round. Not so bad then. Perhaps not to hurt he meant" (p. 380).

By the time Bloom turns to write a message in the sand, his ego has dwindled to a thin, humble, ephemeral thread. "All these rocks with lines and scars and letters" (p. 381) *might*

171

bear some philosophical message, if only we possessed the key to nature's hieroglyphic scrawlings. They might even provide an ontological answer to the eternal, haunting question, "What is the meaning of that other world" (p. 381). Alone on the beach, Bloom senses the helplessness of the individual to write words that will contribute to metaphysical understanding. The tools he possesses—a bit of a stick and paper from an old copybook—are entirely incongruous and of little help to the task at hand. Bloom is reduced to imprinting his ego on sand. He knows that like all the signs of human endeavor, this too is "useless" and will be "washed away" (p. 381).

Bloom writes "I. . . . AM. A." and then gives up. "No room. Let it go" (p. 381). He cannot define himself in the face of an overwhelming, engulfing cosmos. Perhaps there is no room in the universe for Bloom's being-there, his existential *Dasein*. He realizes that all human life is built on sand, and that in the end, "all fades" (p. 381)—life, love, existence, and ego. The conclusion of "Nausicaa" may signal Bloom's conversion to the non-egoic, cosmic sense of self that he will later embrace in "Ithaca." Perhaps he is beginning to understand the stoic need to let go of his claims to conjugal appropriation and egocentric privilege. In a "half dream" he muses: "And she can do the other. Did too. And Belfast. I won't go. . . . It never comes the same" (p. 382).

As Joyce suggested in a letter to Frank Budgen, masturbation may be the herb "moly" that protects Bloom from the assaults of Bella Cohen in Nighttown.[10] Onanism liberates Bloom from erotic obsession, so that he can achieve a heroism that is both literally and figuratively self-actualizing. Molly's coition with Boylan has been just as infertile as Leopold's voyeurism. Molly enjoys Blazes as a bed partner, and Bloom takes pleasure in Gerty as a visual accomplice in masturbation. Bloom empties his seed on the sand; Boylan expels his on the bed sheet. Both men are technically guilty of onanism, for in both cases, the spilled seed is wasted for procreation.

172

"Look at it other way round" (p. 380).

In "Oxen of the Sun," Joyce satirically decries the sins of onanism and contraception that encourage "copulation without population" (p. 423). He facetiously bids that "all Malthusiasts go hang" (p. 423) and mourns the loss of "those Godpossibled souls that we nightly impossibilise. . . . For, sirs, . . . our lust is brief. We are means to those small creatures within us and nature has other ends than we" (p. 389).

In the Holles Street maternity hospital, Bloom encounters the Janus-image of Gerty MacDowell's sentimental romanticism. Here, once again, is the aggression inspired by male bonding— the threatening camaraderie of "Cyclops," now applied to sexuality. *Machismo* is the watchword of the chapter, from Theodore Purefoy's stud performance to Mulligan's vocation as *"Fertiliser and Incubator"* of willing Dublin dames.

For the Trinity medical students, sex entails masturbation *à deux.* The act is a physical "coming together," stripped of spiritual "at-onement." Sex is reduced to phallic friction—a mechanical piston-and-cylinder action performed in the context of penile prowess. The medical Dicks and Davys are just as narcissistic as Gerty MacDowell. Locked in the prison of male egotism, they deny themselves the possibility of human warmth, affection, or compassion. Bloom is glaringly out of place in this boisterous crowd, and his alienation from the younger men further serves to define his androgynous sensibility.

Stephen uses the model of physical reproduction as a paradigm for artistic creation: "In woman's womb word is made flesh but in the spirit of the maker all flesh that passes becomes the word that shall not pass away. This is the postcreation" (p. 391). The young man makes fun of the Catholic doctrine of "virgin birth" that attributes the conception of Christ to the infusion of the Holy Spirit in the womb of the Blessed Virgin Mary. (*"C'est le pigeon, Joseph"* [p. 41]). Like Léo Taxil,

Stephen and the medicals prefer the bawdy, un-biblical theory that Jesus was the illegitimate son of Panther, a Roman centurion. The choice is between Scyllan superstition and Charybdian materialism.

Ironically, Stephen denies the possibility of "virgin birth" at the same time that he demands the right to aesthetic parthenogenesis. At this point in the narrative, he clings to the ideal of autoerotic art. He wants to create by divine infusion, without "coming together" with the real world of men and women. He fears returning to the foul rag and bone shop of the heart, for he is convinced that he will merely encounter solipsistic images of himself: "*If Socrates leave his house today he will find the sage seated on his doorstep*" (p. 213).

Like Gerty MacDowell, Stephen wants to retreat to a "heavenly ideal" where "there are no more marriages, glorified man, an androgynous angel, being a wife unto himself" (p. 213). Mulligan earlier suggested another solution to chastity, a "honeymoon in the hand." So far, Stephen's literary production has been limited to "a capful of light odes" (p. 415) inspired by literal or by figurative masturbation. (His *Portrait* villanelle is written after a wet dream: "O what sweet music! His soul was all dewy wet" [*PA* 217]; and the "Proteus" poem has been cribbed from Douglas Hyde [p. 132]). He seems unaware that his own "Shakespeare theory" implies a need for the genius to be deflowered, "gored" by the tusk of experience, before he can create from the ripe potential of a fertile consciousness. The anima of the artist is metaphorically female and must be fertilized by painful congress with the "world without as actual" (p. 213).

Oxen are appropriate symbols for the barren braggadocio of the medicals, and the sacred cattle provide an ironic commentary on a chapter that ostensibly champions the glories of physical procreation. An ox is a castrated bull, and the medical Dicks are young bulls who spiritually castrate themselves by refusing personal commitment. In a letter to Frank Budgen, Joyce described the idea behind "Oxen" as "the crime committed against fecundity by sterilizing the act of coition."[11] The

174

episode, however, is chiefly concerned with emotional, rather than with physical, prophylaxis. Joyce identifed the crime as "fraud" in the formal sense of "breaking a vow." The young men may "impossibilise" the "Godpossibled souls" denied embodiment by contraception. But their true sin involves egotism—the failure to mitigate a masculine, aggressive persona with feminine sentiment, or to honor vows of amorous attachment. They have embraced life as "a beastly thing and nothing else" (p. 8), to which callous hedonism is a suitable response. The comedy of their banter arises from impersonal brutality. By refusing troths of love, they cut themselves off from the ability to feel, denying the faculty that makes both passion and compassion possible.

Stephen's association with the medical students is a coition that remains barren. It implies male bonding that ignores the anima and excludes androgynous feeling. "Coming together" with the oxen leaves the poet aesthetically sterile and bereft of spiritual progeny. Joyce, in his schema for the chapter, figuratively describes Bloom as the "spermatozoon" that will fertilize Stephen's consciousness.[12] Out of the union of poet and "womanly man," a new artistic vision may be fashioned.

Stephen has made the mistake of turning solely to his literary forefathers for inspiration. Not a single female writer proves worthy of emulation in the "Oxen" episode. Like the Holles Street refectory, the world of literary tradition suggests an exclusively male heritage. After a long gestation and a difficult birth, the literary "word" is born with the utterance of "Burke's." Is it any wonder that the offspring ushers in the misshapen discourse of slang and pidgin English? Out of a homophiliac environment springs a word that perpetuates male camaraderie in a world of booze and phallic prowess.

Stephen has searched so long for his spiritual roots that he momentarily gives way to the temptations of alcohol, paralysis, and ribald jest. Not until the next episode will he respond to Leopold Bloom, the "transubstantial" father who will introduce Stephen to the "real world" from which all genuine creation arises. Bloom, for his part, has already begun to regard

175

the young man with pity and to consider him a surrogate son: "Leopold that had of his body no manchild for an heir looked upon him his friend's son and was shut up in sorrow for his forepassed happiness and as sad as he was that him failed a son of such gentle courage . . . so grieved he also in no less measure for young Stephen for that he lived riotously with those wastrels and murdered his goods with whores" (pp. 390–91). Leopold "bore fast friendship to sir Simon and to this his son young Stephen. . . . Ruth red him, love led on with will to wander, loth to leave" (p. 388). "Now he is himself paternal and these about him might be his sons. Who can say? The wise father knows his own child" (p. 413).

In "Oxen," Joyce satirically celebrates the god Bringforth, a vengeful *dio boia* who "in a very grievous rage . . . would presently lift his arm and spill their souls for their abuses and their spillings done by them contrariwise to his word which forth to bring brenningly biddeth" (p. 396). Fundamentalists like the Purefoys, who go forth and fruitfully multiply, can hardly be considered a Joycean ideal. Theodore Purefoy, by presenting Mina with "hearty annuals," has reduced her to perpetual broodmare. Continual pregnancy is one way to insure female chastity and to certify paternity. But it substitutes animal reproduction for a more humane spousal relationship. Both Theodore and Mina sacrifice individual creativity for the good (or the peril) of the species. They mindlessly continue to copulate and to populate, with the same gesture of mechanical automation that impels the medical students to frictional excitation.

Throughout "Oxen," Joyce scatters examples of perverted fatherhood—of paternal powers frustrated or abused. Phallic prowess can wreak havoc in the lives of others. Consider the consequences of potency in *Ulysses:* a three-day session of torture on the bed of parturition. "Three days imagine groaning on a bed with a vinegared handkerchief round her forehead, her belly swollen out! Phew! Dreadful simply! Child's head too big: forceps. Doubled up inside her trying to butt its way out blindly, groping for the way out. Kill me that would" (p. 161). Mina

176

Purefoy is immolated on the altar of history, and her belly suitably becomes the altar on which a Black Mass is celebrated in "Circe."

From Stephen's musings, we know that the bed of conception is identical with the beds of birth and of death: "Bridebed, childbed, bed of death" (pp. 47–48). And because Bloom has witnessed both a birth and a death resulting from copulation, he is loath to initiate a process that might end in parental anguish and filial loss. We are born, suffer, and die in violence: "The aged sisters draw us into life: we wail, batten, sport, clip, clasp, sunder, dwindle, die: over us dead they bend" (p. 394). And when human suffering adheres to the spectacle of infant mortality, the experience of absurdity becomes too blatant to warrant deliberate collusion. Psychologically, Bloom refuses to abet the enemy death, though his protest entails abstinence from the rites of fertility.

Bloom is genuinely distressed by Stephen's flippant mockery of sex, and he even ventures to object to the young man's blasphemy: "In a recent public controversy with Mr L. Bloom . . . he [Stephen] is reported by eyewitnesses as having stated that once a woman has let the cat into the bag (an esthetic allusion, presumably, to one of the most complicated and marvellous of all nature's processes, the act of sexual congress) she must let it out again or give it life, as he phrased it, to save her own" (p. 420). Bloom's discomfort at Stephen's joke is a function of his own repressed fear of "putting the cat into the bag." He does not want to be responsible for the cat coming out again—for the agonies of labor and delivery, or for the disappointment of frustrated parenthood.

Bloom is so in touch with the anima, the "female" aspect of his psyche, that he has psychosomatic headaches during Molly's menstrual period, and he tries to imagine her experiences of pregnancy and parturition. Although he feels the desire to "have a baby" (and does so in a "Circean" fantasy of multiple births), he finds phallic aggression so distasteful that he is unwilling to *cause* his wife (or anyone else) the futile pain of childbirth. Molly, too, reveals negative feelings about gestation

177

in "Penelope": "nice invention they made for women for him to get all the pleasure but if someone gave them a touch of it themselves theyd know what I went through with Milly . . . Mina Purefoys husband . . . filling her up with a child or twins once a year as regular as the clock . . . not satisfied till they have us swollen out like elephants" (p. 742). Molly practices a primitive form of birth control in her affair with Boylan and is determined not to risk "having another," "not off him [Boylan]" (p. 742).

In the theological argument that transpires in "Oxen," Bloom champions fetal rights. He supports the Catholic doctrine that would spare the life of a newborn child, rather than that of the mother. He facetiously remarks: "it was good for that Mother Church belike at one blow had birth and death pence" (p. 390). Bloom's "dissembling" statement reveals his anguish at the death of Rudy; and it implies that sexual union might inadvertently result in the sacrificial death of the female. Eros could be linked, in morbid horror, to Thanatos. Bloom is apparently agitated, and he may even feel startled by his own willingness to choose fetal survival over the "warm, fullblooded life" of his spouse.

Because Bloom cannot dissociate Thanatos from Eros, he relinquishes both at once. And in so doing, he allies himself with a new, sympathetic vision of reality that provides a cosmic definition of heroism. Bloom has forfeited filial and conjugal ownership to become an "androgynous" artist, taking the whole of humanity under his wing. As we learn in "Ithaca," his mind is populated with pseudo-scientific schemes for the benefit of mankind. He can envision a world in which human beings refrain from killing, in which a social utopia fulfills the economic needs of every man and woman, and in which a love based on agape might be possible.

At this point in *Ulysses,* physiological procreation has been sublimated to the more significant demands of spiritual renewal. Joyce the artist celebrates all those seminal possibilities of consciousness that have not been actualized by historical event. His fiction glorifies the birth of Stephen Dedalus and

Leopold Bloom into a new awareness of themselves as poetic makers of human life. In Joyce's schema for "Oxen," Bloom may indeed function symbolically as the spermatozoon that fertilizes Stephen's embryonic growth in the English literary tradition. At the end of the episode, both Stephen and Leopold prepare to be reborn—Stephen as son to Bloom and nascent fashioner of the aesthetic word, and Bloom as spiritual father to Stephen and compassionate father to all mankind.

1. Fritz Senn, "Nausicaa," in *James Joyce's "Ulysses,"* ed. Clive Hart and David Hayman, p. 284.

2. Mark Shechner, *Joyce in Nighttown,* pp. 161–62.

3. Joyce, *Letters,* 2:427–29.

4. According to Mark Shechner, "Joyce was playing in this chapter, but the game involved his own erotic propensities, his libidinal clichés. . . . The chapter is an act of exorcism that affirms an old commitment even while denying it" (*Joyce in Nighttown,* p. 161).

5. *Irish Times,* 16 June 1904, p. 1, col. 6; p. 3, col. 9.

6. Joyce, *Letters,* 1:135.

7. Shechner, *Joyce in Nighttown,* p. 165.

8. Senn, "Nausicaa,' pp. 281, 294–95. Gifford and Seidman interpret the passage "just as it reads: 'I am A' (the first letter of the alphabet). Also: I am alpha (the first letter in the Greek alphabet) hence, the first or the beginning." They suggest that the assertion reflects the Lord's statement in Revelation 1:8, "I am Alpha and Omega, the beginning and the ending" (*Notes for Joyce,* p. 331).

9. Richard Ellmann, *Ulysses on the Liffey,* p. 133. In contrast, Stanley Sultan declares that "the masturbation at the center of the chapter is not merely a pathetic and sordid act but a representation, on every level of meaning, of Bloom's self-defeat and self-destruction. . . . Bloom is far more pathetic than when he feels frustrated, ashamed, and helpless; for he is depressed, resigned, and spiritually broken" (*The Argument of "Ulysses,"* p. 264).

10. Joyce, *Letters,* 1:147–48.

11. Ibid., 139.

12. Joyce declared in his letter to Budgen that "Bloom is the spermatozoon, the hospital the womb, the nurse the ovum, Stephen the embryo" (*Letters,* 1:140).

9

"Circe": Ulysses in Nighttown

In the shadows of Nighttown, Stephen Dedalus and Leopold Bloom re-create a nightmare history in order to transcend its grasp. By confronting the sins of the past in grotesque, exaggerated caricatures, both men participate in a surrealistic dreamplay tantamount to the ritual of confession. They become aware of unconscious guilt paralyzing volition; and in a process similar to Freudian psychoanalysis, they dramatically exorcise the ghosts that haunt their tortured mindscapes.

In a Circean universe, the hallucinogenic reigns. "To be is to be perceived." Any material object can come alive and talk, animated by the mental energies of a beholding eye. Art is, quite literally, magic. External perception stimulates inner hallucination, and the mind has unrestricted power to concretize illusion. People and events are propelled by the explosive forces of intoxicated fantasy.

Nighttown is populated by personal ghosts and ancestral specters, all of which thunder from the cave of a Freudian unconscious. As Catholicism has long insisted, volition bears the weight of true event in the terrain of the spirit. Guilt adheres to the fabric of "sinful" imaginings, whether or not these thoughts are realized in the world without as actual. Like data stored in a computer, perceptions and fantasies abide in the recesses of the psyche. In "Circe," the computer spews forth its unprogrammed content. Painful memories masquerade as terrifying monsters. Only when the mind succeeds in recognizing, handling, and "naming" the demons can it conquer the horror associated with their presence.

"Circe" unfolds as an elaborate psychodrama enacted by Leopold Bloom, Stephen Dedalus, and all the chimeras that haunt their imaginations. Both men descend into a modern Hades to exorcise their private demons. Neither character fully articulates the dramatic content of the episode. But each is aware of the startling, purgative effects of his tragicomic voyage into the subterranean world of the unconscious. Consumed by the chaos of dream, each emerges, phoenix-like, from the "locomotor ataxia" of psychological repression.

Though readers are often disturbed by the unreality of the episode, "Circe" is ultra-real in its attempt to render several planes of consciousness simultaneously. Its dramatic form simulates the various dimensions of awareness as they present themselves in human experience. Repressed fears and emotional anxieties have just as much impact on the psyche as do historical events. Nighttown exposes to the light of comedy the dark, frightening "shadow" self that most people sublimate in waking life. The experiment has ramifications that go far beyond linguistic or technical game. Each minor drama in the chapter signals an epiphany in the mind of a character. As Mark Shechner suggests, the entire episode might be viewed as an "epiphany gone mad, one hundred and seventy-two pages of sudden spiritual manifestation."[1] The vision and the waking dream of "Circe" hover on the edge of the void, pointing to the content of the abyss.

182

The Nighttown episode is at once a confession and a Mass, a religious sacrament of spiritual expiation. (''You call it a festivity. I call it a sacrament'' [p. 489]). Joyce, like God the Father, stands behind the dramatic creation and calls to mind Stephen's aesthetic theory of the playwright who remains far off, ''paring his fingernails.'' The author is a divine creator, distant like the gods of Lucretius, yet omnipresent in the unfolding epic-drama. Throughout the chapter, Joyce intrudes in the ''mode of absence,'' choreographing the hallucinatory fantasies of his characters.

Consubstantial with Joyce the father, Bloom and Stephen share a unified consciousness with their creator. They become members of a deified Trinity, simultaneously imagining the lurid phantasms that appear in ''Circe.'' Joyce, the principal puppeteer and stage director, is responsible for the expressionistic dramas animated on the Nighttown stage. But the dreamplay scenario unfolds from the minds of Stephen and Bloom, who embellish the day-world of personal experience with concrete embodiments of unrepressed emotion. Ordinarily, the dreamer is an artist whose creation reveals itself on the private stage of the psyche. In ''Circe,'' dream is externalized and made public—though Joyce and the reader are the only spectators who have full access to all the theatrical scenes. The two protagonists enact fantasies and hallucinations that adhere to the deep structure of the unconscious. By the end of the chapter, both men have undergone transforming experiences of psychoanalytic purgation. The fantasy of ''Blephen-Stoom'' precipitates the novel's climax and becomes the basis of compassionate recognition at the conclusion of the Nighttown episode.[2]

In *Portrait*, Stephen ordained himself ''a priest of eternal imagination, transmuting the daily bread of experience into the radiant body of everliving life'' (*PA* 221). Now at the beginning of ''Circe,'' ''*flourishing the ashplant in his left hand*,'' he ''*chants with joy the* introit *for paschal time*'' (p. 431). As principal celebrant of the Nighttown Mass, Stephen takes the place of Christ, the high priest. (''Im sure you are a spoiled priest'' [p. 523]). And Bloom, as victim, becomes Christ the paschal lamb. (''I have sinned! I have suff . . .'' [p. 544]). Stephen is the ''Light of the World'' described in Saint John's gospel, as well as the ''dog-god'' of the Black Mass: *''He flourishes his ashplant shivering the lamp image, shattering light over the world. A liver and white spaniel on the prowl slinks after him, growling''* (p. 432). As in ''Nestor,'' Stephen's sermon is still the testament of ''gesture.'' He longs to convert the world from linear time and space to phenomenal consciousness: ''So that gesture, not music, not odours, would be a universal language, the gift of tongues rendering visible not the lay sense but the first entelechy, the structural rhythm'' (p. 432). Despite the amorous referent of Stephen's proclamation, his statement has serious import. The bard's ''pornosophical philotheology'' chooses the hedonistic loaf and jug of Omar Khayyam over the bread and wine of the Catholic Mass. The rebel priest celebrates a profane ceremony of sensuous delight, exulting in the joys of the ''here and now.''

Bloom the victim appears (''lovelorn longlost lugubru Booloohoom'' [pp. 433–34]), cramming bread and chocolate into his pockets (as opposed to bread and wine), and dragging with him two thousand years of Hebraic guilt. From long acquaintance with persecution, Bloom has formed a criminal self-image: ''What is that? A flasher? Searchlight'' (p. 434). He fears public exposure of the dark, hidden layers of subliminal guilt stored in the chambers of erotic memory. ''On fire'' with a sense of rage and impotence, he entertains the fantasy that Boylan's house may be burning: ''Big blaze. Might be his house. Beggar's bush. We're safe'' (p. 434).

As Bloom enters Nighttown, animated objects suddenly take shape out of the fog. Two cyclists *''swim by him, grazing him, their bells rattling''* (p. 435). Bloom *''halts erect stung by a spasm''* (p. 435). Machines overcome him with sexual force: *''Through rising fog a dragon sandstrewer . . . slews heavily down upon him, its huge red headlight winking, its trolley hissing on the wire''* (p. 435). Mechanical monsters scream at him incomprehensibly: ''Bang Bang Bla Bak Blud Bugg Bloo''

184

(p. 435). Bloom feels as helpless as a bug whose blood is about to be shed in inadvertent sacrifice. As usual, he is treated like a superfluous object and a victim of public scorn: "Hey, shit-breeches, are you doing the hattrick?" (p. 435). The "new womanly man" feels a "bit light in the head. Monthly or effect of the other. Brainfogfag. That tired feeling" (p. 436).

Menacing objects dart out of the mist, and sinister figures hover in the shadows: "Gaelic league spy, sent by that fire-eater" (p. 436). Specters arise from the unconscious, threatening to overwhelm their prey. Like Christ, Bloom is assaulted by the Jews for abandoning the Old Testament tradition: "*A stooped bearded figure appears garbed in the long caftan of an elder in Zion. . . . Yellow poison streaks are on the drawn face*" (p. 437). The elder Rudolph taunts his son with patriarchal vilifications: "I told you not go with drunken goy ever. So. You catch no money. . . . What you making down this place? Have you no soul? . . . Are you not my son Leopold, the grandson of Leopold? Are you not my dear son Leopold who left the house of his father and left the god of his fathers Abraham and Jacob?" (p. 437). Bloom can only respond: "(*With precaution.*) I suppose so, father. Mosenthal. All that's left of him" (p. 437).

Leopold is maligned not only by Rudolph and Ellen Bloom, but by his wife Molly, and by every other female of his acquaintance. The string of charges sets him apart as Jewish reprobate and impotent cuckold. Molly reminds Poldy of his "cold feet" and calls him "a poor old stick in the mud" (p. 440). Bridie Kelly, the whore who introduced Leopold to sex, furtively accosts her one-time customer and "*flaps her bat shawl*" (p. 441) in his wake. Gerty MacDowell claims that this "dirty married man" mentally deflowered her and saw all the secrets of her "bottom drawer" (p. 442). Even Josie Powell Breen, a former sweetheart, accuses Bloom of "humbugging and deluthering as per usual" with a "cock and bull story" (p. 447).

"Caught in the act" (p. 453) of dispensing pity to a stray dog, and apprehended in the guise of Henry Flower, the harried defendant attempts to assert his personal identity rooted in the present. His stammering, confused phrases of self-approbation echo the language of the Old Testament and foreshadow HCE'S claim to be "Missaunderstaid" (*FW* 363): "Gentleman of the jury, let me explain. A pure mare's nest. I am a man misunderstood. I am being made a scapegoat of. I am a respectable married man, without a stain on my character. I live in Eccles street. My wife, I am the daughter of a most distinguished commander" (p. 457). Bloom is desperately trying to abnegate the strain of defilement. His speech combines Isaiah's description of Christ the Lamb with the Pentateuchal language of Yahweh, the God who names Himself "I am Who am." The defendant appeals to the contemporaneous "instant" isolated from historical guilt to demonstrate his subjective innocence. He challenges the "pure mare's nest" of traditional history— the nightmare that J. J. O'Molloy uses in Bloom's defense, claiming that his client suffers from an "aberration of heredity" (p. 463).

Bloom's argument is no more understood by the jurymen than it was by the Irish taverners. "*Bloom, pleading not guilty,*" claims to have been "*branded as a black sheep*" (p. 461). "Mistaken identity. . . . I am wrongfully accused" (p. 456). Bloom insists that all attempts to impose a categorical identity on personal consciousness are fundamentally "mistaken." They restrict and betray the limitless possibilities of the mind to create its own identity in the present. If history is based on fictive archetypes, then why not supplant the legends of racial heritage with projects of the intellectual imagination?

Bloom's self-portrait as a blue-blooded Britisher parodies the expectations of his imperial prosecutors: "I fought with the colours for king and country in the absentminded war under General Gough in the park and was disabled at Spion Kop and Bloemfontein. . . . I did all a white man could" (pp. 457–58). Because genealogical pedigree and chauvinistic ardor both depend on fictional categories of race and nationality, Bloom feels free to invent a history that will ingratiate him with his tormentors. He fabricates an impressive family tree and spins jingoist tales of military glory.

186

During the interrogation, Bloom declares himself a re-nowned "'author-journalist,'" despite the repudiation of "'Blue-bags'" by Myles Crawford, editor of the *Freeman's Urinal* and *Weekly Arsewiper* (p. 458). Philip Beaufoy, author of *Matcham's Masterstroke,* indicts Bloom as a "plagiarist. A soapy sneak masquerading as a literateur" (p. 458). In the magical world of Nighttown, however, secret ambitions have just as much reality as genuine accomplishments. Bloom's talent for the commercial manipulation of words and his fantasies of literary prominence verify his degree from the "university of life" (p. 459). The mind insists on "leading a quadruple existence" (p. 460): consciousness freely embraces the imaginary projects of multiple personalities.

Bloom finds himself on trial in "Circe" for his hang-ups and his obsessions. He is accused of his deepest and most perverted impulses, and he must bear the weight of all the salacious desires that have ever accosted his beleaguered imagination. Hence the charges proffered by Mary Driscoll, scullerymaid: "He surprised me in the rere of the premises" (p. 461). The coprophiliac nature of a court exhibit displaying Bloom's feces, soiled with a "Titbits *back number*" (p. 462) implies prosecution for anal-related fantasies. J. J. O'Molloy must defend his client as a foreigner "of Mongolian extraction and irresponsible for his actions," an Oriental, and a Jewish exile in "the land of the Pharoah" (p. 463). Bloom's ostensible excuse for eccentricity lies in his alienation: he cannot reconcile his own self-image with the foreign identity thrust on him by the nation he inhabits. In effect, his eastern homeland, "Agendath Netaim in faraway Asia Minor" (p. 464), has been mortgaged; the law of the jungle and survival of the fittest have preempted the Mosaic code.

Mrs. Yelverton Barry accuses Bloom of sadomasochistic and adulterous solicitations. Mrs. Bellingham, a "cold potato" of high society, indicts him for fetishistic attachment to furs, silk hose, and expensive lace. The robust Mrs. Talboys, in "amazon costume," relates tales of epistolary exhibitionism: "He implored me to soil his letter in an unspeakable manner, to chastise him as he richly deserves, to bestride and ride him, to give him a most vicious horsewhipping" (p. 467).

The aristocratic amazons threaten to thrash, geld, and vivisect their prey. "I'll flog him black and blue in the public streets" (p. 469). Bloom meekly emulates Severin, the masochistic hero of Leopold von Sacher-Masoch's *Venus in Furs.* (*Venus im Pelz*). He champions "the spanking idea. A warm tingling glow without effusion" (p. 468) for the sake of erotic titillation. But like Severin, Bloom gets more than he bargains for. In the course of "Circe," he becomes Everyman, and a transvestite Everywoman as well. He is Egyptian, Jew, Mongolian, Chinaman, and perpetual scapegoat. "When in doubt persecute Bloom" (p. 464).

His Honour, sir Frederick Falkiner, finds Bloom guilty as "a well-known dynamitard, forger, bigamist, bawd and cuckold and a public nuisance to the citizens of Dublin" (p. 470). The judge sentences this "odious pest" to death by hanging. In self-defense, Bloom pleads the evidence of his own pity. He calls as a character witness Paddy Dignam, who materializes in the form of a ghouleaten beagle, "by metempsychosis. Spooks" (p. 473).

Rescued by the corpse's lugubrious plea, Bloom returns to the land of the living. He meets the prostitute Zoe and luxuriates in a brief erotic fantasy of "*the womancity, nude, white, still, cool*" (p. 477). When Zoe suggests that he "make a stump speech," the womancity melts into the vision of a socialist utopia. Bloom imagines himself as a proletarian Messiah pitted against the evils of capitalism: "Machines is their cry, their chimera, their panacea. Laboursaving apparatuses, supplanters, bugbears, manufactured monsters for mutual murder, hideous hobgoblins produced by a horde of capitalistic lusts upon our prostituted labour" (p. 479).

Even the "world's greatest reformer" cannot refuse the temptations of totalitarian power. The crowd salutes Bloom as "Leopold the First," "undoubted emperor president and king chairman, the most serene and potent and very puissant ruler of this realm" (p. 482). Bloom ascends the Viconian ladder from democracy, to aristocracy, to autocracy and virtual theocracy. He prophesies salvation and beatific bliss in "the golden city which is to be, the new Bloomusalem in the Nova Hibernia of the future" (p. 484). *"Thirtytwo workmen . . . construct the new Bloomusalem. It is a colossal edifice, with crystal roof, built in the shape of a huge pork kidney"* (p. 484).

Like most plans for social revolution, Bloom's beneficent reign of justice and pity is contingent on death, destruction, and a political bloodbath demanding the *"instantaneous deaths of many powerful enemies"* (p. 485). The populace is narcotized with public gifts and *"cheap reprints of the World's Twelve Worst Books"* (p. 485). As a successful demagogue, Bloom dispenses "open air justice," creates *"the new nine muses"* (actually twelve), and suggests a plan for "social regeneration": "I stand for the reform of municipal morals and the plain ten commandments. New worlds for old. Union of all, jew, moslem and gentile. . . . General amnesty, weekly carnival, with masked licence, bonuses for all, esperanto the universal brotherhood. No more patriotism of barspongers and dropsical impostors. Free money, free love and a free lay church in a free lay state" (pp. 489–90). The aims of the Bloomite platform are similar to those proposed by HCE in "The Ballad of Persse O'Reilly":

> He was fafafather of all schemes for to bother us
> Slow coaches and immaculate contraceptives for the populace,
> Mare's milk for the sick, seven dry Sundays a week,
> Openair Love and religion's reform,
> > (Chorus) And religious reform,
> > Hideous in form.
>
> > > *(FW* 45)

Like all regimes on the Viconian wheel, the "Paradisiacal Era" of the new Bloomusalem is doomed to explode in anarchy and chaos. The Dublin populace characteristically betrays its illustrious hero. Father Farley condemns Bloom as "an episcopalian, an agnostic, an anythingarian" (p. 490). Bloom's philosophy of tolerance and equanimity proves to be his political nemesis. He publicly condones "mixed races and mixed marriage"—and possibly "mixed bathing" (p. 490). Purefoy accuses him of sexual prophylaxis; and Alexander Dowie vilifies him as a pervert, a non-Christian, and a worshiper of the Scarlet Woman. The crowd turns against Bloom and deposes him from power. Once again, he faces trial as an "abominable person" and a "fiendish libertine" (pp. 490, 492).

Dr. Malachi Mulligan pronounces the defendant "bisexually abnormal" and an "intact virgin":

> Born out of bedlock hereditary epilepsy is present, the consequence of unbridled lust. . . . There are marked symptoms of chronic exhibitionism. Ambidexterity is also latent. He is prematurely bald from selfabuse, perversely idealistic in consequence, a reformed rake, and has metal teeth. In consequence of a family complex he has temporarily lost his memory and I believe him to be more sinned against than sinning. I have made a pervaginal examination and . . . I declare him to be *virgo intacta*. (P. 493)

Dr. Dixon testifies that "Professor Bloom is a finished example of the new womanly man. His moral nature is simple and lovable. Many have found him a dear man, a dear person" (p. 493). The doctor appeals for clemency on the grounds that Bloom "is about to have a baby" (p. 494).

Bloom immediately verifies his androgyny by giving birth to eight gold and silver male children, in keeping with his Jewish mercantile heritage. He performs miracles of acrobacy, healing, impersonation, and parallax; but the judgment of the irate crowd is confirmed by a supernatural messenger. The sign of a "Deadhand" declares that Bloom is neither savior nor God, but a simple "cod" (p. 496). "Lynch him! Roast him! He's as bad as Parnell was" (p. 492).

Bloom suffers a phantasmagoric martyrdom in which every figure from his past takes on the role of accuser or torturer. History, like a huge hockey ball, has been resurrected in Nighttown to become the overpowering "back kick" of culpability.

Like Humphrey Chimpden Earwicker, Bloom is a Kafkaesque defendant on trial for the heinous crime of existence. Out of this nightmare chaos, he emerges as sacrificial scapegoat. *"In a seamless garment marked I. H. S.,"* Bloom *"stands upright amid phoenix flames"* (p. 498). On the threshold of immolation, he identifies with the phoenix, a mythical symbol of Christ and a figure of Viconian renewal. Like the Arabian bird consumed in its own flames, the holocaust *"becomes mute, shrunken, carbonised"* (p. 499), only to be resurrected as a new and purified Messiah, combating temptations of despair and suicide.

Regeneration is literal, and Leopold, *"in babylinen and pelisse, bigheaded"* (p. 501), appears as an infant before the maternal Zoe. Tempted by the sordid gratifications of a bestial world, Bloom steps to the edge of a sensuous inferno. Drugged *"male brutes,"* *"exhaling sulphur of rut and dung"* (p. 501), accost him. He hesitantly enters the zoological brothel that shelters ape-like men and goosefat whores. Kitty Ricketts *"horses"* her foot and *"snakes"* her neck, in rutting invitation to animal enjoyment.

In the midst of this iniquitous den, Stephen Dedalus raves about poetic rites and pagan hymns celebrated *"round David's that is Circe's or what am I saying Ceres' altar"* (p. 504). He describes the *"greatest possible ellipse. Consistent with. The ultimate return"* (p. 504). *"What went forth to the ends of the world to traverse not itself. God, the sun, Shakespeare, a commercial traveller, having itself traversed in reality itself, becomes that self. Wait a moment. Wait a second. Damn that fellow's noise in the street"* (p. 505).

The bard's prophecy embraces both musical lore and dramatic reality. When Bloom finally catches up with his errant charge, *"extremes meet"* and *"Jewgreek is greekjew"* (p. 504). The pagan priest and the Jewish victim collide in a sacramental encounter. They represent extremes of youth and experience, of art and science, of spiritual virginity and middle-aged impotence. In the Circean Mass celebrated by both, history is sacrificed in a ceremony of psychoanalytic purgation.

The two men who symbolize "the greatest possible ellipse" consistent with an "ultimate return" will meet, interact, and eventually resume attitudes of mutual separation. But through their temporary union, both discover the "not-self" contiguous with subjective self-projection—a foreign consciousness made intelligible by an act of sympathetic understanding. In a moment of "interindividual relations," each will fuse with the alter-ego perceived. Stephen will begin to comprehend the humanistic roots of aesthetic creation; and in so doing, he will transcend the solipsistic prison earlier described in "Scylla and Charybdis."

The meeting of Stephen and Bloom is celebrated in a mock apocalypse heralded by Reuben J. Antichrist. The ruler of the universe appears as a hobgoblin *dio boia* reminiscent of Thomas Hardy's ironic "Player." The joker claims to be *"L'homme qui rit! L'homme primigène!"* (p. 506). He teasingly exhorts the characters to play the game of fate: *"Sieurs et dames, faites vos jeux!"* Yet he knows that *"Les jeux sont faits!"* from the beginning. Apocalypse is inevitable: *"(The planets rush together, uttering crepitant cracks.) Rien n'va plus"* (p. 506). The comic cataclysm parodies in Blakean language Deasy's "tightrope" definition of history: the *"End of the World"* is ushered in *"along an infinite invisible tightrope taut from zenith to nadir"* (p. 507). The vaudeville drama of cosmic annihilation, complete with *"two-headed octopus in gillie's kilts"* (p. 507), adumbrates the true Viconian *ricorso* to occur later in the chapter.

After *"the consummation of all things and second coming of Elijah"* (p. 507), the biblical preacher proves prophetic when he asks: "Are you a god or a doggone clod? . . . Florry Christ, Stephen Christ, Zoe Christ, Bloom Christ, Kitty Christ, Lynch Christ, it's up to you to sense that cosmic force. . . . Be a prism. You have that something within, the higher self. You can rub shoulders with a Jesus, a Gautama, an Ingersoll. Are you all in this vibration?" (pp. 507–8). Dowie-Elijah reiterates the dog-god theme of the Black Mass. He preaches the divinity of human consciousness, the new cult of the Logos that will

192

arise out of the ashes of an immolated history—despite, rather -
than because of, the revival sermon, repentant prostitutes, the
eight British beatitudes, and a theosophical mysticism offering
"esthetics and cosmetics . . . for the boudoir" (p. 510).

Stephen, the Mass celebrant, chants the gospel of self-
awareness in words that echo "Scylla and Charybdis." God the
sun (Joyce), Stephen-Shakespeare (his artistic son), and Bloom
(the commercial traveler) are all united in a trinitarian consciousness. But before Bloom can realize its fullness, he must
first transcend the grasp of psychic memory: "I wanted then to
have now concluded. . . . Past was is today. What now is will
then tomorrow as now was be past yester" (p. 515).

Lipoti Virag appears in the guise of Macintosh, "sausaged"
in several overcoats that bespeak the meaty mind. Pimping for
prostitutes, Virag peruses the brothel with lascivious delight.
Grandpapachi accuses Bloom of losing his "mnemotechnic,"
or sexual memory; and he challenges his grandson to lay a
voluptuous whore, "coopfattened" and endowed with "natural
pincushions of quite colossal blubber" (p. 513). The renowned
sexologist offers remedies for "warts" (syphilitic chancres);
and for impotence—"willpower over parasitic tissues," "the
touch of a deadhand" (p. 514), truffles of Perigord, and Red-
bank oysters. "Those succulent bivalves may help us . . . in
cases of nervous debility or viragitis" (p. 516). "From the
sublime to the ridiculous is but a step" (p. 515); but Virag's
libidinous obsession with a life or "reiterated coition" leaves
little room for sublimity. Grandpa prefers the kinetic titillations
of a salacious imagination. His description of oriental eroticism
is rife with primitive lust, violence, and sexual abuse: "Woman, undoing with sweet pudor her belt of rushrope, offers her
allmoist yoni to man's lingam. Short time after man presents
woman with pieces of jungle meat. . . . Then giddy woman
will run about. Strong man grasps woman's wrist. Woman
squeals, bites, spucks. Man, now fierce angry, strikes woman's
fat yadgana" (pp. 519–20).

The figure of Henry Flower, Virag's alter-ego, is hardly
more enticing. *"He has the romantic Saviour's face"* (p. 517),

193

the face that Gerty MacDowell saw in "Nausicaa." Plucking a dulcimer, this disembodied spirit caresses a *"severed female head"* (p. 522). He has apparently murdered to dissect, choosing soul over sensuous reality.

Taking his cue from Lipoti Virag, Bloom confesses to Bella Cohen that he is only "partly" married: he has "mislaid" his mnemotechnic in a household where "the missus is master. Petticoat government" (p. 527). Complaining of impotence and sciatica, he yields to the "massive whoremistress": "Enormously I desiderate your domination. I am exhausted, abandoned, no more young" (p. 528). Bloom's sexual humiliation by Bella/Bello closely mimics the experiences of Severin in Sacher-Masoch's *Venus in Furs*. The accusations against Bloom build up to a scene of transvestite torture. The sadistic Bello transforms him into a sow, a woman, and a gelded ox—all in retaliation for his crime of sexual impotence and for his unmanly eliminative obsession: "Adorer of the adulterous rump!"; "Dungdevourer" (p. 530).

The new "womanly man" longs to act out the kind of female debasement glorified by the medicals in "Oxen of the Sun." If the sexual encounter can be reduced to virile conquest, then Bloom prefers to play the victim, acted upon rather than acting. But his masochistic fantasies backfire when he is feminized and humiliated: "What you longed for has come to pass. Henceforth you are unmanned and mine in earnest" (p. 535). Clothed in a punishment garment, Bloom confesses his guilt for earlier transvestite experiments. He tried on Molly's clothes "only once, a small prank, in Holles street" (p. 536). Languishing in Mrs. Dandrade's castoff shift, he entertained fantasies of sexual violation by forceful male lovers. Shyly, he admits: "It was Gerald converted me to be a true corsetlover when I was female impersonator in the High School play *Vice Versa*" (p. 536). Like HCE, he guiltily stammers: "I rererepugnosed in rerererepugnant" (p. 538).

Bello promises to "administer correction" with the "nosering, the pliers, the bastinado, the hanging hook" (p. 532). In a parody of "Cyclops," she/he rides Bloom sexually as a "cock-

194

horse," a scapegoat for the whoremaster's loss in the Gold Cup Race. Bloom is expiating the sins of *Ulysses*. Earlier in the day, he lusted after the "moving hams" of a woman. Now Bello reduces him to a fleshly morsel of erotic delectation—a piece of swine-flesh to be devoured in a repast that is definitely non-kosher: "Very possibly I shall have you slaughtered and skewered in my stables and enjoy a slice of you with crisp crackling from the baking tin basted and baked like sucking pig with rice and lemon or currant sauce. It will hurt you" (pp. 532–33). Bloom undergoes complete emasculation at the hands of Bello, who wallows in vindictive amusement at the "smut" or "bloody goodghoststory" (p. 538) of her victim's philandering crimes.

A chorus of personified "Sins of the Past" rises to condemn Bloom-Everyman, who must endure a hell more personalized than Dante's Inferno. Bloom is tried and punished in a psychoanalytic expiation of marital failure. He fawns in lascivious bestiality before Bella Cohen until the "bip" of a trouser button jolts him back to reality. The modern Ulysses will not capitulate either to the allurements of his own deep-seated masochism or to Bello's mirror image, the libidinous nymph who offers phallic castration as "one way out" of the pangs of erotic desire: "Only the ethereal. Where dreamy creamy gull waves o'er the waters dull" (p. 552). With a burst of self-confidence, Bloom retorts: "If there were only ethereal where would you all be, postulants and novices? Shy but willing, like an ass pissing" (p. 553). He responds with similar invective to Bella/Bello, whom he now recognizes as the metamorphosed nymph, "mutton dressed as lamb": "Clean your nailless middle finger first, the cold spunk of your bully is dripping from your cockscomb. Take a handful of hay and wipe yourself" (p. 554). Finally, Bloom rescues from Zoe his sexual talisman, "poor mamma's" potato, to which there is "a memory attached" (p. 555).

Before he can fully recover his autonomy, Bloom must undergo still another trial by fire and subjugate the most pernicious "spook" of all, the ghost of Blazes Boylan. As penance for his refusal to do a "man's job" as fertilizer and incubator of Molly,

195

Bloom is condemned to voyeuristic participation in his own cuckoldry. He imagines himself playing Boylan's flunkey, offering vaseline and orangeflower to facilitate the deed. The sadomasochistic fantasy brings him face to face with the ambivalence of his emotions. He not only visualizes but dramatically participates in the spectacle of his wife's infidelity: "You can apply your eye to the keyhole and play with yourself while I just go through her a few times" (p. 566). As husband and lover, Bloom is deeply wounded by Molly's adultery. But at the same time, he feels genuine relief, as well as voyeuristic pleasure, at having found a stud-surrogate for insemination (though not impregnation) of his spouse.

As Stephen and Bloom gaze in a mirror, *"The face of William Shakespeare, beardless, appears there, rigid in facial paralysis, crowned by the reflection of the reindeer antlered hatrack in the hall"* (p. 567). The figure *"crows with a black capon's laugh"* and warns Bloom: "Thou thoughtest as how thou wastest invisible. Gaze. . . . Iagogo! How my Oldfellow chokit his Thursdaymomun" (p. 567). If Bloom thought himself an "invisible" cuckold, he was mistaken. Nothing is invisible in Nighttown. The Shakespearean apparition taunts him for conjugal failure and laughs at the anguish of marital betrayal. The ghost confirms the aesthetic theory earlier presented in "Scylla." Like Iago, the specter is obsessed with infidelity. Primordial wounds of seduction and adultery have paralyzed the Renaissance bard and locked him in an *idée fixe*. Stephen reflects Shakespeare the artist; Bloom reflects the cuckolded husband. Their mutual vision of antlered infamy reminds us that Joyce, the "invisible" artist supposedly paring his fingernails, is actually choking his drama of Thursday, 16 June 1904, full of convenient fictional coincidences.

Like Freud, Joyce recognized the cathartic possibilities of comedy and its power to expose subliminal threats to the light of playful absurdity. The psychodrama of "Nighttown" enables Bloom to purge his repressions through exaggerated reenactment of psychological horror. Comedy allows him to domesticate the monsters that prowl about his anxious psyche. By

196

facing the specters of the unconscious, he gives fear a local habitation and a name and concretizes the deep structure of inarticulate pain that haunts him. Bloom's dreamwork may seem hyperbolic, but it is far from pathological. In the course of "Circe," he dramatically exposes the erotic perversions that have plagued him in fantasies of morose delectation. He publicly does penance for his "sins" against phallic virility: voyeurism, masturbation, effeminacy, transvestism, masochism, and coprophilia.

Bloom is aware of the social opprobrium attached to his fetishes; and he recognizes, as well, society's mistrust of the feminine virtues of compassion and tolerance. Hence his deep-seated guilt, anxiety, and self-recrimination. In 1904, even Freud had few compunctions about condemning behavior that appeared "uncivilized." Civilization, he insisted, was built on the discontents of psychological repression. Sublimation was the principal building block of the superego and the major bequest of Oedipal transference.

In "Circe," James Joyce, like Shem the Penman, writes from the ink of his own digested experience. Just as he comically portrayed the process of defecation in "Calypso," he now tries to incorporate erotic fantasy into the definition of what it means to be truly human. The author is convinced that libidinous phantasms that might seem outrageous or preposterous in social intercourse constitute a basic dimension of human existence. They ought not to be shunned as deviant aberrations.

Joyce dramatizes repressed desire in a frame of comic absurdity. He asks us to confront the darkest recesses of erotic passion, to accept our sensuous imaginings, and to laugh at human nature in the fuller context of civilized pretension. Beneath the scaffolding of power and romantic love, beneath the pomp and circumstance of political theory, exists a frail and somewhat ludicrous species, *homo sapiens*. By shining the light on Nighttown, Joyce exposes our fears and shows us that they are nothing but painted images, dumb shows that need not harm us.

In "Circe," ego gives way to the instinctual id. Stephen and Bloom encounter the "superhuman" world of myth and super-

197

stition. They unmask all that is dark and incomprehensible, including Bella/Bello, Alexander Dowie, and the ghost of Mary Dedalus. The man-god is also a dog-god—divine and bestial, simultaneously. Under the pressures of exhaustion and inebriation, Stephen acknowledges the subterranean activities that transpire in the unconscious. In order to create a fictional microcosm, he must incorporate into his vision the dark underside of experience, as well as its surface manifestation.

Stephen-Christ, the antihero and priest of *Ulysses,* has to demystify the ghosts of personal history before he can begin to forge a new ''conscience'' for himself and for his race. Specters from *Portrait* rise up in comic guise: Father Dolan's *''bald little round jack-in-the box head''* (p. 561) springs from the piano, recalling the ''coffin'' of a dead Jesuit tradition. Even the fantastic images from Clongowes prove disconcerting. The pandybat's sting has been seared into Stephen's soul, and he winces in confusion: ''Hurt my hand somewhere'' (p. 563). Could it be, once more, the pain of Father Dolan's stick?

As the pageant of Nighttown progresses through the Race of Life to the Dance of Death, the comic phantasma grow less innocuous. When the music stops, Stephen too ''stops dead,'' assaulted by the resurrected image of Mary Dedalus: *''Stephen's mother, emaciated, rises stark through the floor in leper grey with a wreath of faded orange blossoms and a torn bridal veil, her face worn and noseless, green with grave mould. Her hair is scant and lank. She fixes her bluecircled hollow eyesockets on Stephen and opens her toothless mouth uttering a silent word''* (pp. 579–80). ''I was once the beautiful May Goulding,'' the specter declares. ''I am dead'' (p. 580). Stephen screams out against this ''bogeyman's trick,'' but the ghost is a real construct of tortured memory. It taunts its victim with sundered family relations, the grave-green earth of Mother Ireland, and the ''snotgreen sea'' of exile.

Stephen begs his mother to utter that ''word known to all men'' (p. 581), the word of love and of human sympathy. The ghost can only reiterate the judgmental word of God. The apparition is obsessed with linear time: ''All must go through it,

198

Stephen. . . . You too. Time will come" (p. 580). "I pray for you in my other world. . . . Years and years I loved you, O my son, my firstborn, when you lay in my womb" (p. 581). Like Garrett Deasy, Stephen's mother appeals to the weight of compiled time to justify her exhortation. She even claims to have been pregnant for "years and years." Mary Dedalus pleads that her son repent "in time" to escape the fires of hell. She associates penance with temporal remission of punishment in "the other world": "Prayer is all powerful. Prayer for the suffering souls in the Ursuline manual, and forty days' indulgence. Repent, Stephen" (p. 581).

Stephen is horrified by the reproving phantasm and tries to shift his culpability to time itself: "*(Choking with fright, remorse and horror.)* They said I killed you, mother. He offended your memory. Cancer did it, not I. Destiny" (p. 580). Stephen defends himself by accusing destiny of his mother's murder. He blames time, the process of aging, and the fatal disease of cancer. The ghost, however, is not appeased. Mary Dedalus vindicates the "grim Reaper" and continues to excoriate her son: "Repent! O, the fire of hell!" (p. 581).

At the height of mental agony, Stephen cries out against the charges of a guilt-ridden past. Echoing "Telemachus," he yells: "The corpsechewer! Raw head and bloody bones!" (p. 581). Strangled with rage, he answers the admonition "Beware! God's hand!" with the furious retort, "Shite!" "*Ah non, par exemple!* The intellectual imagination! With me all or not at all. *Non Serviam!*" (p. 582).

The ghost of Mary Dedalus constitutes the force of historical enslavement driving Stephen to apocalypse. He raises the cry of the antihero, the *Non Serviam* of Lucifer. Stephen *will not serve* a mental construct of temporal-spatial imprisonment; he refuses to be intimidated by specters of the past. Shouting the word *"Nothung!"*, *"He lifts his ashplant high with both hands and smashes the chandelier. Time's livid final flame leaps and, in the following darkness, ruin of all space, shattered glass and toppling masonry"* (p. 583).

With a single blow, Stephen shatters the foundations of a

nightmare history. His cry *"Nothung!"* is similar to the roar of thunder in *Finnegans Wake*. The Wagnerian gesture initiates a Viconian *ricorso* that salvages "nothing" of the old order. As artist and priest, Stephen ordains a new era of the "intellectual imagination" and exults in the powers of existential consciousness. He celebrates a world of phenomenal reality, a world in which existence precedes and determines essence: the human mind "creates a meaning" for itself and for the earth.

The "ruin of all space" echoes Stephen's earlier ruminations in "Nestor" (p. 24). In contrast to the *Fiat Lux* of Genesis, Stephen's gestures proclaim, "Let there be darkness." Let the road of past history, a "disappointed bridge," be darkened and annihilated. And let each individual emerge from blind tradition to fashion his own reality *ex nihilo* in the present. Stephen's apocalyptic moment symbolically challenges both the Light of the World celebrated in Saint John's gospel and the "allbright" deity worshipped by Garrett Deasy.

Like Vico and like William Blake, Joyce believed that out of chaos comes new energy and, out of anarchy, rebirth. The Wagnerian act of destruction in "Circe" is "nihilistic" in the Sartrian sense. By smashing the chandelier, Stephen is asserting his desire to be God. He is engaged in a process of reverse creation, which at the same time appropriates the object it destroys. If the lamp stands for the light of Western tradition, then Stephen symbolically negates the past in order to fashion a new reality grounded in the epiphanic moment. Plunging the world into darkness, he attempts to annihilate history by making it a controllable object of personal consciousness. Because art demands a postcreation, the artist-hero must destroy the old world in order to posit a revolutionary vision of the cosmos.

Stephen's rebellious gesture constitutes the turning point of "Circe." Like Prospero, the priest whose task is finished, the poet abandons his ashplant and flees from Bella Cohen's whorehouse.[3] The climax of dramatic ritual explodes with the rhythmic intensity of sexual orgasm. Stephen experiences a release from mental bondage and rushes forth impelled by exuberant liberation. History has proved the ultimate victim of

200

the sacrifice: a "transubstantiation" of the past into impotent present memory concludes the purgative ceremony.

Stephen leaves Bella Cohen's with the power to "kill the priest and the king" (p. 589)—to release himself, in Blakean terms, from a lifetime of servitude to church and state.[4] When Edward VII appears as *"a grand elect perfect and sublime mason"* (p. 590), plastering *Défense d'uriner* signs, Stephen clings to his role as "toppler" of masonry. In the face of the mason-king, he begins to preach his gospel to Private Carr in terms of political philosophy: "I understand your point of view, though I have no king myself for the moment. . . . But this is the point. You die for your country, suppose. . . . Not that I wish it for you. But I say: Let my country die for me. Up to the present it has done so. I don't want it to die. Damn death. Long live life!" (p. 591). Stephen rejects the death-dealing philosophy of traditional history—the political "necessity" that has produced the ludicrous Edward VII, who *"levitates over heaps of slain in the garb and with the halo of Joking Jesus, a white jujube in his phosphorescent face"* (p. 591). When Mother Ireland appears as "Old Gummy Granny," Stephen indicts her with the *Portrait* epithet of "old sow that eats her farrow" (p. 595). With one breath he exterminates the figure of Granny, an anachronistic phantasm in a world of intellectual freedom.[5]

Stephen's dialectic has enraged the two British soldiers, who are infuriated by his supposed insolence toward Cissy Caffrey. Private Carr screams: *"(With ferocious articulation.)* I'll do him in, so help me fucking Christ! I'll wring the bastard fucker's bleeding blasted fucking windpipe!" (p. 600). Stephen, the "new Christ," identifies Carr with Judas. But like Christ, he refuses to wield his augur's rod. He echoes both Jesus' answer to Saint Peter and Nietzsche's definition of philosophy: "Stick, no. Reason. This feast of pure reason" (p. 601). It is for the feast of reason that Stephen suffers the martyrdom of an Antichrist. Like Dolph in *Finnegans Wake,* the artist refuses to retaliate and falls victim to the political man of action. "Personally, I detest action" (p. 589), he insists. Carr *"rushes towards Stephen, fists outstretched, and strikes*

201

him in the face. Stephen totters, collapses, falls stunned. He lies prone, his face to the sky, his hat rolling to the wall. Bloom follows and picks it up'' (p. 601).

Struck down by Carr, Stephen undergoes a symbolic decapitation. But Bloom, a witness to the crucifixion, rises as transubstantial father and healer of the Antichrist. He shelters Stephen from the Dublin police, as well as from the ''polite'' invitation of Corny Kelleher, who appears bearing *''a death wreath in his hand''* (p. 603). Wielding the ashplant, Bloom resurrects his charge from death-like immobility. He asserts a commitment to Stephen the only way he knows how—by uttering Masonic phrases that evoke the ''moraculous'' tide of cyclical consciousness and resuscitate the ghost of his lost son Rudy:

> (*He murmurs.*) . . . swear that I will always hail, ever conceal, never reveal, any part or parts, art or arts . . . in the rough sands of the sea . . . a cabletow's length from the shore . . . where the tide ebbs . . . and flows . . .
> (. . . *Against the dark wall a figure appears slowly, a fairy boy of eleven, a changeling, kidnapped, dressed in an Eton suit with glass shoes and a little bronze helmet, holding a book in his hand. He reads from right to left inaudibly, smiling, kissing the page.*)
> Bloom: (*Wonderstruck, calls inaudibly.*) Rudy! (P. 609)

Rudy returns, a child who has retained the Jewish heritage of his twice-converted father. Unlike Virag and the elder Rudolph, little Rudy appears as the reconciled Judaic lamb-figure. He *''gazes unseeing into Bloom's eyes and goes on reading, kissing, smiling. He has a delicate mauve face. On his suit he has diamond and ruby buttons. In his free left hand he holds a slim ivory cane with a violet bowknot. A white lambkin peeps out of his waistcoat pocket''* (p. 609). Revived as a ''dandified'' aesthete, Rudy is the last phantasm to be exorcised from Bloom's psyche. With the apparition of his dead son, Bloom is released from the neurosis of guilt and impotence he has so long associated with the child. The ghost is resurrected, only to become a memory—to relinquish its filial heritage to the new son whose rebellion has negated past history.

By the end of the ''Circe'' episode, Bloom has been liberated from irrational self-hatred. Redeemed from the guilt that has haunted him since Rudy's death, he begins to feel reconciled to his son's loss, and he is able to embrace a new paternity. In an act of mental freedom, he assumes the existential role of adopted parent to Stephen. He becomes the bard's ''transubstantial father'' in a bond of fellowship rooted in the present. Bloom's paternity is a product of the instant—a reality that springs, fully born, from the psychological transformation that occurs in Nighttown. ''Circe'' ends with a reconciliation and with a resurrection: Stephen and Bloom are emancipated from the cloying cerements of historical bondage.

For both characters, the heritage of the flesh is confining, neurotic, and self-annihilating. Stephen is haunted by the ghost of his mother; Bloom is obsessed with memories of Virag and Rudy. By ritual reenactment of the past in ''Circe,'' the two men escape the categories of physical lineage. They transcend history as mentally uninhibited egos, at liberty to form meaningful attachments in the present. Through his meeting with Leopold Bloom, Stephen is able to identify another individual as subject of the gospel of humanism that he earlier expounded in ''Nestor.'' For the first time in *Ulysses,* Stephen begins to make contact with the world of ''interindividual relations.'' He discovers through Bloom that ''word known to all men'' (p. 581), the good word of sympathy that liberates the aesthetic imagination of the artist.

Purged of the ghosts of their past, Stephen and Bloom come together in a new relationship as father and son. For the older man, the incident marks a revitalization of paternity. Stephen is the adopted son he can treat with fatherly solicitude. Bloom acts the part of a man, a competent citizen, though keyless. He creates a momentary kinship that is significant, despite its precarious brevity. In the course of ''Circe,'' Bloom has successfully met and conquered the specters of his dead father; of Rudy, his deceased son; and of Blazes Boylan, the lover who signals the death of a hitherto monogamous relationship with Molly. On this day, Bloom has died as a husband, to be born as a cuckold; or perhaps, like the phoenix, to come full circle and regain his manhood. The hero of *Ulysses* proves himself a man in the most human sense of the word.

Readers too often apply the "fallacy of imitative form" to the conversation later reported in "Ithaca." They assume that Joyce's authorial distance and catechetical style indicate coldness in the meeting of Stephen and Bloom. Joyce declared in a letter to Frank Budgen: "I am writing *Ithaca* in the form of a mathematical catechism. All events are resolved into their cosmic physical, psychical etc. equivalents. . . . Bloom and Stephen thereby become heavenly bodies, wanderers like the stars at which they gaze."[6]

In "Ithaca," both men awake from a nightmare history to cast their shadows, metaphorically, "beyond the farthest star." Unencumbered by guilt and repression, they acknowledge a communal bond of human fellowship rooted in the fullness of the present. Beyond linear time, and beyond the restrictions of historical confinement, they experience mental liberation and the intersubjective discovery of one another.[7]

At this point in "Circe," the two characters have reversed roles. Stephen has become Christ the sacrificial victim; and Bloom functions as Christ the Savior. In "Eumaeus," a drunken Stephen mutters: "*Christus* or Bloom his name is, or, after all, any other, *secundum carnem*" (p. 643). And Bloom echoes the New Testament when he asks Stephen why he left his "father's house" (p. 619). In "Ithaca," Stephen more soberly conjectures that one of Bloom's "concealed identities" is that of a Christ-figure: "The traditional figure of hypostasis, depicted by Johannes Damascenus, Lentulus Romanus and Epiphanius Monachus as leucodermic, sesquipedalian with wine-dark hair" (p. 689). The narrator is progressively engaged in "substituting Stephen for Bloom Stoom" and "Bloom for Stephen Blephen" (p. 682), until both men are united in a sympathetic moment of shared perception: "Silent, each contemplating the other in both mirrors of the reciprocal flesh of theirhisnothis fellowfaces" (p. 702).

204

In the course of "Circe," Stephen and Bloom undergo a revolutionary alteration in consciousness. They conquer the ghosts of the past and stand open to "interindividual relations" in the future. Their radical transformation of mental perspective gives evidence of a psychoanalytic encounter that proves both cathartic and liberating. When private absurdity is confronted in exaggerated guise, the mind gains control over terror and guilt. Comic distance gives birth to cosmic awareness.

In the gospel of *Ulysses,* Joyce is bringing us the good news of the "word." Each individual has within himself the powers of the Logos—the "moraculous" potential of the psyche to absorb, transcend, and re-create experience through the artistic capaciousness of the intellectual imagination. The human mind can shatter the nightmare of history and challenge the specters of psychological enclosure. Past memory functions as an *ekstasis* of the present moment. Through a radical act of existential creation, consciousness fashions a new reality from present, epiphanic revelation. "This is the postcreation."

1. Shechner, *Joyce in Nighttown,* p. 105.

2. Mark Shechner suggests that the characters in the episode "hallucinate their reality. Boundaries evaporate; inner and outer interpenetrate, and idenity becomes a flux of interlocking possibilities" (ibid., p. 120). In contrast, Marilyn French asserts that "Bloom and Stephen are not hallucinating. The hallucinations are hypostatizations of their hidden feelings; on the naturalistic level, the characters are simply feeling. The hallucinations are production numbers staged by the author for the audience. . . . Circe is a nightmare sent by god-Joyce to the reader" (*The Book as World*, p. 187). French's explanation of the chapter's dramatic action fails to account for the revolutionary alteration in consciousness that Stephen and Bloom experience, a change comprehensible only in the light of psychoanalytic confrontation and mental exorcism.

3. For a further discussion of the significance of Stephen's ashplant in the "Circe" episode, see Morris Beja's article "The Wooden Sword: Threatener and Threatened in the Fiction of James Joyce."

4. In his recent study *The Consciousness of Joyce,* Richard Ellmann also interprets the climactic scene in "Circe" as the destruction of space and time, and as a political act of defiance against the authority of priest and king. "The priest lays claim to an eternity of time, as the king if he could would rule over infinite space; and against these forces, anthropomorphized in earthly authorities, Stephen and Bloom have to muster their own forces" (pp. 79–80).

5. Granny is an obvious parody of the "Old Woman" who appears in Yeats's play *Cathleen ni Hoolihan: "(Thrusts a dagger towards Stephen's hand.)* Remove him, acushla. At 8:35 a.m. you will be in heaven and Ireland will be free" (p. 600). Unlike Michael Gillane, Stephen will not remove "the strangers" by force.

6. Joyce, *Letters,* 1:159–60.

7. In his essay "*Ulysses:* A Structuralist Perspective," Robert Scholes suggests that in the last chapters of *Ulysses* Joyce was moving toward "the collapse of individuated characterization" and "a radical redefinition of the world itself and man's place in it." "As his career developed, he accepted less and less willingly the notion of characters bounded by their own skins, and of actions which take place at one location in space-time and then are lost forever. . . . Joyce attacked the ego itself, beginning with his own. . . . The cybernetic serenity of his later work was long coming and hard won. . . . Stephen Dedalus is Joyce's bioenergetic self-portrait, while Leopold Bloom is his cybernetic self-portrait" (Robert Scholes, *Structuralism in Literature: An Introduction,* pp. 181, 183).

206

"Eumaeus" and "Ithaca": *Nostos*

After the experiences of Nighttown, Stephen and Bloom accompany one another first to a cabman's shelter, then to 7 Eccles Street. The significance of their encounter and the question of Bloom's fatherhood have long been debated by readers of *Ulysses*. Are the two men destined to become lifetime companions, solacing one another in exile? Will Stephen return to give Molly Italian lessons and win her affections? Or do the characters separate, never to meet again? These are questions that Joyce refuses to answer, and to which no reading of *Ulysses* will supply a clue. The author defeats our expectations of a traditional denouement: the knot is wound up, but never unraveled. Joyce deflates our assumptions of progressive linear development. He will not model his book on *a priori* structures of realism or observe the traditional novel plot.[1] Rather than speculating beyond the novel or fabricating extraliterary lives for its characters, we must concentrate on what does occur in the

207

Nostos section of *Ulysses*. We are forced to turn our gaze directly toward the aesthetic object presented to us by the author.

In "Eumaeus," Bloom leads his inebriate charge to a cabman's shelter, buys him coffee, tries to engage him in conversation, and finally invites him home. The entire episode is characterized by confusion, incertitude, ambiguity, and coincidence. Events are unpredictable, appearances unreliable. Things may not be what they seem: the conflict between appearance and reality is central to the chapter. W. B. Murphy speaks of "Simon Dedalus," a marksman in Hengler's circus. Bloom unconsciously identifies with Murphy, the *Pseudangelos* who will return home to discover "his better half, wrecked in his affections" (p. 624). Tales of Murphy, Enoch Arden, Ben Bolt, and Rip van Winkle reinforce Bloom's "hesitency" to recover his beleaguered domicile. "Bow to the inevitable," he muses. "Grin and bear it. I remain with much love your brokenhearted husband" (p. 625).

Bloom is preoccupied and despondent; Stephen is lost in a drunken stupor. Little communication occurs between the two men, who seem to talk at cross purposes whenever they speak. Bloom defines the soul as "brainpower," "convolutions of the grey matter" (p. 633). Stephen retorts with a cynical parody of Aristotle, Aquinas, and Thomas Hardy; he insists that the soul is "simple" and incorruptible, but subject to the whimsical caprice of a *dio boia*. The two characters are "poles apart"—or so it would seem. Bloom stumbles toward the articulation of an agnostic philosophy, a gospel of humanism, and a Marxist view of political economy. Although Stephen mockingly expounds Catholic dogma, he shares the older man's perspective: his apparent disclaimer is actually a skeptical mode of agreement.

Similarly, Bloom feels rebuked when Stephen insists that Ireland "belongs to him" as an aesthetic subject. The younger man refuses to join Bloom's socialist utopia. He repudiates Irish "propaganda literature" and the Celtic Renaissance. Stephen declines to play the role of Gaelic "bard" to Ireland, though he *will* function as her cynical and Socratic conscience, emulating

208

the Renaissance fool who tattoos tales of wisdom on the foolscap of his body and speaks to humanity through stories of comic import.

Like Antonio, the artist who emblazons his face onto Murphy's tattoo, Joyce is writing himself into the novel through satirical involution. The figure "sixteen" appears on the sailor's chest: "And what's the number for?" (p. 632). Murphy never responds, and neither does Joyce. Sixteen is associated with homosexuality in erotic numerology. Bloom thinks of the number when he meditates on the Criminal Law Amendment Act (though not on the section that prohibits the "love that dare not speak its name"). And the reader is aware that this is the sixteenth chapter of the novel. The number may be a clue to secret mysteries, or it may simply function as a red herring. There may not be "one vestige of truth in it" (p. 621). As Stephen warns: "Sounds are impostures. . . . Like names" (p. 622).

"Eumaeus" unfolds in a style of clichéd, inscrutable, and exasperating prose. What is the figure in Joyce's intricate carpet? After the verbal experiments of "Sirens," "Oxen of the Sun," and "Circe," Joyce returns to "narrative, old." He gives us a parodic rendition of nineteenth-century fiction, full of circumlocution, inflated bombast, and fustian elegance. Joyce titillates our hopes and our curiosity. At precisely the moment of heightened expectation, he refuses to allow us the satisfaction of emotional release.

When Stephen and Bloom come together, they are locked in separate, private worlds. Bloom is procrastinating and Stephen is confused. One man must "act" by returning to conjugal disappointment; the other must determine to set out on a path of artistic exile. The prose of the chapter is not imitative, but descriptive. Despite emotional preoccupation and drunken stupefaction, the two men are attempting to get acquainted. Each makes brief forays out of solipsistic reverie toward some kind of friendly exchange. The style of the episode forces us to recognize the difficulties involved in communication. Stephen and Bloom must wade through an abyss of fortune and of

209

temperament, using the only tools their society has to offer—a cumbersome vocabulary, restrictive cliché, political opinion, and vacuous rhetoric. The process is tedious, often labyrinthine—yet a necessary prelude to understanding.

The excess baggage of "Eumaeus" suggests the kind of impediments that hinder genuine fellowship. The words at our disposal are usually inadequate; the "language of gestures" gives hope, but not assurance. We traverse the formidable gulf between private consciousness and public communication with tremendous vicissitude. Like the builders of Babel, we all murmur in different tongues. We talk at cross-purposes, and usually to ourselves. Each person alludes to universals that actually depend on a private vocabulary; language is conditioned by previous experience and by present state of mind. We ascribe diverse connotations to the same words or use different words as synonyms for analogous apprehensions. We may argue rhetorically with someone whose feelings we share; or we may attach entirely incongruous referents to identical linguistic symbols. Personal relationship is never facile: it is demanding, even improbable. We must grope through the disorderly muddle of human life toward sympathy, understanding, and compassion. The quest for "interindividual relations" is arduous indeed. And Joyce will not spare us any of the tedium or irritation involved.

In "Eumaeus," Stephen is "not yet perfectly sober" (p. 614), and Bloom feels apprehensive about returning to his wife. Nevertheless, something significant *does* happen: the two men recognize their mutual concern for humanism and the similarity of their day's experiences. Bloom recounts his heroic action in the face of the bigoted Citizen and proposes a philosophy of universal tolerance:

> —Of course, Mr. Bloom proceeded to stipulate, you must look at both sides of the question. It is hard to lay down any hard and fast rules as to right and wrong but room for improvement all round there certainly is. . . . It's all very fine to boast of mutual superiority but what about mutual equality? I resent violence or intolerance in any shape or form. It never reaches anything or stops anything.

210

A revolution must come on the due instalments plan. It's a patent absurdity on the face of it to hate people because they live round the corner and speak another vernacular, so to speak.

—Memorable bloody bridge battle and seven minutes' war, Stephen assented, between Skinner's alley and Ormond market.

—Yes, Mr. Bloom thoroughly agreed, entirely endorsing the remark. . . .

All those wretched quarrels, in his humble opinion, stirring up bad blood . . . were very largely a question of the money question which was at the back of everything, greed and jealousy, people never knowing when to stop. (P. 643)

As usual, Bloom is the "allround man" with stereoscopic vision. He insists on looking at "both sides of the question" and defends the philosophy that he earlier elaborated before the mob in Kiernan's pub. Remembering the unfavorable reception of his afternoon speech, Bloom is hesitant to mention love, "the opposite of hatred." He cloaks his argument in circumlocutions such as "on the face of it" and "so to speak." But he continues to defend an ethic of humanistic inclusion: those who are alien must be brought within the circle of compassion. Barriers of race, language, religion, and geography are senseless. It is absurd to hate one's fellows on the basis of arbitrary contingencies, "because they live round the corner" (p. 643).

Despite his inebriation, Stephen responds to Bloom's speech with a shock of recognition. He recalls his own experience in "Nestor" and murmurs assent: "Memorable bloody bridge battle and seven minutes' war" (p. 643). Bloom is preaching the same gospel that Stephen proposed to Garrett Deasy. All history is a "disappointed bridge," a series of Pyrrhic victories that only perpetuate violence. Bloom waged his "seven minutes' war" with the Citizen to defy a nightmare history composed of "bloody bridge battles."

In a moment of drunken connection, Stephen identifies Bloom as a "comrade in arms" who challenges Irish nationalism, chauvinism, and blind intolerance. Bloom's boast of his Odyssean victory over the Citizen functions as an epiphany for Stephen, who remarks: "*Christus* or Bloom his name is, or, after all, any other, *secundum carnem*" (p. 643). Bloom is

211

shown forth as a messianic figure, the new "lamb of God": "People could put up with being bitten by a wolf but what properly riled them was a bite from a sheep" (p. 658).

Amid tales of wonder and infamy, Stephen and Bloom begin to establish a rapport based on mutual trust and sympathetic good will. As Bloom grows more candid with Stephen, he becomes increasingly honest with himself. Bloom contemplates adultery, but he avoids the pain of direct confrontation. He twice recounts to himself the story of Parnell's affair with Kitty O'Shea; and in so doing, he moves from public condemnation to private understanding. As a kinetic poet, Bloom considers the political scandal in terms of emotional compulsion. He tries to rationalize the motives for conjugal infidelity and to comprehend the forces of extramarital attraction. By confronting the "unknown" dimensions of Parnell's adultery, Bloom is desperately attempting to resign himself to the "known" case of Molly's infidelity. History functions as a thinly veiled metaphor for introspective analysis.

Cloaking his own grief in a tribute to Parnell, Bloom concludes that adultery should be considered "a case for the two parties themselves" (p. 655). He wants to be "honest and aboveboard about the whole business" and to avoid "the same old matrimonial tangle alleging misconduct" (p. 654). ("Why cant we all remain friends over it instead of quarrelling," Molly asks [p. 777]). Bloom has little patience with the melodrama of Victorian sex scandals. He offers a searing "naturalistic" account of the affair: "Whereas the simple fact of the case was it was simply a case of the husband not being up to the scratch with nothing in common between them beyond the name and then a real man arriving on the scene. . . . The eternal question of the life connubial, needless to say, cropped up. Can real love, supposing there happens to be another chap in the case, exist between married folk?" (p. 651). It is precisely this "connubial question" that haunts Bloom throughout "Eumaeus."

By way of Parnell and the nightmare of history, the "cuckolded" husband circuitously rearrives at a tolerant understanding of human frailty. Bloom knows that beauty and power are

212

tenuous, that political and romantic heroes *do* have mundane roots. He champions Parnell against the Irish populace and vilifies the fickle crowd for dehumanizing its leader: "they discovered to their vast discomfiture that their idol had feet of clay, after placing him upon a pedestal" (p. 654). Bloom refuses to make the same mistake with Molly. He does not place his wife "on a pedestal" or insist that she be "stonecold" and dispassionate, like the Junonian statues in the National Museum. In fact, he admires her Mediterranean temperament: "it was just the wellknown case of hot passion, pure and simple, . . . she also was Spanish or half so, types that wouldn't do things by halves, passionate abandon of the south" (p. 652).

Bloom shows Stephen Molly's photo, hoping it will "speak for itself" (p. 653). But what does Bloom want the picture to *say*? Critics have suggested that he is "pimping" for Molly, offering her to Stephen in a covert homosexual liaison. Like the number sixteen and old Antonio, the hint is a false clue. Joyce is playing with our expectations, manipulating the traditional sentiments we associate with male friendship.

Molly is so conspicuously a part of Bloom's identity that he *must* allude to her in order to establish intimacy with Stephen. Bloom is proud of his wife's beauty and accomplishments. He hopes that the younger man will respect him for winning this "Oriental prize of Dublin." But more importantly, Bloom wants to share with Stephen his own passionate admiration for the "mother-wife" and "earth-goddess" at the focal point of his consciousness. This is the one gift that Bloom can offer his newfound son.

Molly later thinks: "what is he driving at now showing him my photo . . . I wonder he didnt make him a present of it altogether and me too after all why not . . . they all write about some woman in their poetry well I suppose he wont find many like me . . . then hell write about me lover and mistress" (pp. 774–76). Molly might serve Stephen as a muse of beauty and inspiration; and she might introduce him to the "warm, fullblooded life" of human affection. Presenting Molly's graven image, Bloom offers her for public worship.

By the end of "Eumaeus," the two protagonists are locked in a familiar "*tête-à-tête*." Stephen, unused to physical contact of any kind, is leaning on his companion and touching the "strange kind of flesh of a different man" (p. 660). Throughout the chapter, Joyce has strewn prolific allusions to "six sixteen," "old Antonio," and the Criminal Law Amendment Act. By interpolating lines from "The Low-Backed Car" in the episode's concluding paragraph, he portrays the two men on their way *"to be married by Father Maher"* (p. 665). Joyce is deliberately challenging archaic responses to the range of human relationship. The friendship between Stephen and Bloom is based on agape rather than on Eros. The cabman or the narrator may see something queer about the homophiliac embrace, which calls to mind the unrequited sexual desire celebrated in an Irish ballad. Such a perspective, however, adheres to the fabric of Victorian melodrama. It implies a traditional resolution of plot through erotic union, marital intrigue, or the discovery of blood relationship. In actuality, Stephen and Bloom have done little more than "get acquainted." They have initiated a humane connection based on sympathy and genuine good will.[2]

Bloom is about to face the dilemma of conjugal displacement. He hopes that Stephen will provide him with distraction, consolation, and support in the impending crisis. In the "Ithaca" episode, Stephen and Bloom proceed to 7 Eccles Street and partake of cocoa and cream as part of a eucharistic communion. The event acknowledges a bond between the two men, who share a nocturnal feast in celebration of their fortuitous meeting. The potation of "god-food" (*theobroma*) is a love-offering. Bloom relinquishes the symposiarchal right to his moustache cup and drinks from a mug similar to Stephen's. He serves "extraordinarily to his guest and, in reduced measure, to himself the viscous cream ordinarily reserved for the breakfast of his wife Marion" (p. 677). The communion is momentary, without promise of future significance. But in a world of ever changing phenomena, only the "instant" can point to the minor victories of human life.

214

During their conversation, Stephen and Bloom discover other "common factors of similarity between their respective like and unlike reactions to experience": "Both were sensitive to artistic impressions musical in preference to plastic or pictorial. Both preferred a continental to an insular manner of life, a cisatlantic to a transatlantic place of residence. Both indurated by early domestic training and an inherited tenacity of heterodox resistance professed their disbelief in many orthodox religious, national, social and ethical doctrines. Both admitted the alternately stimulating and obtunding influence of hetero-sexual magnetism'' (p. 666). As Helmut Bonheim notes, the two men rebel against the "crooked ess" of society and abjure "the power of the family at the personal level, the church at the religious, and the state at the political level."[3]

Leopold Bloom feels "recurrent frustration" at his inability to "amend many social conditions, the product of inequality and avarice and international animosity" (p. 696). Neverthe-less, he recognizes the limitations of the human situation. Life is *not* "infinitely perfectible." One must deal with "the generic conditions imposed by natural, as distinct from human law, as integral parts of the human whole: . . . the painful character of the ultimate functions of separate existence, the agonies of birth and death: . . . catastrophic cataclysms which make terror the basis of human mentality: . . . the fact of vital growth, through convulsions of metamorphosis from infancy through maturity to decay'' (p. 697). Bloom's all-encompassing sympathy stems from his observation of the temporal-spatial conditions that circumscribe freedom. Each person is born, lives, and dies in isolation: he cannot alter the functions of separate existence, nor can he change the course of a generative process that hurls him toward annihilation. Bloom acknowledges that "from inexis-tence to existence he came to many and was as one received: . . . from existence to nonexistence gone he would be by all as none perceived" (pp. 667–68). As a "scientific observer," Bloom cannot modify the absurdity of the human situation. He is helpless to "substitute other more acceptable phenomena in place of the less acceptable phenomena to be removed" (p.

697). His only recourse is a stoic attitude in the face of inexorable circumstance.

Through meditations "increasingly vaster," Bloom moves toward a cosmic perspective. He contemplates "the parallax or parallactic drift of socalled fixed stars, in reality evermoving from immeasurably remote eons to infinitely remote futures in comparison with which the years, threescore and ten, of allotted human life formed a parenthesis of infinitesimal brevity" (p. 698). Bloom thinks of the infinite spaces surrounding the world and of an eternity devouring the life-span of each individual. Like Pascal, he is fascinated by the "two infinites" defining existence. The universe is bounded by endless space, yet the void penetrates into the center of every particle of matter. In "obverse meditations of involution increasingly less vast," Bloom thinks "of the incalculable trillions of billions of millions of imperceptible molecules contained by cohesion of molecular affinity in a single pinhead: of the universe of human serum constellated with red and white bodies, themselves universes of void space constellated with other bodies," all divisible until, "if the progress were carried far enough, nought nowhere was never reached" (p. 699).

It seems probable that Bloom's philosophical musings have been inspired by the *Pensées* of Pascal, who writes:

> The whole visible world is only an imperceptible atom in the ample bosom of nature. No idea approaches it. We may enlarge our conceptions beyond all imaginable space; we only produce atoms in comparison with the reality of things. It is an infinite sphere, the centre of which is everywhere, the circumference nowhere. . . .
>
> Returning to himself, let man consider what he is in comparison with all existence; let him regard himself as lost in this remote corner of nature. . . What is man in the Infinite?
>
> But to show him another prodigy equally astonishing, let him examine the most delicate things he knows. Let a mite be given him, with its minute body and parts incomparably more minute, . . . blood in the veins, humours in the blood, drops in the humours, vapours in the drops. Dividing these last things again, let him exhaust his powers of conception. . . . I will let him see therein a new abyss. I will paint for him not only the visible

216

universe, but all that he can conceive of nature's immensity in the womb of this abridged atom. . . .

For in fact what is man in nature? A Nothing in comparison with the Infinite, an All in comparison with the Nothing, a mean between nothing and everything.[4]

Pascal offers a theological solution to the terrors of the void: "These extremes meet and reunite by force of distance, and find each other in God, and in God alone."[5] The seventeenth-century philosopher appeals to a metaphysical noumenon to unite the two infinites.

Leopold Bloom leaves no room for a deity in his cosmic speculations. He looks only to the phenomena of the visible world, and he rejects traditional metaphors that describe the expansive "heavens." For Bloom, the sky is "not a heaventree, not a heavengrot, not a heavenbeast, not a heavenman" (p. 701). Alone in an unconscious and indifferent universe, the individual must confront the terrors of finite existence. Bloom is willing to acknowledge the "parenthesis of infinitesimal brevity" that punctuates human life:

> Alone, what did Bloom feel?
> The cold of interstellar space, thousands of degrees below freezing point on the absolute zero of Fahrenheit, Centigrade or Réaumur: the incipient intimations of proximate dawn. (P. 704)

Unlike Stephen Dedalus, Bloom cannot affirm "his significance as a conscious rational animal proceeding syllogistically from the known to the unknown and a conscious rational reagent between a micro and a macrocosm ineluctably constructed upon the incertitude of the void" (p. 697). The micro and the macrocosm refer to the two infinites in Bloom's meditation. As Pascal explains:

> The nature of our existence hides from us the knowledge of first beginnings which are born of the Nothing; and the littleness of our being conceals from us the sight of the Infinite.
> This is our true state; this is what makes us incapable of certain knowledge and of absolute ignorance. We sail within a vast sphere, ever drifting in uncertainty, driven from end to end.[6]

217

Both extremes are constructed on the "incertitude of the void," with the human individual as sole mediator between two worlds he cannot fully understand.

Stephen Dedalus is aware of his own importance as a thinker who can proceed syllogistically from observed phenomena to the contemplation of abstract truths. He is satisfied with his role as philosopher and artist. In contrast, Leopold Bloom, the "competent keyless citizen," proceeds "energetically from the unknown to the known through the incertitude of the void" (p. 697). A man of action, Bloom goes from the abstract to the concrete. From the two extremes that define human existence, he contemplates the unalterable phenomena of the "known" world around him. He regards birth, love, and death from a cosmic perspective that evokes universal compassion for mankind. Scientific speculation leads him back to sympathy for his fellowmen, who must endure the cold of interstellar space without possible reprieve.

From the point of view of eternity, no human victories are permanent, no relationships complete. Nevertheless, the individual must proceed energetically through incertitude to creative action. He cannot "cease to strive," as Stephen is tempted to do at the end of "Scylla and Charybdis." Within the ephemeral "instant," the human being is obliged to *act* and to develop the full potentials of existence. He must work toward self-creation, as well as toward an intersubjective understanding of his fellowmen.

In "Ithaca," Stephen and Bloom eat together, chat, and urinate in the garden. The events of the episode appear to be inconsequential, until we consider Bloom's recollection of other "nocturnal perambulations in the past." He realizes that this is the first time he has enjoyed "interindividual relations" with anyone since Rudy's death:

> What reflection concerning the irregular sequence of dates 1884, 1885, 1886, 1888, 1892, 1893, 1904 did Bloom make before their arrival at their destination?
>
> He reflected that the progressive extension of the field of individual development and experience was regressively accompanied

218

by a restriction of the converse domain of interindividual relations. (P. 667)

Bloom's conversation with Stephen marks the first genuine "communication" he has enjoyed since 1893. For the past eleven years, he has inhabited a shell of neurotic isolation. His meeting with Stephen consitutes a significant change in his mode of existence. Bloom overcomes a decade of mourning for his consubstantial infant son by establishing a transubstantial relationship of paternity with Stephen. Bloom conquers emotional impotence and is able to bring his "adopted son" in contact with the active world of social understanding. He is satisfied: "To have sustained no positive loss. To have brought a positive gain to others. Light to the gentiles" (p. 676). Bloom's newly discovered paternity will later give him the courage to realize that he has "sustained no positive loss," either in the Gold Cup race, or in the case of Molly's adultery.

As Stephen and Bloom emerge "silently, doubly dark, from obscurity" (p. 698), they make a liturgical exodus, with Stephen as deacon and Bloom as acolyte. The "doubly dark" figures eschew the evangelical light and turn to the glimmer of the stars. Earlier, when Bloom chanted phrases from the Jewish anthem, Stephen heard in the "profound ancient male unfamiliar melody the accumulation of the past" (p. 689). Bloom puts Stephen in touch with Hebraic and with Celtic history: he shares with his guest the burden of racial identity, now celebrated in the context of transcendence. Stephen clings to the role of aesthetic priest and Irish exile; and Bloom sees in his companion's "quick young male familiar form the predestination of a future" (p. 689).

The obscure catechetical style of "Ithaca" locates Stephen and Bloom in a rapidly expanding context of cosmic awareness. It provides a vast frame for their sacramental meeting. Joyce filters the events of the evening through an abstract mathematical perspective that diffuses sentimental and emotional resonances. Surrounded by the infinite spaces of the universe, the protagonists are transformed into "heavenly bodies, wanderers like the stars at which they gaze."[7] Suspended between two infinites, they nevertheless affirm the dignity of human consciousness.

Despite the debris of scientific and technical detail in "Ithaca," Stephen and Bloom manage to utter the "good word" of fellowship that resounds through interstellar space. They symbolically merge in the shared identity of "Stephen Blephen" and "Bloom Stoom" (p. 682), each projecting his subjective consciousness into the foreign "life-world" of the other. They stand "silent, each contemplating the other in both mirrors of the reciprocal flesh of theirhisnothis fellowfaces" (p. 702). Through momentary "Adamic" fusion, they transcend the limits of the isolated ego and escape the solipsistic prison of the self. Each is aware that the "fellowface" into which he stares is at once "his" and "not his." Both men are united in their common humanity, in their "mutable (aliorelative)" (p. 708) relations with each other and with the rest of society. Yet each is forever bound to a "solitary (ipsorelative)" (p. 708) physiological microcosm.

Stephen has apparently been immolated, consenting, in the Jew's "secret infidel apartment" (p. 692). Like Little Harry Hughes, he experiences ritual annihilation of the ego and escapes from the intellectual bondage of his own head. He proves receptive to matters of the heart, to the intimate friendship and affection offered him by Leopold Bloom. Physically diminished in an overwhelming universe, Stephen and Bloom nevertheless appear heroic, aggrandized by a consciousness that apprehends the need for universal sympathy, the "inanity of extolled virtue," the limitations of egocentric desire, and the "apathy of the stars" (p. 734).

In the "creative" act of urination, both men pay homage to the mystical light of benediction that emanates from Molly's window. Bloom elucidates "the mystery of an invisible person, his wife Marion (Molly) Bloom, denoted by a visible splendid sign, a lamp": "With indirect and direct verbal allusions or affirmations: with subdued affection and admiration: with description: with impediment: with suggestion" (p. 702). In an

220

aspect of meditation, the two men behold the symbol of an unseen muse presiding over their nocturnal encounter: "their gazes, first Bloom's, then Stephen's, elevated to the projected luminous and semi-luminous shadow" (p. 702). As they stand in an attitude of worship, a "celestial sign" confirms the sacramental nature of their momentary communion: "A star precipitated with great apparent velocity across the firmament from Vega in the Lyre above the zenith beyond the stargroup of the Tress of Berenice towards the zodiacal sign of Leo" (p. 703). The auspicious omen would seem to predict future good fortune for both men in the realms of love and lyrical creation. Yet we realize that the stars are apathetic and that the illusory "heaventree" is a utopia of nescient matter, "there being no known method from the known to the unknown" (p. 701).

After Stephen leaves, Bloom continues to contemplate his personal insignificance in the material universe. Like the Stoics, he looks at human life from a detached perspective. He smiles amusedly at the fact that each man believes himself to be a woman's first lover, when in reality "he is neither first nor last nor only nor alone in a series originating in and repeated to infinity" (p. 731). Adultery becomes a single term in a mathematical series, and marital intercourse takes its place alongside pre- and post-conjugal relations. Bloom describes the act of sex in scientific, mechanical terms, as "energetic human copulation and energetic piston and cylinder movement necessary for the complete satisfaction of a constant but not acute concupiscence" (p. 732).

Bloom refuses to adopt the categorical response of marital outrage at his wife's infidelity. He examines his cuckoldry as a "natural phenomenon": "As natural as any and every act of a nature expressed or understood executed in natured nature by natural creatures. . . . As not as calamitous as a cataclysmic annihilation of the planet in consequence of collision with a dark sun. As less reprehensible than theft, highway robbery, cruelty to children and animals, . . . manslaughter, wilful and premeditated murder. As not more abnormal than all . . . processes of adaptation to altered conditions of existence. . . . As more than inevitable, irreparable'' (p. 733). Bloom reasons that adultery is a natural act; not criminal or socially harmful; and, as an event belonging to the past, irremediable. The ''cuckold'' decides that what's done is done, and that perhaps it was not so reprehensible after all. Ironically, Bloom's mental arguments are precisely those that Molly will use to justify her affair with Boylan. Molly later thinks: ''theyre not going to be chaining me up . . . for stupid husbands jealousy . . . her husband found it out what they did together well naturally and if he did can he undo it hes coronado anyway whatever he does'' (p. 777). She tells herself that sex is ''only natural''; that her husband's lack of erotic interest has forced her into adultery; and ''if that's all the harm we did in our lives,'' the world would be a much more habitable place.

Neither Molly nor Leopold can speak of ''adultery'' directly. Molly uses a demonstrative pronoun, ''that,'' to designate her infidelity. And Bloom cloaks the deep structure of the sentences ''He fucked her'' and ''She was fucked by him'' in elaborate verbal rhetoric:

> By what reflections did he, a conscious reactor against the void incertitude, justify to himself his sentiments?
> The preordained frangibility of the hymen, the presupposed intangibility of the thing in itself: . . . the variations of ethical codes: the natural grammatical transition by inversion involving no alteration of sense of an aorist preterite proposition (parsed as masculine subject, monosyllabic onomatopoeic transitive verb with direct feminine object [He fucked her]) from the active voice into its correlative aorist preterite proposition (parsed as feminine subject, auxiliary verb and quasimonosyllabic onomatopoeic past participle with complementary masculine agent [She was fucked by him]) in the passive voice: . . . the futility of triumph or protest or vindication: the inanity of extolled virtue: the lethargy of nescient matter: the apathy of the stars. (P. 734)

In a materialistic universe, the astrological deities are apathetic. Man, the most conscious being in the cosmos, finds himself powerless to change the condition of nonthinking matter. Nor can he alter the stasis of the past. In ''Ithaca,'' Bloom is surrounded by a world of things—events and data enumerated with scientific exactitude. He regards the facts of his past life clearly, from a realistic and detached perspective. Heroically transcending his situation, Bloom reaches a state of emotional equanimity. In an absurd world, he performs an existential act of mind that liberates him from psychological imprisonment. Bloom consciously *chooses* himself and his destiny, despite the limitations imposed by past history and by his present situation.

Molly's infidelity is a *fait accompli*. Ulysses-Bloom exercises the liberty of deciding "at each moment the *bearing* of the past" on present experience.[8] He mentally slays his wife's suitors through an act of conscious acceptance. He draws the lens of his perception *so* far back that he attains a "god's-eye" view. By considering his cuckoldry in a cosmic frame of reference, he methodically dismisses "antagonistic sentiments" and achieves a state of emotional balance consisting of "more abnegation than jealousy, less envy that equanimity" (p. 733).[9] Bloom exercises a "negative capability" that allows him to feel compassion and tolerance for his spouse. Reconciled to her adultery, he seeks animal security in the sensual warmth of Molly's buttocks:

> In what final satisfaction did these antagonistic sentiments and reflections, reduced to their simplest forms, converge?
>
> Satisfaction at the ubiquity in eastern and western terrestrial hemispheres . . . of adipose posterior female hemispheres, redolent of milk and honey and of excretory sanguine and seminal warmth, reminiscent of secular families of curves of amplitude, insusceptible of moods of impression or of contrarieties of expression, expressive of mute immutable mature animality. (P. 734)

Bloom goes to sleep, drifting into the night world of unconscious dream that Joyce portrays in *Finnegans Wake:* "Going to a dark bed there was a square round Sinbad the Sailor roc's auk's egg in the night of the bed of all the auks of the rocs of Darkinbad the Brightdayler" (p. 737). We are left with nothing but a large black dot on the page, an instant that culminates our vicarious participation in Leopold's consciousness.

223

Bloom has reached a promised land "redolent of milk and honey," the land of dream and mythic imagination. Joyce refuses to tell us whether or not he has won the impossible "auk's egg" of conjugal harmony.[10] The author frustrates our hopes that Bloom and Molly will resume normal intercourse and end the novel as a "happily married couple."

Despite the propensity of critics to interpret the eggs that Bloom demands from Molly on the morning of 17 June as ovular archetypes, the text of "Ithaca" would seem to contradict such optimistic speculations. Bloom realizes that at this point in time, it would be "absurd" for him and Molly "to reunite for increase and multiplication." And he knows that it is impossible to "form by reunion the original couple of uniting parties" (p. 726). Furthermore, Bloom recognizes the futility of his dreams of departure in search of fame and fortune. Though intellectually he may wander "selfcompelled, to the extreme limit of his cometary orbit, beyond the fixed stars" (p. 727), advancing age cuts him off from fantastic physical adventures in the macrocosm. He is forced to acknowledge an "unsatisfactory equation between an exodus and return in time through reversible space and an exodus and return in space through irreversible time" (p. 728).

At the end of "Ithaca," readers are apt to feel that Joyce has left them "in the dark" concerning the Bloom ménage. Critics speculate relentlessly as to the outcome of events on 17 June 1904. Such conjecture is futile. As we know from our Joycean catechism, the past is irreparable and the future unpredictable: the circus clown was not Bloom's father; the notched florin never came back. "Ithaca," that lame duck of a chapter, deals a *coup de grâce* to the traditional reader eager to "know everything and know it in the baldest, coldest way."[11]

Leopold Bloom is one of those rare literary heroes whom we have recently learned to admire as androgynous. He has a "touch of the poet" about him and a "touch of the woman," as well. In "Circe," Bloom is described as the "new womanly man" who will redeem the wasteland of twentieth-century society. He exhibits such "female" characteristics as compas-

224

sion, empathy, and nurturance. He appears at times to suffer from a conspicuous dearth of masculine *libido*, and he finds himself attracted to forceful women who complement his vulnerability.

With some "hesitency," Joyce stutters the theme of sexual fall throughout his fiction. Leopold-Ulysses is both the man that Joyce was and the husband that he feared to be. From Joyce's 1909 correspondence with Nora, we know that the author was capable of unfounded, irrational jealousy. He was terrified of being cuckolded; and subconsciously, at least, he feared giving his wife cause for adultery through impotence. The key is there: we have never discovered it. "His loss is our gain." James Joyce and D. H. Lawrence both conceal beneath prodigious literary creation a masculine terror of sexual failure. They use art to compensate for their own "man-womanliness," to "hide themselves from themselves."[12] Lawrence creates sexual dynamos; Joyce retreats into the Rabelaisian refuge of comedy.

Most critics declare Leopold Bloom heroic in his psychic slaughter of the suitors and magnanimous in his equanimity. They assume that Molly's affair with Boylan is both reprehensible and forgivable. Yet Joyce may have had in mind still another possibility: Molly Bloom's adultery, like Leopold's onanism, could have an affirmative, liberating, and redemptive function in the novel. Intercourse with a virile lover frees Molly from erotic frustration and conjugal resentment. It allows her to relate to her husband as an individual whom she loves and wants to protect. As if in emulation of her spouse, Molly will achieve equanimity by the end of the "Penelope" episode.

Molly is indeed a Gea-Tellus, a primordial earth-mother, "fulfilled, recumbent, big with seed" (p. 737). And since the death of Rudy, Bloom has served as all of Molly's "daughtersons," her "manchild in the womb." She offers her husband enough maternal warmth of breast and buttocks to satisfy the most perverse of polymorphous desires. And in so doing, she rewards him with satisfactions that make heterosexual copulation superfluous. Bloom may well harbor an "incest taboo" against intercourse with mother Molly. Such a psychological

225

fixation would explain his apparent castration complex, a fear of putting the phallus "out of sight" in the vagina lest it be destroyed. Since the death of his son, Bloom has been unwilling or unable to engage in "complete carnal intercourse": he confesses that he "could never like it again after Rudy" (p. 168). Not only does he fear disappointed procreation, but he seems to have relinquished his phallic role in order to *become* a surrogate for Rudy, arrested in infantile sexuality. Bloom is fascinated by his wife's "large soft bubs, sloping within her nightdress like a shegoat's udder" (p. 63); and he nightly worships at the "altar of the adulterous rump," kissing "the plump mellow yellow smellow melons . . . on each plump melonous hemisphere, . . . with obscure prolonged provocative melonsmellonous osculation" (pp. 734–35). He ends his day "reclined laterally" in embryonic position, his head at Molly's feet. He rests in a peace that re-creates uterine security for "the childman weary, the manchild in the womb" (p. 737).

Even Freudian critics have neglected to explore the full implications of Bloom's Oedipal attachment. Leopold demands of his spouse a primordial "mother's love": "*Amor matris,* subjective and objective genitive, may be the only true thing in life" (p. 207). As a surrogate son-husband, he can freely bestow on his wife the unmitigated devotion of filial attachment. Beyond the jealousy of Eros lies the fertile terrain of agape. Loss of erotic obsession allows Bloom to achieve a higher, more liberated sympathy for his spouse. Molly is the "earth-mother" fertilized by the "blazin' and boilin' heat of the sun"—a heat that Bloom has learned to "fear no more." She treats Leopold with protective care and maternal solicitude, resolving that "theyre not going to get my husband again into their clutches if I can help it" (p. 773). "*Amor matris*" is the "only true thing in life" because of its utter gratuity. It resembles neither the reward of patriarchal approval nor the prize of amorous devotion. Mother-love is unconditional: it implies a deep, unshakable, personal faith, independent of performance or activity. Like the humanistic agape, the ideal of Christian charity, maternal affection is soul-directed and non-judgmen-

226

tal. It concerns *being* rather than *doing;* and as such, it is the closest thing on earth to divine beneficence.

Once Molly has committed adultery, she frees Bloom to pursue the path of agape, leaving Eros to lesser lights. Bloom rests in the assurance that his satisfied spouse can now fully delight in the physical and spiritual attentions of her impotent son-husband. Proof of sexual performance is no longer essential to marital harmony. Disarmed of a lover's conjugal demands, Molly can accept her husband with full respect for his humanity, his uniqueness, and even his kinkiness.

Molly is "true" to Leopold despite herself. She enjoys playing sexual games with Boylan; but ultimately, she returns to the "big memory" of Howth for spiritual sustenance. Her personal affection survives adultery. She recognizes that from the first moment of consummation, Bloom "understood or felt what a woman is" (p. 782).

> Take thou no scorn to wear the horn;
> It was a crest ere thou wast born.
>> *As You Like It* 4.2

Whatever his private fears of sexual betrayal, Joyce was enough of an artist and enough of a genius to recognize the absurdity of sexual obsession. His comic vision outguessed and out-prophesied the lyrical fiction of D. H. Lawrence: one need only compare the two "unfaithful women," Constance Chatterley and Molly Bloom. Garrett Deasy may blame adulterous females for the sins of mankind, from Eve and Pandora to Kitty O'Shea. But Joyce knows better, and he tells us so. Despite the greed and jealousy of human nature, men and women must strive for equanimity in their love relationships. This is the truth that Joyce envisioned in *Exiles* and finally realized in *Ulysses*.

Joyce was at once fascinated and repelled by the Catholic doctrine of conjugal possession. The sacrosanct Irish family, with its assumptions of domestic ownership and female chastity, conspired with the church to stultify individual creativity. Joyce so despised the "trap" of bourgeois marriage that he and

227

Nora postponed their wedding ceremony until 1931. The author put his own opinions about love and marriage into the mouth of his protagonist in *Stephen Hero:* "The Roman Catholic notion that a man should be unswervingly continent from his boyhood and then be permitted to achieve his male nature, having first satisfied the Church as to his orthodoxy, financial condition, [and] prospects and general intentions, and having sworn before witnesses to love his wife for ever whether he loved her or not and to beget children for the kingdom of heaven in such manner as the Church approved of—this notion seemed to him by no means satisfactory" (*SH* 203–4). Stephen Dedalus declares to Lynch:

> I like a woman to give herself. . . . These people count it a sin to sell holy things for money. But surely what they call the temple of the Holy Ghost should not be bargained for! Isn't that simony?
> . . . A woman's body is a corporal asset of the State: if she traffic with it she must sell it either as a harlot or as a married woman or as a working celibate or as a mistress. But a woman is (incidentally) a human being: and a human being's love and freedom is not a spiritual asset of the State. . . . A human being can exert freedom to produce or to accept, or love to procreate or to satisfy. Love gives and freedom takes. (*SH* 202–3)

Rationally, Joyce shared with Lawrence the ideal of man and woman "being free together." He was convinced that twentieth-century society must grow beyond the infantile demands of sexual ownership. Yet he knew the visceral compulsions of jealousy, the conviction of betrayal, and the emotional need for marital fidelity. Only by transcending the desire for possession can human beings get beyond the ever-present threat of amorous betrayal. Hence Shakespeare's mature wisdom in "Scylla and Charybdis," Richard Rowan's acceptance of conjugal ambiguity in *Exiles,* and Leopold Bloom's cosmic equanimity in "Ithaca." By conquering the "pain of loss," Joyce's cuckold achieves the freedom of non-possession.[13]

James Joyce, for the first time in the history of English literature, has given us a portrait of an "open marriage" that works. No longer dependent on sexual union, the conjugal bond has shed it erotic compulsion. Molly and Bloom have escaped the limits of sexual obsession and are free to relate as full, self-actualizing human beings. Despite masturbatory and adulterous activities, they remain faithful to one another in their fashion.

Molly enjoys the company of the well-endowed red-haired gentleman who plows and pleases her amid crumbs of Plum-tree's Potted Meat. But her love affair is largely a *jeu d'esprit,* a game that brings her closer to her husband. Molly gives little heed to concealing her afternoon frolic from Bloom. She energetically moves furniture, but she fails to change the sheets soiled with Boylan's "spunk" (p. 780). Molly never takes her adultery too seriously. She feels that "if thats all the harm ever we did in this vale of tears God knows its not much doesnt everybody only they hide it I suppose" (p. 780). There will always be stallion-studs around to oblige a willing lady. But Bloom is something special. He understands and feels what a woman is. And when all the Blazes have burned themselves out, Bloom will still be there to kindle the flame of love. Why should we assume, after all, that impotence makes him less of a "man" in any sense of the word?

At the end of "Ithaca," Bloom becomes a semi-mythic figure, a "heavenly body" who wanders in the track of the sun and the paths of the stars. The chapter conquers the limits of time and space: it plunges into the atemporal realm of the unconscious, that "Utopia" which is "not a heaventree, not a heavengrot" (p. 701), but a "nowhere."

The question of "When? is answered by a mythic allusion to Sinbad the Sailor and Darkinbad the Brightdayler—imaginary figures associated with the "auk's egg" that symbolizes the impossible. The narrative defies linear history and culminates in a timeless dream world, a world that embodies the collective consciousness of the race. Our location, "Where," is designated by a large black dot, an isolated point independent of surrounding space. We are "everywhere" and "nowhere." Just as the "moment" transcends chronological time, the "point" suggests disembodied matter. The single, round geometrical figure is free-floating and unlimited: it offers a "transspatial" connection with the infinite.

By the end of "Ithaca," we have discovered the cosmic freedom of conscious detachment and the liberated utopia of unconscious dream. We embrace that timeless, non-spatial world of myth and collective fantasy that Joyce alludes to in "Penelope" and fully explores in *Finnegans Wake*.

1. As Richard Ellmann observes in *Ulysses on the Liffey*, Joyce scholars frequently attempt to supply the novel with an "ending." "What then does happen to Bloom and Stephen? One critic declares that Stephen goes out into the night and writes—*Ulysses*. But *Ulysses* is not the work of Stephen, . . . it issues from that mind of which Stephen, Bloom, Molly, and even Mulligan and Boylan are only aspects. . . . William Empson remembers that Stephen . . . agrees to exchange with Mrs. Bloom Italian for singing lessons, and proposes that Stephen returns on 17 June. . . . The mutual instruction then takes a predictable turn. . . . The other theory for 17 June is exactly opposite. According to it, Bloom, instead of relaxing further his marriage tie, tightens it and becomes a proper husband. Edmund Wilson proposed this idea some years ago in an uncharacteristic burst of optimism." Ellmann notes that all these critics "suffer from a desire, vestigial even among modern readers of novels, to detain the characters a little longer in their fictional lives" (pp. 159–61).

2. Ellmann suggests that in the *Nostos* section of *Ulysses:* "The 'fusion' that Joyce spoke of now occurs between Stephen and Bloom—not atomic but Adamic fusion: together they must form between them the new Adam and convey intimations of a terrestrial paradise" (ibid., p. 150).

3. Bonheim, *Joyce's Benefictions*, pp. 32–33.

4. Blaise Pascal, *Pensées*, trans. W. F. Trotter, pp. 16–17. Since the original composition of this text, several other critics have noted the similarity between Bloom's meditation and Pascal's philosophical writing. I chose to quote extensively from the *Pensées*, however, because Pascal's influence on Bloom is so germane to my argument.

5. Pascal, p. 19.

6. Ibid.

7. Joyce, *Letters*, 1:160.

8. As Sartre explains in *Being and Nothingness*, "the formula 'to be free' does not mean 'to obtain what one has wished' but rather 'by oneself to determine oneself to wish' (in the broad sense of choosing). In other words success is not important to freedom. . . . Now the meaning of the past is strictly dependent on my present project. . . . I alone in fact can decide at each moment the *bearing* of the past" (pp. 483, 498).

9. According to Robert Scholes, "the final lesson of the 'Ithaca' chapter is one of the most deeply imbedded meanings in the entire book. At the end of the chapter, after a day of anxiety, Bloom rearrives at an equilibrium which is not merely that of a body at rest but that of a self-regulated system operating in harmony with other systems larger than itself" (Scholes, *Structuralism in Literature,* p. 190). Throughout *Ulysses,* Joyce seems to indicate that Bloom is responsible for "bearing in his arms the secret of the race, graven in the language of prediction" (p. 676).

10. Cf. *Finnegans Wake:* "Lead, kindly fowl! . . . What bird has done yesterday man may do next year, be it fly, be it moult, be it hatch, be it agreement in the nest" (p. 112). The "auk's egg" may be the last item in the catalogue.

11. Joyce, *Letters,* 1:159–60. The following discussion of "Ithaca" was first published under the title of "Joyce's Bloom: Beyond Sexual Possessiveness," *American Imago,* vol. 32, no. 4 (1975), pp. 329–34; reprinted by permission of *American Imago* and Wayne State University Press. Several months later, Marilyn French's study *The Book as World* again stressed the importance of *caritas* and of Joyce's philosophy of conjugal non-possession. Working separately, and without knowledge of each other's writing, French and I both devised similar theories concerning the "Ithaca" chapter. I suspect that the apparent confluence of ideas may be the result of a shared "androgynous" perspective applied to the interpretation of *Ulysses.*

12. The quotations are paraphrased from Stephen's portrait of Shakespeare in the "Scylla and Charybdis" episode and from Joyce's description of Bloom as the "new womanly man" in "Circe."

13. The stoic repudiation of sexual ownership may be compensatory, but it is nevertheless valid. I am by no means suggesting that Joyce had "feminist" sympathies in his rejection of patriarchal privilege and conjugal appropriation. In fact, he tended to ridicule Francis Sheehy-Skeffington's commitment to the cause of women's rights. Joyce's rebellion against the bourgeois, commercial exchange of sexual favors had other roots. It was part of his attempt to cast off the paralytic "enslavement" to priest and king sanctioned by Irish religious and political authorities. In *Stephen Hero,* Joyce describes marriage as "a mark of ordinariness" (p. 201). Echoing Thomas Hardy's *Jude the Obscure,* he insists that "a man who swears before the world to love a woman till death part him and her is sane neither in the opinion of the philosopher who understands what mutability is nor in the opinion of the man of the world" (p. 201). He declares that the modern poet must treat love ironically because "we cannot swear or expect fealty" in an age in which "we recognise too accurately the limits of every human energy" (p. 174). Joyce disdained Irish Catholic puritanism, which he took to be the "cause of all the moral suicide in the island" (p. 200). He embraced his own interpretation of Ibsen's spirit of "free love" and explored the theory of sexual "non-possession" in *Stephen Hero,* in *Exiles,* in *Ulysses,* and in *Finnegans Wake.*

"Penelope": The Flesh Made Word

While Joyce was composing the final episode of *Ulysses,* he wrote to Frank Budgen that Molly's soliloquy would be "the indispensable countersign to Bloom's passport to eternity." "*Penelope* is the clou of the book. The first sentence contains 2500 words. There are eight sentences in the episode. It begins and ends with the female word *yes.* It turns like the huge earth ball slowly surely and evenly round and round spinning, its four cardinal points being the female breasts, arse, womb and [cunt] . . . expressed by the words *because, bottom* (in all senses bottom button, bottom of the class, bottom of the sea, bottom of his heart), *woman, yes.*"[1]

In 1922, when *Ulysses* was published, most readers were scandalized by Joyce's "Penelope." A few intellectuals viewed the episode as the final liberation of literature from Victorian prudery. And students of Freud applauded Molly for her outspoken frankness, her earthiness, and her unprecedented attitude toward sex. Carl Jung congratulated Joyce on the verisimilitude of his description of the female psyche: "I suppose the devil's grandmother knows so much about the real psychology of a woman. I didn't." In contrast, a number of critics, from Nora Joyce to the present, have skeptically observed that the author knew "nothing at all about women."[2]

Whether Molly Bloom is a convincing mimetic representation of woman remains to be seen. As Philip Toynbee explains, "Within the limits of the judgment we are making we need not decide whether this *is* the female mind or not; it is, in any case, the *anima,* the female image in the mind of the male, sensual, intuitive, submarine."[3] For Joyce, Molly seems to be Woman writ large, imbued with all the mythic qualities of Goethe's eternal feminine.

Critics eager to defend Molly as "true to life" often forget that she exists as a female projection of the male psyche, encumbered with a "farraginous" cargo of sexual fantasy and erotic illusion. She is the life-giver mysteriously in touch with the waters of fertility and the soil of excrement, the one muck from which both artist and lover take their creative powers. James Joyce, with his sentimental, artistic yearning for fulfillment by and through an extraordinary woman, wanted for Leopold Bloom nothing less than a "mother's love"—a gratuitous affection that could transcend all tragedy, even the marital affliction of chronic impotence.

Molly Bloom was made to fit Joyce's psychological model: she was preconceived and brought forth under the aegis of Nora Joyce. If Stephen Dedalus is all "head," then Molly is the concupiscent body—a fluid form that embraces the flowers and the mud of existence, that gives birth to the poetry of reverie and the song of experience. Molly is mythically fertile, in touch with the amorphous, Heraclitean reality that so eluded Stephen in his quest for the Protean mysteries. The young philosopher might ponder the thoughts of Aristotle and Aquinas; but his bit of a poem, plagiarized from Douglas Hyde, is little better than Bloom's "dreamy, creamy gull" or Garryowen's Celtic doggerel. Molly, by the poetry of her consciousness, mocks

234

Stephen's scholarly pride and the infamy of his sterile meditation. Ironically and inadvertently, she informs Joyce's Hamlet that there is more to life than he dreams of in his philosophy.

Molly Bloom is *such* an anti-Stephen—so much a corrective to literary erudition—that her formal knowledge is limited to the emanations of popular culture. Like Gerty MacDowell and Leopold Bloom, she has been fed a steady diet of pornography and penny papers. She interprets even the classics in terms of kinetic sensation. Molly believes, for instance, that Aristotle was the author of an obscene picture-book on embryology; that Daniel Defoe created a lascivious namesake quite unlike our present Moll; and that Rabelais was a French hack writer who specialized in grotesque accounts of gestation. She paradoxically sits in moral judgment of these scandalous authors who offend her sense of decency. Molly surely would have been one of the readers shocked by Joyce's fictional *sindbook:* she may well have censored her own titillating ruminations as unfit for public consumption.

James Joyce never gives Molly Bloom the scope or the breadth he attributes to his male characters. Her monologue is fascinating, but limited to the libidinous preoccupations that men have traditionally projected onto women to the exclusion of all else. Joyce remarked to Frank Budgen that he considered Molly "to be perfectly sane full amoral fertilisable untrustworthy engaging shrewd limited prudent indifferent *Weib. Ich bin der Fleisch der stets bejaht.*"[4] Ultimately, Molly Bloom is far more interesting as an abstraction than as a mimetic character. The subject of observation in "Penelope" becomes the stream of human consciousness rooted in the flesh, poetically transforming the phenomena of the external world.

The "Penelope" episode is impelled by the cyclical rhythms of Molly's mind. Her thoughts move like the tide—flowing forward, breaking, rolling back upon one another. In the words of Frank Budgen, her "monologue snakes its way through the last forty pages of *Ulysses* like a river winding through a plain, finding its true course by the compelling logic of its own fluidity and weight.''[5] Leopold Bloom is appropriately a "waterlover, drawer of water, watercarrier" (p. 671), who exalts both the element and his spouse as "paradigm and paragon" (p. 672). In contrast, Stephen is a hydrophobe who distrusts "aquacities of thought and language" (p. 673), despite his Aquarian birth sign.

In choosing an unpunctuated style for "Penelope," Joyce selected a literary form closest to the "stream of consciousness" described by William James.[6] Molly is the precursor of Anna Livia Plurabelle, a mythic embodiment of the river Liffey in *Finnegans Wake*. Emulating time's moving stream, Molly's thought flows perpetually onward: it never stops to reflect on itself, to qualify, or to rationalize. Hence Molly's pervasive illogic. She frequently makes a statement, then contradicts herself. She suggests that if women were involved in politics, there would be no more wars: "itd be much better for the world to be governed by the women in it you wouldnt see women going and killing one another and slaughtering . . . because a woman whatever she does she knows where to stop" (p. 778). A few moments later, Molly claims that women are so catty they are always fighting with one another: "its some woman ready to stick her knife in you I hate that in women no wonder they treat us the way they do we are a dreadful lot of bitches" (pp. 778—79). Molly scoffs at the idea of sadomasochistic arousal: "flagellate sure theres nothing for a woman in that all invention" (p. 752). But she later admits to having entertained a desire to "flagellate" her husband publicly after a boating accident (p. 765). Penelope complains of her spouse's prolonged absence from home, despite its obvious convenience: "then leaving us here all day you never know what old beggar . . . might be a tramp and put his foot in" (p. 765). Molly is never concerned with the inconsistency of her remarks. Like Walt Whitman and Buck Mulligan, she feels that if she contradicts herself, well then, she contradicts herself. She contains multitudes.[7]

We might compare the "Penelope" soliloquy to a Cubist painting: the blotches of thought appear to be incompatible, but

236

together they constitute a perceptual whole.[8] Joyce gives us in "Penelope" the associative stirrings of a mind as it takes in the "stuff of life." If Molly dwells on phenomenal appearances, it is because no interior distance separates objects of perception from her perceiving ego. Her consciousness consists of a "turning toward" intentional objects. Molly embraces the reality of vital sensation. She clings to the moment, holding "to the now, the here, through which all future plunges to the past" (p. 186). Her consciousness turns in a continuous, all-embracing present, like the huge earth ball itself, round and round spinning. The episode is, in effect, "timeless." Joyce refused to assign the chapter an hour of the day.

Molly draws the past into the present in the mode of creative memory. She frequently thinks about past events, but her mind manipulates duration and suppresses distance. She never differentiates past from present: the contiguous images of her life appear simultaneously before her gaze. All three modes of time flow together and are contained in a spatial continuum. Gibraltar and Dublin, Mulvey and Bloom, are present contemporaneously as objects of mental perception. Molly's memories are localized, connected to a system of places.[9] Her recollection of Mulvey, for example, is always fused with thoughts of Gibraltar. "I was thinking," she says, "of so many things he didnt know of Mulvey and Mr Stanhope and Hester and father and old captain Groves and the sailors playing all birds fly and I say stoop . . . and the Spanish girls laughing in their shawls and their tall combs" (p. 782).

Molly recalls "how he kissed me under the Moorish wall and I thought well as well him as another and then I asked him with my eyes to ask again yes" (p. 783). The first "he" refers to Mulvey ("Jack Joe Harry Mulvey was it" [p. 761]), the third to Leopold, and the second both to Mulvey on the occasion of Molly's first kiss and to Bloom just before his "seduction" and marriage proposal. Molly is saying "yes" to the kiss, to sex, and to matrimony—all at once. Adverbs of time, such as "then" and "again," give the illusion of temporal progression. The sequence of events actually occurs entirely in the present.

Molly shifts her focus from one area of the canvas to another, but the whole, expansive "painting" never escapes her gaze. The speaker wants to look at everything simultaneously—at all past events coexisting in a present, spatial medium.

Molly Bloom is so eager to embrace the whole of experience that she has no time for punctuation. The comma indicates a pause; the period, a full stop. Both are signs of a mental sequence that differentiates past from present, a completed thought from thought in process. Molly fails to recognize such a distinction. For her, life is continually in process, but always in the present. Like a spider weaving its web, she moves in circles without losing sight of the egoic unity informing consciousness.[10] Grammatical punctuation acknowledges the temporal nature of literature as "*nacheinander,*" one thing coming *after* another according to the "ineluctable modality of the audible" (p. 37). In defiance of Gotthold Lessing and of Stephen Dedalus, Molly wants to convert the sequential nature of both time and literature into a unified spatial continuum—things existing *nebeneinder,* one *beside* the other, in the "ineluctable modality of the visible" (p. 37). Because her soliloquy is without punctuation, our ultimate impression of the "Penelope" episode is spatial rather than temporal. We see the words side by side on the page, without periods and with few capital letters. Numbers are represented photographically: Molly thinks about what she did at "¼ after 3" (p. 747) and remembers that "Milly is 15" (p. 775). The entire chapter is a visual *tour de force,* an attempt to spatialize the temporal medium of language.

Joyce depicts in "Penelope" a pre-intellectual, poetic consciousness that delights in naming. Molly Bloom celebrates the wonders of physical experience; and in the final pages of her monologue, she recites a paean to Nature that might well be transcribed as poetry:

> God of heaven
> theres nothing like nature
> the wild mountains
> then the sea
> and the waves rushing

238

then the beautiful country
with fields of oats and wheat
and all kinds of things
and all the fine cattle going about
that would do your heart good to see
rivers and lakes and flowers
all sorts of shapes and smells and colours
springing up even out of the ditches
primroses and violets
nature . . .
the sun shines for you he said
the day we were lying
among the rhododendrons
on Howth head . . .
the day I got him to propose to me
yes
first I gave him the bit of seedcake
out of my mouth
and it was leapyear
like now
yes
16 years ago
my God
after that long kiss
I near lost my breath
yes
he said I was a flower of the mountain
yes
so we are flowers all
a womans body
yes . . .
and O that awful deepdown torrent
O and the sea
the sea crimson sometimes like fire
and the glorious sunsets
and the figtrees in the Alameda gardens
yes
and all the queer little streets
and pink and blue and yellow houses
and the rosegardens
and the jessamine and geraniums and cactuses
and Gibraltar as a girl
where I was a Flower of the mountain

yes
when I put the rose in my hair
like the Andalusian girls used
or shall I wear a red
yes
and how he kissed me under the Moorish wall
and I thought
well
as well him as another
and then I asked him with my eyes
to ask again
yes
and then he asked me
would I
yes
to say yes
my mountain flower
and first I put my arms around him
yes
and drew him down to me
so he could feel my breasts all perfume
yes
and his heart was going like mad
and yes
I said yes
I will
Yes.

(Pp. 781–83)

The soliloquy moves with passionate vitality toward a lyrical crescendo. Molly associates the word "yes" with her husband's proposal and love-making "among the rhododendrons on Howth head." Her recollection of the scene is suffused with nostalgia for Gibraltar and her youth. But in the last few lines of the monologue, she focuses exclusively on Bloom and on her first experience of sexual consummation. The interval between "yeses" grows shorter until Molly is panting with excitement. Her staccato repetition of "yes" gathers momentum, linguistically simulating erotic agitation. The orgasmic rhythms come to a climax with Molly's sexual surrender to Bloom; and the

240

language explodes in a burst of pleasure, joy, and amorous intensity at Penelope's final "Yes." Our last impression of Molly is that of consenting, "fertilisable . . . *Weib*."

In discussing Molly Bloom, Joyce told his friend Harriet Weaver: "I tried to depict the earth which is prehuman and presumably posthuman"[11]—but always superhuman and superwomanly. Frank Budgen notes that Molly "dwells in a region where there are no incertitudes to torture the mind and no Agenbite of Inwit to lacerate the soul, where there are no regrets, no reproaches, no conscience and consequently no sin."[12]

When Bloom tells his wife about Stephen, Molly begins to invent a capricious affair with the young poet. In her imagination, Stephen has *already* become her lover; she sees herself as his muse and inspiration, even though the two may actually never meet as adults. True to form, Molly pictures Stephen in terms of narcissistic desire, thinking it would be nice "to have an intelligent person to talk to about yourself" (p. 775).[13] She tries to imagine Stephen's "young body," and her attention quickly shifts to other examples of the male figure:

> besides hes young those fine young men I could see down in Margate strand bathing place from the side of the rock standing up in the sun naked like a God or something and then plunging into the sea with them why arent all men like that thered be some consolation for a woman like that lovely little statue he bought . . . theres real beauty and poetry for you I often felt I wanted to kiss him all over also his lovely young cock there so simply I wouldnt mind taking him in my mouth if nobody was looking as if it was asking you to suck it so clean and white he looked with his boyish face I would too in ½ a minute even if some of it went down what its only like gruel or the dew theres no danger besides hed be so clean (Pp. 775–76)

Molly conflates Stephen with Narcissus, and both with the "fine young men" on the strand: all are part of a single, abstract maleness. She longs to "suck" their "lovely young cocks," and at the same time, to suck all men into herself. The words "gruel," "dew," and "suck" suggest images of viscosity. For

241

Joyce, the female represents a principle of fecundity and natural creation. But like the ocean, she is also dangerous, a figure of the "agony of water" that "draws me . . . sucks at me."[14]

In "Proteus," Stephen compared the flow of the ocean's tide with female menstruation. Here Joyce puts the same analogy into the mouth of Molly Bloom: "O Jesus wait yes that thing has come on me yes . . . have we too much blood up in us or what O patience above its pouring out of me like the sea anyhow he didnt make me pregnant as big as he is . . . O Jamesy let me up out of this pooh sweets of sin" (p. 769). Molly feels disgruntled, but nevertheless relieved, by the onset of her menstrual period. She has enjoyed the "sweets of sin" this time, without paying the bittersweet price of pregnancy.

Toward the end of the episode, Molly's fantasies become wilder and more unselective: "I was thinking would I go around by the quays there some dark evening where nobodyd know me and pick up a sailor off the sea thatd be hot on for it and not care a pin whose I was only to do it off up in a gate somewhere or one of those wildlooking gipsies in Rathfarnham . . . that blackguardlooking fellow with the fine eyes peeling a switch attack me in the dark and ride me up against the wall without a word or a murderer anybody" (p. 777).[15] In her erotic musings, Molly associates sex with violence and feels titillated by images of punishment at the hands of a "wild gipsy" or a "murderer," though she is aware that "half of those sailors are rotten again with disease" (p. 778).

One of Molly's favorite words is "up," the message on Denis Breen's insulting postcard. Among her strongest instincts is the desire to feel "full up" with the phallus of the male—to contain, nurse, and assimilate her lovers. Joyce declared that he wanted to portray women as more "whole" than men; and since he was so fond of puns, he probably intended an allusion to the homonym "hole," as well.[16] Thus Molly observes: "no I never in all my life felt anyone had one the size of that to make you feel full up . . . whats the idea making us like that with a big hole in the middle of us like a Stallion driving it up into you because thats all they want out of you with that

242

determined vicious look in his eye . . . nice invention they made for women for him to get all the pleasure'' (p. 742); ''your vagina he called it'' (p. 770); ''then if he wants to kiss my bottom Ill drag open my drawers and bulge it right out in his face as large as life he can stick his tongue 7 miles up my hole as hes there my brown part'' (p. 780). Molly seems to be obsessed with holes. For her, sexual intercourse consists in ''filling up'' the ''big hole in the middle of us.''[17]

Although Joyce denied being influenced by Freudianism, ''the new Viennese school Mr Magee spoke of'' (p. 205), he appears to have set out in ''Penelope'' to disprove Freud's assertion that the ''libido is invariably and necessarily of a masculine nature.''[18] The stream of consciousness in ''Penelope'' reveals a bold feminine ego, stripped of the responsibilities imposed by a superego, and strongly controlled by the instinctual desires of the id. Molly Bloom is all woman and all libido, impelled by the passionate forces of concupiscent desire.[19]

Molly is wholly ''Flesh,'' sometimes to the point of comic absurdity. She strips words of their spiritual and emotional connotations and interprets them in a literal, physical way. She declares that her daughter Milly ''cant feel anything deep yet,'' then adds, ''I never came properly till I was what 22 or so it went into the wrong place always only the usual girls nonsense and giggling'' (p. 767). Molly tells us that ''Poldy has more spunk in him'' than Boylan, but we later discover that by ''spunk'' she means ''semen'': Boylan's ''spunk'' has left a stain on the bed sheet. Molly uses the word ''tongue'' figuratively when she complains that Milly's ''tongue is a bit too long for my taste'' (p. 767); but she believes that Bloom's tongue is literally ''too flat'' (p. 773) for the proper performance of cunnilingus. ''Soul'' has the connotation of ''passion,'' as does ''heart'': Molly feels glad that Boylan ''put some heart up'' into her (p. 758). And ''sensitivity'' apparently refers to the need for amorous approval. ''Of course a woman is so sensitive,'' Molly remarks, as she devises a plan for ''sticking'' Boylan for expensive presents, ''after what I gave'' (p. 749).

Molly has little patience with maudlin, sentimental notions of romance: "in Old Madrid silly women believe love is sighing I am dying" (p. 758). Yet her own desire for a "loveletter," one that "fills up your whole day and life," indicates her need for sexual affirmation beyond animal friction. "Fleshly" Molly is contradictory even in her longing for spiritual renewal and intellectual companionship. She wants love to be "like a new world" (p. 758). And with a Beckettian sense of resignation, she observes: "were never easy where we are . . . waiting always waiting" (p. 757).

Molly Bloom is Joyce's portrait of the sensuous woman: she looms larger than life, invested with all the mythic qualities of female *Weib*. Ultimately, she fails as a mimetic character because she represents Joyce's abstract concept of *femina sensualis*. As Frank Budgen remarked, "Perhaps she is so superwomanly because a man created her out of feminine elements only. Nature is rarely so exclusive."[20]

Critics of *Ulysses* have inveterately applied nineteenth-century values to the novel—first condemning Molly as immoral, then liberally forgiving her sexual prodigality. They judge Molly as a latter-day Emma Bovary; and they tend to ignore the fact that both James Joyce and Leopold Bloom not only forgive but genuinely admire Molly's insatiability. Bloom paradoxically boasts of his wife's allurements and numbers among her suitors all those men who have ever glanced lasciviously at Molly's voluptuous bottom.

Molly Bloom is Joyce's "darling." She is positive, yea-saying, and life-affirming. She is psychologically rich and poetically fertile, in touch with the "awful deepdown torrent" of universal vitality. Predecessor to Anna Livia Plurabelle, Molly exhibits what D. H. Lawrence would have called the pure "desire-stream." She wants to feel "full up" with an infinite variety of imaginary lovers. And it is precisely the catholicity of her appetites that Joyce finds so appealing. Molly offers her sexual dynamism to all the men who come within the circle of her opulent curves. In the lush terrain of her psyche, the earth mother mythically energizes

244

her suitors and unites them with the waking dreams of the collective unconscious.

Molly dissolves her *enamorata* in a torrent of cosmic eroticism. By embracing their racially common "maleness," she elevates her lovers to the level of archetypal significance: "each one who enters imagines himself to be the first to enter whereas he is always the last term of a preceding series even if the first term of a succeeding one" (p. 731). It is Molly who finally unites Stephen and Bloom in their shared humanity: she brings hero and antihero together in the lyrical fluidity of romantic meditation. Molly will flow, quite naturally, into her sister and mother, ALP, who offers to all men the warmth and security of *amor matris*: "where would they all of them be if they hadnt all a mother to look after them" (p. 778).

Although Molly contemplates Stephen with erotic interest, her reverie goes beyond physical desire to an expression of maternal solicitude. Thinking of the young man as a possible lover, she assures herself: "Im not too old for him if hes 23 or 24" (p. 775). But she later muses, with parental fondness, "I suppose he was as shy as a boy he being so young hardly 20" (p. 779). Molly attributes Stephen's homelessness to his mother's death: "thats why I suppose hes running wild now out at night away from his books and studies and not living at home" (p. 778). She longs for "a fine son like that," for she felt instinctively after Rudy's death that she would "never have another . . . we were never the same since" (p. 778). For both the Blooms, Stephen functions symbolically as the lost son who reunites the couple. He differs so radically from Boylan that his visit to 7 Eccles Street prompts "for the hostess" a "disintegration of obsession" (p. 695)—Molly's rejection of "Hugh the ignoramus that doesn't know poetry from a cabbage . . . sure you might as well be in bed with what with a lion" (p. 776). Stephen basks in the light of Molly's affection and joins her son-husband Leopold in womb-weary adoration of Venus-Gea-Tellus.

Leopold Bloom takes a certain pride in enumerating the long line of male worshipers who have paid homage to Molly's sexuality. By composing the impressive list of fictitious lovers at the end of ''Ithaca,'' he attempts to put his wife's afternoon adventure into the context of earlier masculine attraction. Molly's affair with Boylan appears to be her first ''technical'' experience of adultery. She speculates that ''its only the first time after that its just the ordinary do it and think no more about it'' (p. 740).[21] Molly has evidently dallied flirtatiously with a number of male admirers. She engaged in extensive ''petting'' with Mulvey before her marriage, and possibly with Gardner and others in her sixteen years of wedlock. But despite lascivious desires, her intrigue with Boylan on 16 June 1904 seems to mark her first extramarital affair completed with ''ejaculation of semen within the natural female organ'' (p. 736). Hence her extreme turbulence and agitation in ''Penelope.''

Molly's ultimate return, like Bloom's, is to Ithaca and to the mythic moment of consummated love among the rhododendrons of Howth. In the fullness of imaginative reverie, Molly comes back to the ''masculine feminine passive active'' (p. 674) figure of Bloom. She believes that the majority of males consider the phallus ''1 of the 7 wonders of the world'' (p. 753) and harbor ''not a particle of love in their natures'' (p. 767). But Molly respects her husband and appreciates his uniqueness. He ''knew the way to take a woman'' during courtship (''I liked the way he made love then'' [p. 747]); and he still does. He ''takes'' Molly by *not* taking her—by allowing her to gyrate in liberated equilibrium around a central core of passionate affection. Bloom refuses to emulate ''that idiot in the gallery hissing the woman adulteress'' (p. 769). He knows that Gea-Tellus, the great earth mother, will spin round and round perpetually; but that she has chosen *him* as axis and focal point, the center of affection around which her thoughts eternally circulate.

At the end of ''Penelope,'' Molly comes back to her son-husband as ''flower of the mountain'' and nurturant mother, giving him ''the bit of seedcake'' out of her mouth and feeling again ''that awful deepdown torrent'' (pp. 782–83). In the realm of the psyche, all experience exists simultaneously, as a dimension of present consciousness. Molly imaginatively im-

246

bues her husband with mythic and heroic stature. Her monologue celebrates his timeless act of potency, an act inundating
and fertilizing the amorous memory of Gea-Tellus. The theme
of lovemaking on Howth recurs like a musical motif throughout
Ulysses. The final paragraph of the novel achieves, both
literally and figuratively, the effect of a symphonic climax.

Against the perils of the void, Molly thrusts an affirming
challenge of hope and belief. She, too, exhibits a "touch of the
artist." Out of the stuff of daily life, she weaves and unweaves
the material of myth: she elevates quotidian experience to the
plane of poetry. Molly's "day-mare," the waking dream that
precedes night sleep, is a Janus image of the historical nightmare that threatens Stephen and Bloom. Her mind is free to
roam through a landscape peopled by all the men and women
she has ever encountered. A thin thread of consciousness asserts
the "moraculous" power of the imagination to associate and to
recombine—to delight, exult, and fantasize on the sensual
pleasures of human existence.

For Joyce, the concupiscent senses are doors to perception.
They stimulate the mind to multiply fictional images of itself in
joy and pain, in suffering and contentment. Molly creates
"worlds" of fantasy captured only in shadow by the words that
reach the linguistic surface of meditation. In contrast to
Bloom's staccato monologue, Molly's thoughts are characterized by verbal opulence. Her soliloquy is full and voluptuous. As soon as Molly calls up a photographic image, a three-
dimensional, spiraling reality develops from the single point of
her recollection. The "unstoppable" prose of "Penelope"
suggests a life energized by unquenchable passion.

Of all the characters in *Ulysses,* Molly Bloom most clearly
exhibits a genuine talent for *being*—for existing in the present,
as the moment takes shape and creates itself from the temporal
interface between sensuous perception and transcendental consciousness. Molly dismisses the "nightmare past" and, with a
spirit of desire and adventure, she turns her gaze toward the
seductive horizons of an unknown future.

Molly's consciousness unfolds with amazing fertility, and

247

her prodigious discourse is truly open-ended. She dallies with the idea of seducing Stephen and of becoming his poetic muse. She momentarily thinks about eloping with Boylan, but she quickly rejects the proposal because "hes not a marrying man" (p. 749). (Molly takes care to select lovers who are *not* the marrying kind: Gardner was about to be shipped to South Africa, and Boylan is a perennial bachelor). Molly's projects include a startling list of outrageous and unladylike acts. She considers hiring a young boy as a gigolo and teaching him *ars amoris*. She entertains masochistic fantasies of thrilling coition with a sailor, a gipsy, or a dangerous criminal. She contemplates the pleasures of *fellatio* with the fine young men on the strand, the statue of Narcissus, and the unwashed body of Stephen Dedalus. She speculates about erotic experiences with a black lover. And she wonders what ever happened to a railway worker she met on the trip to Howth sixteen years ago. Molly thinks about cutting her pubic hair, both to startle Boylan and to cool her body in the summer heat. She contemplates rising early and going to the vegetable market. And she even considers preparing breakfast for Poldy, while he sits in bed like a "king of the country" (p. 764).

"Why does Molly Bloom menstruate?" critics ask quizzically. The answer is obvious: Joyce wants to assure us that Molly is not pregnant, despite the prophecies of Bella Cohen ("Wait for nine months, my lad! Holy ginger, it's kicking and coughing up and down in her guts already! That makes you wild, don't it? Touches the spot?" [p. 541]). Molly's frolic with Boylan has been infertile, and Bloom's worst fears have not been substantiated. At the end of *Ulysses,* we at least know that the Bloom ménage is still intact. Molly maps out a plan for rekindling her husband's sexual interests by appealing to fetishes of gloves and drawers, to jealousy, and to erotic titillation. "Ill just give him one more chance" (p. 780). She contemplates arousing his coprophiliac obsession by spouting lascivious obscenities: "Ill tighten my bottom well and let out a few smutty words . . . or the first mad thing comes into my head . . . now make him want me" (p. 781). And who can say

248

which, if any, of these colorful projects Molly–Penelope–Gea-Tellus will execute on 17 June 1904?

Molly's approach to life is that of a wondrous child. By filtering the present through a dense net of past experience and future possibility, she arrives at a new, exciting, parallactic perspective that eludes the more intellectual *penseur*. Lying in the bed of birth, conception, and death, Molly becomes the female equivalent of Rodin's symbolic ''thinker.'' To cerebral meditation, she adds the ''warm, fullblooded life'' of sensuous and emotional perception. An artist of her own imaginings, she manipulates reality by embellishing and re-creating actual events. Hence her infamous multiplication of the number of times that she and Boylan ''did it'' from ''3 or 4 times'' (p. 742), to ''4 or 5 times locked in each others arms'' (p. 763), to ''5 or 6 times handrunning'' (p. 780). Whereas the fictional craftsman organizes material toward an aesthetic ideal of stasis, the artist of life alters experience according to the dictates of kinetic desire. Desire kindles passion, and passion makes art.

Molly defies the nightmare of history by drawing the past into the present in a transcendent moment of ecstasy. Like the poet Wordsworth, she creates from recollection, but in a moment of agitation rather than of tranquility. Dreams, associations, and fantasies allow her to construct the fascinating world of ''Penelope''—a world of words usually articulated for an audience of one in somnolent, solipsistic splendor. The ''post-human'' Molly proves to embody the ''postcreation'' of the artist-god.

In the final episode of *Ulysses,* Joyce reminds us that we all possess the magical capacity to transform flesh into word, life into Logos. As the lights of the day-world are nightly extinguished, we enter the dark underside of consciousness, to join the mythic company of Moses and Sinbad. We fashion our lives anew, re-creating ourselves in terms accessible to post-diurnal, pre-nocturnal fantasy.

Like Shem the Penman, we give symbolic meaning to the quotidian surface of life, writing the mysteries of ourselves with the furniture of words in the haunted inkbattlehouse of the

249

psyche. We fictionalize personal history by scratching parables over the malleable integument of private consciousness. By inflating the content of our own experience, by exalting joy and compensating for pain, we become artists of the imagination, creating a private legend that gives us the strength to endure.

The mind, reflecting on itself, fashions poetic myths of happiness or despair, of glory or opprobrium. In the moments before sleep, we describe ourselves to ourselves with the fictional trappings of ecstatic desire. The eternal imagination, that "feminine" dimension of the psyche, draws us forward into the future with visions of meaning and self-transcendence. We create myths of identity from a collective racial consciousness, elevating an otherwise mundane personal history to the level of the sublime. The anima puts us in touch with a Jungian substratum of image and symbol that gives us faith in the heroic potential of our own existence.

Of all the characters in *Ulysses,* Molly Bloom alone perceives the cyclical nature of recurrent personal history. Her soliloquy presages *Finnegans Wake,* a work in which Joyce moves toward a broader mythic perspective. In both "Penelope" and the *Wake,* Joyce posits the simultaneity of human experience. He conquers time and space by making all events contemporaneous aspects of consciousness, accessible to the mind through impassioned perception. Molly Bloom may have been conceived as wholly "flesh"; but through her poetic fantasy life, she embodies the flesh made word—the Logos that arises from sensuous experience and perpetually affirms existence in a yea-saying moment of transcendent *ekstasis.*

1. Joyce, *Letters,* 1:160,170. Stuart Gilbert suggests in a footnote that the fourth "cardinal point," which I have supplied, is "unprinted here but easily imagined by adult readers" (*Letters,* 1:170). Cf. Molly's comment on reading Rabelais: "her a--e as if any fool wouldnt know what that meant I hate that pretending of all things" (*Ulysses,* p. 751).

2. Joyce, *Letters,* 3:253; Ellmann, *James Joyce,* p. 642.

3. Philip Toynbee, "A Study of James Joyce's *Ulysses,*" in *Two Decades of Criticism,* p. 282.

4. Joyce, *Letters,* 1:170.

5. Frank Budgen, *James Joyce and the Making of "Ulysses,"* p. 262.

6. William James, *The Principles of Psychology,* 1:239.

7. Phillip Herring notes that Molly Bloom "is more complex than her classic ancestor and fickle in many more ways. . . . On a 'Penelope' notesheet Joyce wrote 'MB jealous of men, hates women'. . . . This essential ambiguity (in two senses), like the circular imagery in the episode, contributes to the universality of Molly as female principle in *Ulysses*" ("The Bedsteadfastness of Molly Bloom," p. 56). For further discussion of Molly's contradictions, see Marilyn French, *The Book as World,* chap. 7; and James Van Dyck Card, "'Contradicting': The Word for 'Penelope,'" pp. 17–26.

8. As Everett Knight explains in *Literature Considered as Philosophy:* "Modern art since Cézanne, like literature since the symbolists, has been a return to things in themselves. . . . Perception is not guided by the intelligence, it is warped by it. This is the insight upon which the vision of Cézanne is based. His whole endeavour is to capture objects before his intelligence has organized them into something quite different from what they really are" (p. 73).

9. Georges Poulet, in *L'Espace Proustien,* makes a number of similar observations about the work of Marcel Proust.

10. Joyce wrote to Carlo Linati that in "Penelope," "the past sleeps." And in the Gorman-Gilbert schema, Joyce cites "web" and "movement" as correspondences for the "Penelope" episode (Ellmann, *Ulysses on the Liffey,* Appendix). Phillip Herring tells us that "phrases in the *Ulysses* notesheets in the British Museum which reflect Joyce's view of Penelope are these: 'Penelope—her body possessed'; 'learn-unlearn, build-destroy, Penelope'. . . . Other phrases indicate that he saw a parallel between Penelope as weaver/enchantress and the nursery rhyme about the spider and the fly" ("The Bedsteadfastness of Molly Bloom," 56 *n*).

11. Joyce, *Letters,* 1:180. We might compare Joyce's description of Molly Bloom to Stephen's earlier admiration for the "monk-errants, Ahern and Michael Robartes," encountered in Yeats's *Tables of the Law.* Stephen declares that "their morality was infrahuman or superhuman," and he feels that "they live beyond the region of mortality, having chosen to fulfil the law of their being" (*SH* 178). Certainly Molly Bloom, like the Nietzschean superman, fulfills the "law of her own being."

12. Budgen, *James Joyce and the Making of "Ulysses,"* p. 265.

13. Molly inadvertently hints at Stephen's growth when she says: "I hope hes not that stuck up university student sort no otherwise he wouldnt go sitting down in the old kitchen with him taking Eppss cocoa" (p. 775). In the early episodes of *Ulysses,* Stephen appeared to be an intellectual prig, the "stuck up university student sort." Now Joyce seems to indicate, through Molly, that Stephen's friendly associations with Bloom signify a definite change in character.

14. Sartre, *Being and Nothingness,* pp. 607, 609.

15. While writing "Penelope," Joyce asked Frank Budgen to send him "Fanny Hill *Memoirs* (unexpurgated)" (*Letters,* 1:171). Here Joyce seems to be drawing on an incident from John Cleland's *Fanny Hill.* Fanny, tired of being a "kept woman" to an impotent gentleman, finds excitement by "picking up a sailor off the sea."

16. Cf. Leopold Bloom's remark in "Circe": "Man and woman, love, what is it? A cork and bottle" (p. 499). In *Finnegans Wake,* Joyce frequently puns on the "whole"-"hole" homonym in referring to Anna Livia Plurabelle.

17. Sartre writes in *Being and Nothingness* that the female sex "is an appeal to being as all holes are. In herself a woman appeals to a strange flesh which is to transform her into a fullness of being by penetration and dissolution" (pp. 613–14).

18. Sigmund Freud, "Three Essays on the Theory of Sexuality," 1905, in *Complete Psychological Works,* 7:219. In *The Consciousness of Joyce,* Richard Ellmann offers proof of Joyce's early familiarity with Freud by citing the presence of Freud's pamphlet *A Childhood Memory of Leonardo da Vinci* in Joyce's Trieste library. Joyce later purchased a copy of Freud's *Psychopathology of Everyday Life* in Zurich during World War I (p. 54 and Appendix, p. 109).

19. Joyce claims in *Finnegans Wake* to have been "jung and easily freudened"; and two of the *Wake* commandments advise: "Sell not to freund. . . . Let earwigger's wivable teach you the dance!" (*FW* 579).

20. Budgen, *James Joyce and the Making of "Ulysses,"* p. 265.

21. Like David Hayman and Marilyn French, I subscribe to the "single lover" theory of "Penelope" and assume that Molly's comment refers to the first time that she has ever committed adultery. See David Hayman, "The Empirical Molly," in *Approaches to "Ulysses": Ten Essays,* ed. Staley and Benstock; and Marilyn French, *The Book as World,* chap. 7.

252

Bibliography

Adams, Robert Martin. *Common Sense and Beyond*. New York: Random House, 1966.

———. *Surface and Symbol*. New York: Oxford University Press, 1962.

Auerbach, Erich. *Mimesis: The Representation of Reality in Western Literature*. Trans. Willard R. Trask. Princeton, N.J.: Princeton University Press, 1953.

Bacca, Juan David Garcia. "E. Husserl and J. Joyce or Theory and Practice of the Phenomenological Attitude." *Philosophy and Phenomenological Research* 9 (March 1949): 588–94.

Bachelard, Gaston. *The Poetics of Space*. Trans. Maria Jolas. 1958; rpt. Boston: Beacon Press, 1969.

Beach, Sylvia. *Shakespeare and Company*. New York: Harcourt, Brace, & World, 1959.

Beckett, Samuel. *Proust*. New York: Grove Press, 1931.

———. *Three Novels: Molloy, Malone Dies, The Unnamable*. New York: Grove Press, 1958.

———, et al. *Our Exagmination Round His Factification for Incamination of Work in Progress*. London: Faber & Faber, 1929.

Beja, Morris. *Epiphany in the Modern Novel*. Seattle: University of Washington Press, 1971.

———. "The Wooden Sword." *James Joyce Quarterly* 2 (Fall 1964): 33–41.

Blake, William. *The Complete Writings of William Blake*. Ed. Geoffrey Keynes. London: Nonesuch Press, 1957.

Bonheim, Helmut. *Joyce's Benefictions*. Berkeley: University of California Press, 1964.

Brivic, Sheldon R. "James Joyce: From Stephen to Bloom." In *Psychoanalysis and Literary Process*. Ed. Frederick C. Crews. Cambridge, Mass: Winthrop Publishers, 1970.

Brown, Norman O. *Closing Time*. New York: Random House, 1973.

Budgen, Frank. *James Joyce and the Making of "Ulysses."* 1934; rpt. Bloomington: Indiana University Press, 1967.

Burgess, Anthony. *ReJoyce*. New York: Ballantine Books, 1966.

Campbell, Joseph, and Henry Morton Robinson. *A Skeleton Key to "Finnegans Wake."* New York: Harcourt, Brace, & World, 1944.

Card, James Van Dyck. "'Contradicting': The Word for 'Penelope.'" *James Joyce Quarterly* 11 (Fall 1973): 17–26.

Cixous, Hélène. *The Exile of James Joyce*. Trans. Sally Purcell. New York: David Lewis, 1972.

Crews, Frederick C., ed. *Psychoanalysis and Literary Process*. Cambridge, Mass.: Winthrop Publishers, 1970.

Cronin, Anthony. A *Question of Modernity*. London: Secker & Warburg, 1966.

Daiches, David. *The Novel and the Modern World*. 1939; rev. ed. Chicago: University of Chicago Press, 1960.

Damon, S. Foster. "The Odyssey in Dublin." In *James Joyce: Two Decades of Criticism*. Ed. Seon Givens. 2d ed. 1948; rpt. New York: Vanguard Press, 1963.

De Beauvoir, Simone. *The Second Sex*. Trans. and ed. H. M. Parshley. 1949; rpt. New York: Bantam Books, 1964.

Eliot, T. S. "*Ulysses,* Order and Myth." In *James Joyce: Two Decades of Criticism*. Ed. Seon Givens. 2d ed. 1948; rpt. New York: Vanguard Press, 1963.

Ellmann, Richard. *The Consciousness of Joyce*. Toronto and New York: Oxford University Press, 1977.

———. *James Joyce*. New York: Oxford University Press, 1965.

———. *Ulysses on the Liffey*. London: Faber & Faber, 1972.

Frazer, Sir James George. *The New Golden Bough*. Ed. Theodor H. Gaster. 1890; rpt. Garden City, N.Y.: Doubleday & Co., 1961.

French, Marilyn. *The Book as World: James Joyce's "Ulysses."* Cambridge, Mass.: Harvard University Press, 1976.

Freud, Sigmund. *Complete Psychological Works*. 24 vols. Ed. James Strachey. Vol. 7. London: Hogarth Press, 1953.

———. *General Psychological Theory: Papers on Metapsychology*. Ed. Philip Rieff. 1911–38; rpt. New York: Collier Books, 1963.

———. *New Introductory Lectures on Psychoanalysis*. Trans. and ed. James Strachey. 1933; rpt. New York: W. W. Norton, 1965.

Gifford, Don, and Robert S. Seidman. *Notes for Joyce*. New York: E. P. Dutton, 1974.

Gilbert, Stuart. *James Joyce's "Ulysses."* 1930; rpt. New York: Random House, 1952.

Givens, Seon, ed. *James Joyce: Two Decades of Criticism*. 2d ed. 1948; rpt. New York: Vanguard Press, 1963.

Goldberg, S. L. *The Classical Temper: A Study of James Joyce's "Ulysses."* London: Chatto & Windus, 1961.

Goldman, Arnold. *The Joyce Paradox: Form and Freedom in His Fiction*. Evanston, Ill.: Northwestern University Press, 1966.

Gorman, Herbert. *James Joyce*. Rev. ed. New York: Rinehart, 1948.

Hanley, Miles L., ed. *Word Index to James Joyce's "Ulysses."* 1937; rpt. Madison: University of Wisconsin Press, 1951.

Hart, Clive. *James Joyce's "Ulysses."* Sydney, Australia: Sydney University Press, 1968.

———, and David Hayman, eds. *James Joyce's "Ulysses": Critical Essays*. Berkeley: University of California Press, 1974.

Hayman, David. *The Mechanics of Meaning.* Englewood Cliffs, N.J.: Prentice-Hall, 1970.

Heidegger, Martin. *Being and Time.* Trans. John Macquarrie and Edward Robinson. 1926; rpt. New York: Harper & Row, 1962.

Henke, Suzette A. "Joyce's Bloom: Beyond Sexual Possessiveness." *American Imago,* vol. 32, no. 4 (1975), pp. 329–34.

Herring, Phillip. "The Bedsteadfastness of Molly Bloom." *Modern Fiction Studies* 15 (1969): 42–62.

Humphrey, Robert. *Stream of Consciousness in the Modern Novel.* Berkeley: University of California Press, 1962.

Husserl, Edmund. *Cartesian Meditations.* Trans. Dorion Cairns. 1950; rpt. The Hague: Martinus Nijhoff, 1960.

———. *The Phenomenology of Internal Time-Consciousness.* Ed. Martin Heidegger. Trans. James S. Churchill. 1928; rpt. Bloomington: Indiana University Press, 1964.

Huxley, Aldous, and Stuart Gilbert. *Joyce the Artificer: Two Studies of Joyce's Method.* London: private circulation, 1952.

Irish Citizen. 22 May 1915.

Irish Times. 16 June 1904.

James, William. *The Principles of Psychology.* 2 vols. 1920; rpt. New York: Dover Publications, 1950.

Joyce, James. *Chamber Music.* Ed. William York Tindall. New York: Columbia University Press, 1954.

———. *Collected Poems.* 1937; rpt. New York: Viking Press, 1963.

———. *The Critical Writings of James Joyce.* Ed. Richard Ellmann and Ellsworth Mason. New York: Viking Press, 1959.

———. *Dubliners.* 1914; rpt. New York: Viking Press, 1963.

———. *Exiles.* 1918; rpt. New York: Viking Press, 1961.

———. *Finnegans Wake.* 1939; rpt. New York: Viking Press, 1968.

———. *The Letters of James Joyce.* Vol. 1. Ed. Stuart Gilbert, 1957; rev. Richard Ellmann, 1966. New York: Viking Press, 1966. Vols. 2 and 3. Ed. Richard Ellmann. New York: Viking Press, 1966.

———. *A Portrait of the Artist as a Young Man.* 1916; rpt. New York: Viking Press, 1966.

———. *Selected Letters of James Joyce.* Ed. Richard Ellmann. New York: Viking Press, 1975.

———. *Stephen Hero.* 1944; rpt. New York: New Directions, 1963.

———. *Ulysses.* 1922; rpt. New York: Random House, 1966.

Joyce, Stanislaus. *Dublin Diary.* Ed. George Harris Healey. Ithaca, N.Y.: Cornell University Press, 1962.

———. *My Brother's Keeper.* 1958; rpt. New York: McGraw-Hill, 1964.

Kain, Richard M. *Fabulous Voyager: James Joyce's "Ulysses."* 1947; rpt. New York: Viking Press, 1966.

Kenner, Hugh. *Dublin's Joyce*. Boston: Beacon Press, 1962.

———. *The Stoic Comedians*. Berkeley: University of California Press, 1974.

Klein, A. M. "The Black Panther." *Accent* 10 (1950): 139–55.

Knight, Everett W. *Literature Considered as Philosophy: The French Example*. 1957; rpt. New York: Collier Books, 1962.

Kronegger, Maria Elisabeth. *James Joyce and Associated Image Makers*. New Haven, Conn.: College and University Press, 1968.

Lawall, Sarah N. *Critics of Consciousness: The Existential Structures of Literature*. Cambridge, Mass.: Harvard University Press, 1968.

Lessing, Gotthold Ephraim. *Laocoön: An Essay upon the Limits of Painting and Poetry*. Trans. Ellen Frothingham (1873). 1766; rpt. New York: Noonday Press, 1969.

Levin, Harry. *James Joyce: A Critical Introduction*. 1941; rpt. New York: New Directions, 1960.

Lewis, Wyndham. *Time and Western Man*. London: Chatto & Windus, 1927.

Litz, A. Walton. *The Art of James Joyce: Method and Design in "Ulysses" and "Finnegans Wake."* London: Oxford University Press, 1961.

Loehrich, Rolf. *The Secret of "Ulysses": An Analysis of James Joyce's "Ulysses."* 1953; rpt. London: Peter Owen, 1960.

Magalaner, Marvin, and Richard M. Kain. *Joyce: The Man, the Work, and the Reputation*. 1956; rpt. New York: Collier Books, 1962.

McGuire, Rev. Michael A. *The Catholic Catechism*. Baltimore Edition. New York: Benzinger Bros., 1953.

McLuhan, Herbert Marshall. "Joyce, Mallarmé and the Press" and "James Joyce: Trivial and Quadrivial." In *The Interior Landscape: The Literary Criticism of Marshall McLuhan, 1943–1962*. Ed. Eugene McNamara. New York: McGraw-Hill, 1969.

Merleau-Ponty, Maurice. *The Primacy of Perception*. Ed. James M. Edie. Evanston, Ill.: Northwestern University Press, 1964.

Modern Fiction Studies: James Joyce Number 4 (Spring 1958).

Modern Fiction Studies: James Joyce Number 15 (Spring 1969).

Molina, Fernando. *Existentialism as Philosophy*. Englewood Cliffs, N.J.: Prentice-Hall, 1962.

Morse, J. Mitchell. *The Sympathetic Alien: James Joyce and Catholicism*. New York: New York University Press, 1959.

Muller, Herbert J. *Modern Fiction: A Study of Values*. New York: McGraw-Hill, 1937.

Murillo, L. A. *The Cyclical Night: Irony in James Joyce and Jorge Luis Borges*. Cambridge, Mass.: Harvard University Press, 1968.

Nietzsche, Friedrich. *Joyful Wisdom*. 1882; rpt. New York: Frederick Ungar Publishing Co., 1960.

———. *The Portable Nietzsche*. Trans. and ed. Walter Kaufmann. New York: Viking Press, 1960.

Noon, William T. *Joyce and Aquinas*. New Haven, Conn.: Yale University Press, 1957.

O'Brien, Darcy. *The Conscience of James Joyce*. Princeton, N.J.: Princeton University Press, 1968.

O'Connor, Frank. "Joyce and Dissociated Metaphor." In *The Mirror in the Roadway: A Study of the Modern Novel*. New York: Knopf, 1956; rpt. *American Scholar* 36 (1967): 466–90.

Pascal, Blaise. *Pensées*. Trans. W. F. Trotter. 1670; rpt. New York: E. P. Dutton, 1958.

Plato. *Republic*. Trans. B. Jowett. New York: Random House, 1961.

Poole, Roger C. "Structuralism and Phenomenology: A Literary Approach." *Journal of the British Society of Phenomenology* 2 (May 1971): 3–16.

Poulet, Georges. *L'Espace Proustien*. Paris: Editions Gallimard, 1963.

———. *The Interior Distance*. Trans. Elliott Coleman. 1959; rpt. Ann Arbor: University of Michigan Press, 1964.

———. *Studies in Human Time*. Trans. Elliott Coleman. 1956; rpt. New York: Harper & Bros., 1959.

Pound, Ezra. "James Joyce et Pécuchet." *Mercure de France* 156 (1 June 1922): 307–20.

———. "Paris Letter." *Dial* 72 (June 1922): 623–29.

———. *Pound/Joyce: The Letters of Ezra Pound to James Joyce, with Pound's Essays on Joyce*. Ed. Forrest Read. New York: New Directions, 1967.

Prescott, Joseph. *Exploring James Joyce*. Carbondale, Ill.: Southern Illinois University Press, 1964.

Ricoeur, Paul. *The Symbolism of Evil*. Trans. Emerson Buchanan. Boston: Beacon Press, 1969.

Ryan, John, ed. *A Bash in the Tunnel: James Joyce by the Irish*. London: Clifton Books, 1970.

Ryf, Robert S. *A New Approach to Joyce: "A Portrait of the Artist" as a Guidebook*. Berkeley: University of California Press, 1962.

Sartre, Jean-Paul. *Anti-Semite and Jew*. Trans. George J. Becker. 1946; rpt. New York: Grove Press, 1962.

———. *Being and Nothingness*. Trans. Hazel E. Barnes. New York: Philosophical Library, 1956.

———. *Existential Psychoanalysis*. Chicago: Henry Regnery, 1969.

———. *Intimacy*. New York: New Directions, 1948.

———. *Literary and Philosophical Essays*. Trans. Annette Michelson. 1955; rpt. New York: Collier Books, 1962.

———. *Nausea*. Trans. Lloyd Alexander. 1938; rpt. New York: New Directions, 1964.

257

————. *Réflexions sur la question juive*. Paris: Paul Mroihien, 1946.

————. *Saint Genet: Actor and Martyr*. New York: George Braziller, 1963.

————. *The Transcendence of the Ego*. Trans. Forrest Williams and Robert Kirkpatrick. New York: Farrar, Straus & Giroux, 1956.

Scholes, Robert. *Structuralism in Literature: An Introduction*. New Haven, Conn.: Yale University Press, 1974.

Seidel, Michael. *Epic Geography: James Joyce's "Ulysses."* Princeton, N.J.: Princeton University Press, 1976.

Shaw, Bernard, and Archibald Henderson. "Literature and Science." *Fortnightly Review* 122 (1933): 504–23.

Shechner, Mark. *Joyce in Nighttown*. Berkeley: University of California Press, 1974.

Spender, Stephen. *The Struggle of the Modern*. Berkeley: University of California Press, 1963.

Spitzer, Leo. *Essays on English and American Literature*. Ed. Anna Hatcher. Princeton, N.J.: Princeton University Press, 1962.

————. *Linguistics and Literary History: Essays in Stylistics*. Princeton, N.J.: Princeton University Press, 1948.

Staley, Thomas F., and Bernard Benstock. *Approaches to "Ulysses."* Pittsburgh: University of Pittsburgh Press, 1970.

Strong, L. A. G. *The Sacred River*. New York: Pellgrini & Cudahy, 1951.

Sullivan, Kevin. *Joyce among the Jesuits*. New York: Columbia University Press, 1958.

Sultan, Stanley. *The Argument of "Ulysses."* Columbus: Ohio State University Press, 1964.

Svevo, Italo. *James Joyce: A Lecture Delivered in Milan in 1927*. Trans. Stanislaus Joyce. New York: New Directions, 1950.

Thornton, Weldon. *Allusions in "Ulysses."* Chapel Hill: University of North Carolina Press, 1968.

Tindall, William York. *James Joyce: His Way of Interpreting the Modern World*. New York: Charles Scribner's Sons, 1950.

————. *A Reader's Guide to James Joyce*. New York: Noonday Press, 1959.

Tolstoy, Leo. "The Death of Ivan Ilych" (1886). Trans. Aylmer Maude. In *"The Death of Ivan Ilych" and Other Stories*. New York: New American Library, 1960.

Toynbee, Philip. "A Study of James Joyce's *Ulysses*." In *James Joyce: Two Decades of Criticism*. Ed. Seon Givens. 2d ed. 1948; rpt. New York: Vanguard Press, 1963.

Wheelwright, Philip, trans. and ed. *Aristotle*. New York: Odyssey Press, 1951.

Wilson, Edmund. *Axel's Castle: A Study in the Imaginative Literature of 1870–1930*. New York: Charles Scribner's Sons, 1931.

258

Woolf, Virginia. *A Room of One's Own*. London: Hogarth Press, 1929.
———. *The Waves*. 1931; rpt. in *Jacob's Room* and *The Waves*. New York: Harcourt, Brace & World, 1959.
Yeats, William Butler. *Collected Poems*. New York: Macmillan Co., 1956.
———. *Selected Plays*. Ed. Norman Jeffares. London: Macmillan, 1966.

Index

Artist: Bloom as, 6–8, 10, 67, 75–79, 86–87, 129, 203, 212, 224; as god, 3, 6, 9, 24, 42, 49–50, 56–57, 64–73, 183, 200, 249; as hero, 6, 71, 200; Joyce as, 3, 10–12, 73, 114, 193, 196–97; of life, 10, 12; Stephen as, 4–6, 10, 15, 20, 56, 67–73, 196, 201, 203, 218; Stephen's view of, 4, 64–73; Molly as, 9, 10, 234, 247–50

Automation, human (mechanization), 5, 21, 25–27, 33, 42, 116–21, 138–39, 176

Barnacle, Nora. *See* Joyce, Nora Barnacle

Beauvoir, Simone de. *See Second Sex, The*

Beckett, Samuel, 91, 244

Being (existence), 3, 10–11, 24, 34, 48, 65, 91, 106, 120–21, 128, 137, 172, 200, 215–19, 221, 247; annihilation of, by death, 107–10, 112–13

Being-for-itself (*pour-soi;* Sartre), 51 nn. 8 and 10

Being-for-others (Sartre), 21, 33, 78

Being-in-itself (*en-soi;* Sartre), 50 n. 3, 51 n. 8, 56

Being-in-the-world (Heidegger), 61–62, 113

Being-there (*Dasein;* Heidegger), 10, 31, 78, 110, 121 n. 5, 172

Being-toward-death (Heidegger), 113, 121 n. 5

Berkeley, George (bishop), 55, 56

Blake, William, 50–51, 66, 200–201; "Vision of the Last Judgment," 38

Bloom, Leopold, 61, 70, **75–230,** 235–37, 240–41, 244–48; as artist, 6–10, 67, 79, 86, 129, 212, 224; as father, 7, 73, 99–100, 103, 135, 159, 166, 175, 178–79, 202–3, 207, 219; as son-husband to Molly, 213, 226, 245–46

Bloom, Milly, 31, 77, 82, 85, 99, 100, 132, 135 n. 3, 178, 243

Bloom, Molly, 8, 76–77, 80–90, 92, 100–102, 128, 130–33, 142, 172, 177–78, 219–22, 227, **231–50;** as artist, 9–10, 234, 247; Bloom's memory of, 80, 82, 86–87, 97, 114, 136, n. 4, 185, 195–96; as Gea-Tellus, 225–26,

244–47, 249; as mother figure, 83, 102, 213, 226, 245; as muse, 213, 220–21

Bloom, Rudolph Virag (Bloom's father), 103–4, 185

Bloom, Rudy: death of, 84, 99–100, 103–4, 132, 178, 218, 225–26, 245; ghost of, 202–3

Bonheim, Helmut, 151 n. 5, 215

Boylan, Blazes, 82, 84–86, 92, 100–101, 126, 128, 130–31, 170, 172, 178, 195–96, 203, 227, 229, 243, 246, 248–49

Brivic, Sheldon, 99

Budgen, Frank, 156, 172, 174, 179 n. 12, 204, 233, 235, 241, 244

"Calypso" episode, **75–87,** 197

Caritas (charity), 7, 8, 44, 104, 114, 146–48, 226, 231, n. 11

Christ, 28–30, 44, 71, 90, 110–11, 173–74; Bloom as, 89, 92, 148–50, 162, 184–86, 191–92, 202–4, 211; Stephen as, 49, 65, 183, 192, 201, 204

Church. *See* Roman Catholic Church.

"Circe" episode, 6, 89, 92, 118, 168–69, 177, **181–205,** 224, 252

Citizen, the, 98, 101, 116, 139–50, 159, 210, 211

Claritas ("radiance"; Stephen's aesthetic theory), 4, 6, 56

Clifford, Martha, 88–89

Cohen, Bella, 157, 172, 194–95, 198, 201, 248

Confession, 46, 89–90, 163, 181, 183

Consciousness, 7, 23–24, 54, 57–58, 74 nn. 2–4, 77, 182, 186, 202; collective, 8, 229, 249; creative, 5, 6, 8, 10, 39, 48–49, 55, 68–69, 71–72, 128, 175, 178, 183, 187, 192, 205; "criticism of," 11; existential, 184, 200, 223; freedom of, 48, 127; Joyce's revolutionary view of, 101, 205; Molly's poetic stream of, 9, 234–38, 246–50; negativity of, 65, 120; subjective, 115, 186, 210, 220; transcendent, 11, 48–49, 56, 93, 109–10, 127, 146

Creation, artistic, 6, 12, 49, 56–58, 62, 65–73, 79, 104, 119, 128, 192, 221;

analogous to procreation, 68–72, 100, 173, 175, 178; godlike, 183, 200, 249
"Cyclops" episode, 47, 98, 101, 117, 130, **137–52,** 156, 159, 173

Dante Alighieri, 35, 195
Dasein. See Being-there
Das Man ("the crowd"; Heidegger), 7, 34 n. 2, 76, 91, 110, 121
Deasy, Garrett, 5, 40, 43–47, 49, 55, 199–200, 211, 227
Death, 40, 45, 59–61, 72–73; 95–114, 118–19, 140, 149, 198, 215; bed of, 63, 177, 249; Bloom's attitude toward, 81–82, 99–100, 103–13, 123, 171; of Rudy Bloom, 84, 99–100, 103–4, 178, 218, 225–26, 245; Stephen's attitude toward, 18–20, 24, 34 n. 6, 60
Death-in-life, 49, 109, 111, 113–14, 118–21, 134–35
Dedalus, Mary (May Goulding), 16–17, 19–20, 24, 33, 58, 60, 198–99, 203
Dedalus, Simon, 28, 63, 97–100, 111, 131
Dedalus, Stephen, 3–10, 15–65, 75, 78, 98, 99, 117, 119, 146, 159, 173–74, 178–79, 181–205 passim, 214–21 passim, 234–35, 238, 241
Determinism, 5, 6, 15, 20, 33, 39–40, 49, 120
Dignam, Paddy, 95, 97–98, 105, 111, 116, 188
Dio boia, 120–21, 176, 192, 208
Dionysus, 107, 121
Dublin, 67–68, 97, 115, 117, 137

Earwicker, Humphrey Chimpden (HCE), 186, 189, 191
Edward VII, 43, 201
Ego, 7, 22–23, 31, 61, 72, 131, 171–72, 197, 206 n. 7, 220, 231, 243; alter-, 78, 192–93; transcendental, 68, 102, 110, 119, 127, 203, 220
Egotism, 23, 173, 175
Ekstasis (Sartre), 8–9, 48–49, 51 n. 10, 132, 205, 250
Ellmann, Richard, 13 nn. 4, 6, and 9, 34 n. 8, 51 n. 9, 170, 205 n. 4, 230 nn. 1–2

Empson, William 230 n. 1
Epiphany: artistic, 4, 6, 10, 48–49, 56, 86, 205; Circean, 182, 200; negative 27, 60, 81–82, 118–19; transcendent, 48–49, 56, 200
Eros, 82–83, 126, 129, 178, 214, 226–27
Eucharist, 19, 30, 34, 60, 90–92, 138; as love communion, 128–29, 214
"Eumaeus" episode, 204, **208–14**
Everyman, 7, 109, 169, 188, 195
Existence. *See* Being
Existentialism, 6, 10–11, 14, 50 n. 3, 127–28

"Facticity" (Sartre), 50 n. 3, 57
Fenianism, 139, 141–43, 147
Fleischmann, Martha, 154
"Flower, Henry," 78, 88, 92, 100, 185, 193
Frazer, Sir James, 121
Freedom, 30, 48–49, 215, 228; aesthetic, 15, 48, 71; existential, 6, 12, 32–33, 71, 127–28, 132, 146, 200, 203–5, 215, 223, 230 n. 8, 249–50; intellectual, 64–65, 71, 201, 203; personal, 75, 127–28, 132–33, 228
French, Marilyn, 121 n. 7, 205 n. 2, 231 n. 11, 252 n. 21
Freud, Sigmund, 12, 17, 41, 181, 196–97, 226, 233, 243, 252 n. 18
Future, 51 n. 10, 66, 109, 127, 132, 237, 249

Gea-Tellus: Molly as, 9, 61, 225–26, 244–47, 249
Geneva School, the, 11–13, 14 n. 10
Gifford, Don, 35 n. 15, 179 n. 8
Gigantism, 137–38
Gilbert, Stuart, 108, 250 n. 1
God, 26–28, 30, 40, 43–45, 48, 71–72, 90, 142, 147, 159, 186, 191, 198, 217; artist as, 3, 6, 9, 24, 42, 49–50, 64–65, 71–73, 183, 200, 249; Joyce as, 183, 193; Stephen as, 200
Guilt: Bloom's, 103–4, 132, 184–86, 197, 202–3; historical, 44–47, 144, 184–85; primordial, 17, 43, 181; Stephen's, 5, 15–17, 40, 59–60, 199; transcendence of, 10, 204–5

263

Libido (Freudian), 195, 197, 225, 243

Life-world (*Lebenswelt*), 10–11, 18, 53, 95, 110, 220

Linati, Carlo, 47, 51 n. 9, 108, 251 n. 10

Logos, 3, 8–9, 65–66, 68, 72, 74 n. 6, 192, 205, 249–50. *See also* Word

"Lotus-eaters" episode, 87–93

Love, 7–9, 17, 70, 87, 127, 134, 150, 172, 221, 231 n. 13; as agape (Christian charity), 7–8, 114, 129, 178, 214, 226–27; Bloom's, for Molly, 127–29, 132, 236, 240, 244–48; conjugal, 70, 126–27, 212, 228; as Eros (erotic), 8, 80, 82–83, 118–19, 126, 129, 157, 178, 214, 226–27; free, 127, 189, 228, 231 n. 13; homosexual, 71, 209, 213–14; maternal (*amor matris*), 17–18, 40, 226, 234, 245; "opposite of hatred," 146–48, 211; Platonic, 164; romantic, 80, 147, 155–64, 169, 197; universal, 146–48, 198, 218; word of, 62

Lucifer (Satan) 6, 64, 199

MacDowell, Gerty, 17, 153–70, 185, 194, 235

Machismo, 173

Mangan, James Clarence, 48

Marriage: Joyce's attitude toward, 225, 227–29; "open," 228; Stephen's attitude toward, 228

Masochism, 77, 194–95, 197

Mass: "Circean," 183, 191, 193; Catholic, 30, 34 n. 7, 91, 184; Black, 60, 177, 183–84, 191–93

Masturbation, 70, 156, 164, 173–74; as artistic paradigm, 72, 174; Bloom's 152–53, 166–72, 179, 197, 225

"Medusa gaze" (*le regard*), 27, 46, 51 n. 8, 127

Mephistopheles: Mulligan as, 20, 34

Messiah, 28–29, 110, 191; artist as, 6; Bloom as, 148–50, 188, 212

Metamorphosis, 31–33, 195, 215

Metempsychosis, 83, 188

Miller, J. Hillis, 11

"Moly," 172

Moment, 56, 229; epiphanic, 9–10, 48, 51 n. 10, 200, 214; present, 4–5, 9–10, 40, 51 n. 10, 66, 145–46, 205, 247, 249–50

Moore, George, 66

Mulligan, Buck, 16, 20–25, 27–30, 32–35, 65, 72, 98, 174, 190

Mulvey, Sergeant, 99, 237, 246

Myth, 45, 49, 81, 107, 158, 197; collective, 9, 12, 230, Greek, 28, 84, 121 n. 3, Molly's artistic construction of, 9, 247–50; nationalistic, 142

Narcissism: Gerty's, 154–55, 173; Molly's, 241

Nation. *See* State

Nationalism, 57–58, 116–17, 134–35, 139, 142–43, 211

Naturalism: Mulligan's defense of, 20; Zolaesque, 20–21

"Nausicaa" episode, **153–72,** 194

"Negative capability," 147; artistic, 6; Bloom's, 7, 67, 76, 105, 223

"Nestor" episode, **37–50,** 53, 60, 184, 200, 203, 211

Nietzsche, Friedrich, 6, 26, 32, 60, 64, 201, 251 n. 11; *Joyful Wisdom*, 13 n. 4; "Thus Spoke Zarathustra," 13 n. 5

Nihilation (Sartre), 50 n. 3, 54, 79, 120, 200

Nihilism, 82, 200

Noman (*Outis*): Bloom as, 7, 13 n. 6, 169

Oedipal complex, 64, 166, 197, 226, 245–46

One, the (*das Man*), 34, 76, 91, 110, 121

Ordeal of Richard Feveral, The (Meredith), 16, 134

Other, the (*l' autre*), 7, 22, 45–46, 58, 71, 96, 110, 141

Outis. See Noman

"Oxen of the Sun" episode, **173–79,** 194

Parallax, 6, 8, 78, 140, 190, 216, 249

Parnell, Charles Stewart, 111, 117, 190, 212–13

Pascal, Blaise, 216–17; *Pensées,* 216, 230 n. 4

265

Past, the, 5, 9, 40, 43, 49–50, 59–60, 66, 98, 171, 193, 195, 199, 201, 203, 219, 230, 237; memory of, 68, 160; as stasis (*en-soi*), 20, 41, 57–59, 109, 126–28, 131–32, 138, 200, 222, 247

"Penelope" episode, 85, 87, 178, 225, 230, **233–50**

Phenomenology, 11–12

Phenomenon, 140–41, 151 n. 5, 221

Plato, 38, 65; *Republic,* 76, 93 n. 1

Plurabelle, Anna Livia (ALP), 110, 236, 244–45, 252 n. 16

Poole, Roger, 14

"Postcreation," 3, 6, 11, 42, 49, 65, 200, 205; Molly as embodiment of, 9, 249–50

Present, the, 20, 48, 66, 71, 146, 186, 200–201, 203–5, 247–50; continuous, 9, 128, 237–38, 247–50

Procreation, 125–26, 172–79

Projection (psychoanalytic), 106, 109, 187, 195

"Proteus" episode, **53–65,** 78, 174

Psychoanalysis: Freudian, 41, 181; as mode of criticism, 12, 226; as purgation, 183, 195–98, 205

Rabelais, François, 137, 139, 235

Reality, phenomenal, 38, 41, 48, 56, 65–66, 110, 120, 128, 132–33, 153, 175, 184, 215, 217–18

Regression, infantile, 83, 92, 102

Relationship, 61, 113, 227; "interindividual," 6, 67, 192, 203–5, 210, 218; personal, 9, 210, 214, 218–19

Repression, psychological, 73, 157, 182, 197, 204

Resurrection, 39, 202; Christian, 106, 110; myth of, 39, 107, 112–13, 121 n. 3

Ricoeur, Paul, 50 n. 51 n. 6

Ricorso, Viconian, 39, 200

Roman Catholic Church, 5, 15, 18, 30, 44, 63, 69, 73, 90–91, 111, 117–18, 178, 182, 201, 215, 227–28

Russell, George (A.E.), 65–66, 68

Sacher-Masoch, Leopold von, 118, 188; "Venus in Furs," 188, 194

Sadomasochism, 77, 79, 88–89, 187, 196, 236

Sartre, Jean-Paul, 11, 200; *Anti-Semite and Jew,* 151 nn. 4, 7; *Being and Nothingness,* 50 n. 3, 51 nn. 8 and 10, 74, 230 n. 8, 252 n. 17; *Huis Clos,* 113; *Nausea,* 34 n. 9; "The Wall," 121 n. 6

Satan, 29, 35 n. 14

Scapegoat: Bloom as, 126, 141, 143–44, 148–50, 185–88, 190–91, 195; Irish as, 144; Jew as, 44–46, 144–45, 148–49; patriotic, 134–35

Scholes, Robert, 207 n. 7, 231 n. 9

"Scylla and Charybdis" episode, **65–73,** 218, 228

Second Sex, The (Beauvoir), 34 n. 6

Seidel, Michael, 35 n. 16, 93 n. 6

Seidman, Robert J., 35 n. 15, 179 n. 8

Senn, Fritz, 154

Sentimentality: Bloom's, 132–33; Citizen's parody of, 147; of Dubliners, 106, 130–31, 134–35; Gerty's, 154–57, 166–67, 173; Molly's dismissal of, 244; Mulligan's, 16–17; Simon Dedalus', 97–98

Sexuality, 7, 69–70, 99, 157, 177; aggressive, 78–80, 126, 173, 184; Bloom's, 76–89 passim, 93 n. 3, 129, 145–46, 193–94; Gerty's, 162–64, 168–69; Joyce's attitude toward, 225–27; as infantile regression, 85, 92, 102, 226–27; mechanical (impersonal), 118–19, 176, 221; Molly's, 86–87, 222, 233–50 passim; Molly's attitude toward, 87, 133, 237, 240–43

Shakespeare, William, 8, 191; *Hamlet,* 27, 29, 67, 108 (Stephen's theory about, 7, 27, 29, 67–72, 174, 196, 228)

Shechner, Mark, 154, 169, 179 n. 7, 182, 205 n. 2

Sheehy-Skeffington, Francis, 151 n. 10, 231 n. 13

Shem (*Finnegans Wake*), 66, 106, 197, 249

Sin, 10, 45–46, 61, 163, 182, 190, 195, 197, 241; original, 44, 47, 62, 143; "sweets of," 242

"Sirens" episode, **130–35,** 138

266

Solipsism, 23, 55, 69, 72, 164, 174, 192, 209, 220

Space, 11, 38–40, 67, 78, 171, 184, 224; cosmic, 8, 216–20; definition of, 53–55, 66, 74 n. 2; physically enclosed, 4, 15–16, 23, 25, 31; psychologically enclosed, 4, 9, 19, 23, 25, 30, 37, 59–60; transcendence of, 48, 118, 120, 200, 250

Staley, Thomas F., 33 nn. 1, 3

State, the, 5, 116, 150, 189, 201, 215, 228

Stoicism, 103, 172, 221, 231

Suicide: of Bloom's father, 103–4; moral, 231 n. 13

Sultan, Stanley, 179 n. 9

Superman (*Übermensch*), 26, 32, 65, 251 n. 11

Swinburne, Algernon Charles, 20

Sympathy, quality of, 3, 10, 12, 111, 173, 192, 198; in Bloom, 7–8, 67, 76, 80, 86–87, 101–6, 109, 114, 126, 130, 167, 210–11, 214–15, 218, 223–26; creative, 6, 128, 104–5, 203; Gerty's, for Bloom, 159–60

"Telemachus" episode, 4, **15–33,** 53

Thanatos, 178

Theosophy, 65–66

Time, 37–50, nn. 1 and 4, 67, 74 n. 4, 127, 171, 224; destructive effects of, 76, 86–87, 199; linear, 9, 38, 40, 47–48, 184, 198–99, 204; serial nature of, 53–55, 118; as stasis, 131, 137–38, 170; transcendence of, 11, 49, 200–204, 229, 238, 250. *See also* Future; Past; Present

Tolstoy, Leo: "Death of Ivan Ilych, The," 109–10

Toynbee, Philip, 234

Transcendence: amorous, 9, 129; Bloom's, of his situation, 132, 223; creative, 11, 49, 56, 247, 249–50; existential, 109, 127, 150, 203, 219, 247, 249–50

Übermensch (superman; overman), 6, 26, 32, 65, 251

Ulysses (in Homer), 75, 89

Unconscious, 18, 61, 80, 168, 182–83, 197–98, 223, 229; collective, 229, 245

Utopia, 188, 208, 221, 229–30

Vico, Giambattista, 39, 47, 188–89, 191–92, 200

Virag, Lipoti, 92, 193–94

Virgin Mary, 29, 90, 157, 162–63, 173

Voyeurism, 92, 168–70, 196–97

"Wandering Rocks" episode, 118–21

Woolf, Virginia: *The Waves,* 51

Word: artistic, 3, 6, 65, 68, 72–73, 74 n. 6, 175, 179, 205, 249–50; "flesh made," 9, 61, 249–50; "good," 104, 220; "known to all men," 3, 62, 65, 72, 198, 203; "made flesh," 8, 72–73. *See also* Logos

Yeats, William Butler, 28; "Easter, 1916," 111; *Kathleen ni Houlihan* 142, 151 n. 6; *Tables of the Law, The,* 251 n. 11

267